THE UNITED STATES
AND LATIN AMERICA

OUTLINE MAP
OF THE
AMERICAS

 The American Assembly, *Columbia University*

THE UNITED STATES AND LATIN AMERICA

Second Edition

Prentice-Hall, Inc., *Englewood Cliffs, N.J.*

A SPECTRUM BOOK

LIBRARY OF CONGRESS CATALOG CARD NO.: 63-8966

Printed in the United States of America

93840-C

Preface

This is the second edition of THE UNITED STATES AND LATIN AMERICA, revised under the supervision of Herbert L. Matthews. The original edition, in the fall of 1959, comprised the background for the Sixteenth American Assembly, at Arden House, Harriman, New York and for all subsequent Assemblies on the same topic. It was also designed, as is this edition, for general readership.

The chapters which follow reflect the views of the individual authors and not those of The American Assembly, which takes no position, or The Ford Foundation, which generously supported the Assembly program on Latin America.

Henry M. Wriston
Chairman
The American Assembly

Table of Contents

Herbert L. Matthews, Editor
Introduction: Understanding Latin America   1

1

Frank Tannenbaum
Toward an Appreciation of Latin America   8

   Land and People, 12
   The Limits of the Conquest, 18
   Religion, 27
   The Hacienda, 32
   Education, 41
   Leadership, 48

2

K. H. Silvert
Political Change in Latin America   61

   Political Likenesses and Diversities, 63
   Political Values and Types of Politics, 65
   The Uses of Force, 69
   Parties and Pressure Groups, 75
   International Echoes of Internal Politics, 83

3

Reynold E. Carlson
The Economic Picture   86

   Diversities and Growth Rates, 88
   Latin American Trade and the United States, 94
   Inflation, 99
   Foreign Capital, 102
   Income Distribution, 116
   Alliance for Progress, 118

4

Herbert L. Matthews
Diplomatic Relations   121

   The Monroe Doctrine, 122
   The Era of Imperialism, 125
   Imperialism Fades Away, 130

The Doctrine of Nonintervention, 133
Pan-Americanism and the United States, 136
The Cold War in the Hemisphere, 140
Economic Policies, 147
From Nixon to Castro, 155
Present and Future, 167
The United States and Latin America, 171

THE UNITED STATES
AND LATIN AMERICA

Herbert L. Matthews, Editor

Introduction:

Understanding Latin America

When the first of the American Assembly meetings on "The United States and Latin America" was held at Arden House, Harriman, New York, Oct. 15-18, 1959, a sense of crisis was in the air. Since then, the Cuban revolution moved dramatically into its self-proclaimed "Marxism-Leninism" and the United States, backed by the other nineteen nations of Latin America, responded with the Alliance for Progress.

The crisis has gathered intensity. It struck with stunning force in mid-October, 1962, when the Soviet Union tried, secretly and swiftly, to introduce nuclear missile bases in Cuba and thus to upset the precarious "balance of terror" on which peace and survival now depend. A startled United States learned that the seeds of war could be sown in a Latin American country only 90 miles from our shores. This century has taught us that local wars tend to escalate into world wars, and that revolution in one country tends to spread, like an epidemic of disease, to other countries and regions where the same social, economic and political forces are at work.

We live in the most revolutionary period in all history. Latin America has the highest rate of population growth in the world and it is a region that economists and sociologists characterize as underdeveloped. As a result of the new techniques of mass communications, the prevailing nationalism, the agitation of radicals (especially of the Marxist variety),

---

HERBERT L. MATTHEWS *has been on the Editorial Board of* The New York Times *since 1949. Before that he was war correspondent and foreign correspondent for nineteen years in Europe, Africa and Asia for* The Times. *In the last thirteen years Mr. Matthews has specialized in Latin American affairs for* The Times *as editor and on occasion as correspondent. He won the Maria Moors Cabot Award in 1956. He is the author of the following books:* Eyewitness in Abyssinia, Two Wars and More to Come, The Fruits of Fascism, The Education of a Correspondent, Assignment to Austerity (*co-author with Mrs. Matthews*), The Yoke and the Arrows, *and* The Cuban Story.

1

the steady growth of egalitarianism, and the convictions and teachings of earnest, patriotic citizens who feel a burning resentment against the social injustices that their people suffer, there is a challenging atmosphere of revolution in Latin America.

This has been recognized and proclaimed by our leaders, among them President John F. Kennedy, Secretary of State Dean Rusk, Under Secretary Chester Bowles, Ambassador Adlai Stevenson. They agree that there must be revolution or its equivalent in Latin America. The masses are, for the first time in hempisheric history, aware that if they are poor, ignorant and diseased, it is not the will of God or due to the misfortune of having been born in a hovel, or on the Peruvian plateau, or in the Brazilian Northeast, or because their skins are dark.

We now see these masses demanding social justice with a determination that will not be denied. Yet, every student of Latin America, every economist, every sociologist knows that it is beyond the techniques of modern society, whether capitalistic or totalitarian, quickly and efficiently to satisfy these demands.

Thus, the revolutionary pressures come to all of us in the Western hemisphere as a dangerous challenge. The problem is to give the people of Latin America the hope that they, or at least their children, will have a better life, a life that will offer them, and not just a privileged few, land, jobs, decent homes, decent clothes, schools, hospitals and a simple sense of human dignity. To do this, there must be industrialization of their essentially agrarian and mineral economies; there must be diversification of these economies, which are often dependent on one or two commodities; there must be a better distribution of wealth through tax reforms, land reforms, higher wages; there must be education—far better education—for all; and there must be efficient, honest government.

These, of course, are absolutely staggering goals. They are, in fact, utopian in terms of one or perhaps even two generations. They are literally impossible of fulfillment in the ten years that the Alliance for Progress is giving itself. Yet they are goals that a now articulate middle class intelligentsia and an aggressive industrial working class and peasantry demand in Latin America.

Because we have such wealth and power, because we are the "Colossus of the North," they either look to us to help them achieve these goals or they blame their underdevelopment and their miseries on us. We, on our part, feel that we are not to blame. We can help and we want to help, but we are convinced that most of what needs to be done will have to be done by Latin Americans, not by us.

We cannot transform Latin American society; we cannot create honest and efficient civil services, collect taxes, divide the land, impose democracy. We can provide financial aid, capital investments and technical know-how but, as Secretary Rusk said, nine-tenths of the cost of the Alliance for Progress must be raised in Latin America by Latin Americans.

President Dwight D. Eisenhower put the dilemma with brutal frankness: evolution or revolution. This has been repeated more elaborately and even more insistently by President Kennedy and leaders in his Administration. Many of the outstanding democratic statesmen of Latin America have echoed the sentiments.

What do they all mean? This is where the impact of the Cuban revolution is felt. While Latin America was culturally linked to Western Europe, politically the Latin constitutions and forms of government were modelled on the United States, and in this century, when business, banking and the growth of urban centers and of the middle classes assumed such great importance, the economic model was also the United States. At least, the effort was to construct a democratic, capitalistic, free-enterprise economic system like ours, despite much government control and planning.

In the field of power, we had a hegemony in the Western hemisphere and in the field of economics, a monopoly. Now both the hegemony and the monopoly are threatened, and the break came with the Cuban revolution.

That revolution has been an effort to put into effect a totalitarian socialistic system, which the Cubans now call Marxist-Leninist and we call simply Communist. The fact that the system has been working very badly in Cuba is no guarantee that some of its worst mistakes will not be corrected in a technical sense, presuming that the Castro regime survives for any length of time. If the revolution succeeds, even partially, credit will be claimed for the "socialistic" system; if it fails, United States "imperialism" will be blamed by a large body of Latin Americans who will not cease to strive for the social justice that—however distorted in practise—was and is the goal of the Cuban revolutionaries.

The challenge we face was put in these words by President Kennedy to the Latin American diplomatic corps in Washington soon after he took office:

> Our unfulfilled task is to demonstrate to the entire world that man's unsatisfied aspirations for economic progress and social justice can best be achieved by free men working within a framework of democratic institutions.

And it was Ambassador Stevenson who added:

> We must honestly confess that not enough of us saw how great an effort was required until it was brought home to us by the tragedy of Cuba.

When the Arden House Assembly was held in October, 1959, the issues were not as clear as they became later. Yet, in the "Final Reports" of that Assembly and of the regional meetings held in the succeeding sixteen months, the challenges and the basic problems to be faced in our relations with Latin America were all foreshadowed.

Those who had, or acquired, an understanding of what Latin America was like could not have been surprised by the developments after they held their meetings. History does not operate in a vacuum. Today's occurrences are links in a long chain of events and traditions, of racial and national characteristics, of geographic and economic, political and social conditions. These provide the setting into which developments like the Cuban revolution and the Alliance for Progress must fit.

This was understood at all the American Assembly meetings on Latin America. After the National Assembly at Arden House there were held:

The Caribbean Assembly, in Puerto Rico, with the University of Puerto Rico—a bilingual, international meeting of Latin Americans and North Americans.

The Southern Assembly, in Biloxi, Mississippi, with Tulane University.

The Minnesota High School Assembly, in Minneapolis, for gifted high school students, with the Minnesota World Affairs Center.

The Pittsburgh Assembly, with the Foreign Policy Association of Pittsburgh.

The Arizona Assembly, in Tucson, with The University of Arizona.

The Midwest Assembly, at Wingspread, Racine, Wisconsin, with the North Central Association and The Johnson Foundation.

The San Francisco Assembly, with the World Affairs Council of Northern California.

At the Arden House Assembly which started the series, it was stated in the final report that "we must identify ourselves with the aspirations of the Latin American peoples for social reforms, higher standards of living and greater educational opportunities." This, with variant wordings in other Assemblies, was an argument for what has now been formulated as the Alliance for Progress.

The dangers of communism in Latin America were noted in all the Assemblies, but there was also a recognition of the fact that the attraction and growth of communism are reactions to grave social and economic deficiencies and that therefore the best answer to communism is to correct those weaknesses and distortions by positive measures of social and economic reform and not by the negative process of an exclusive anti-communism. Every gathering warned that indigenous movements of social reform (or as the Pittsburgh Assembly put it, "a wish for a better future in the Americas") should not be confused with communism.

At several of the meetings it was agreed, as the Arizona Assembly expressed it, "that the United States should not resort to punitive measures [the Minnesota Assembly said "unilateral intervention by the United States"] in order to combat communism in Latin America."

Since October, 1959, when the first Assembly was held, more emphasis, importance and study has been given to the global problem of dealing with underdevelopment, and especially the growing gap between the few rich nations and the many poor nations. Latin America is an economically underdeveloped area, and it is true that as the United States has grown richer, the Latin American nations, on the whole, stagnated or retrogressed. It is also true that nowhere in the world is there such a shocking disparity in standards of living between the small ruling classes and the great mass of the people as there is in Latin America. The San Francisco Assembly spoke of "the few rich and the many poor."

These economic and social divisions are gradually breaking down. The middle classes are developing strongly and irresistibly. The younger generations of Latin Americans now coming into power in politics, business, land-owning and in the armed forces are more enlightened, progressive and civic-minded than their fathers. They are going to transform their world, and it is our task to help them make the transformation by voluntary, peaceful, democratic and evolutionary methods.

Latin America undoubtedly faces years of attempted revolutions and counter-revolutions. The historic power of the military has already been broken in Mexico, Costa Rica, Uruguay, Chile, Bolivia, Cuba and Colombia, but it will take decades or generations to break it down in Latin America as a whole.

The tradition of personalism (the assumption of power by a man, a general, a dictator, a *caudillo*) has such deep roots in Latin American history and psychology that it will surely also take generations to eliminate it. The example of Fidel Castro in Cuba is characteristic.

Yet, the signs pointing to the years ahead need not be too alarming. They could become so only if we tried to insist that Latin America go our way—a democracy like ours, a free-enterprise, capitalistic system like ours —or if we chose to support Right-wing, militaristic dictatorships out of fear of Left-wing revolutions. Latin Americans are totally unsuited to the disciplines that communism requires and they are, by history, culture and religion wholly committed to the free world, or as we say now, to the West.

No one can predict what the future will bring to Latin America, but we are safe in saying that the Latin American countries will be like neither the United States nor the Soviet Union. The trends now are toward a system of strong presidents, much governmental control of the economy, an intense drive for economic development and industrialization, a breaking down of social imbalances, a fairer distribution of wealth, sovereign dignity and independence.

These are not goals we need fear—on the contrary. They can all be absorbed into a program like the Alliance for Progress. But they cannot be achieved quickly or without much travail. In the process, we are undoubtedly going to be hurt at different places and in different ways. Yet, in the long run, a Latin America where there is social justice and a decent standard of living for all is clearly to our benefit.

The first requisite is understanding, which, as The Southern Assembly pointed out, is "essential . . . to guide future hemispheric relations."

At all the Assemblies, attention was called to the deficiencies of the American press with regard to the publication of news from and about Latin America. In a paper prepared for the original Assembly at Arden House, Dean Edward W. Barrett and Prof. Penn T. Kimball of the Graduate School of Journalism, Columbia University, wrote:

> With a few notable exceptions, newspapers give relatively little space to news of the world and minute space to news of the other Americas. Whether this be cause or effect, the level of interest in and the knowledge of Latin Americans among even educated United States citizens appears shockingly low. . . .
>
> In the United States there is widespread feeling that North Americans do not know or care very much about Latin American news. Some editors say that is why they do not supply more coverage for their audience. This produces a vicious circle: first, the claim is made that Americans are not interested; next, the failure to provide the news perpetuates ignorance; finally, ignorance leads to the lack of interest described by the editors.

"With respect to the mass communication media," the Arizona Assembly concluded (and this was typical of all the meetings), "it was strongly recommended that greater coverage of Latin American affairs is needed in order to improve our understanding of the area. At the present time most of the coverage tends to feature revolutions or violence."

It is perhaps no longer necessary to persuade North Americans that Latin America, as the Midwest Assembly stated, "is of critical importance to the United States" and "must be given a high priority in United States foreign policy." Twenty-five or thirty years ago this would have been a truism, but the Second World War, the cold war, a complacent sense of our own supreme power and wealth, and a mistaken belief that Latin America was not changing significantly, all contributed to a neglect and an underrating of the area. A generation in the United States, one might say, had forgotten the importance of Latin America—until the shock of the Cuban revolution awakened us.

Here is a world at our doorstep on which, to a considerable degree, we depend for our existence as a world power. If we were deprived of the raw materials of the area or its markets, our economy and security would be gravely—perhaps vitally—affected. It is an area where no hostile power can be allowed to gain a foothold for, strategically, this is our "soft underbelly." That is why the Kennedy Administration reacted so forcibly to Soviet intervention in Cuba. We cannot win the cold war in Latin

America, but we can lose it there. Neutralism or an intense Yankeephobia could hurt us badly.

In terms of United States trade and investment, Canada and Latin America outweigh all the rest of the world put together. Yet our foreign policy interests, expressed in the cold war, have been directed far more to Europe and Asia. So we see the paradox of a financial and economic axis running north and south, and a political and military axis running east and west.

The field of study embraced here is a vast and complicated one. Latin America is a region of twenty countries as different from each other as France, Italy and Spain, and at different stages of political, economic and social progress. Yet, there is such a thing as "Latin America." It has common denominators.

A book of this nature can only be an invitation to learning and discussion. Its aim is to provide basic facts and to give an idea of what Latin America is like—its physical make-up, its people and their ways of life, its political movements, its economy. There is also an account and discussion of our diplomatic relations with Latin America which is necessarily controversial and provocative, for it is a field where interpretation and opinions are open to dispute. No effort has been made to eliminate minor differences of opinion between the contributors. This is not a scientific textbook. Sociology, politics, economics and diplomacy are not sciences.

Yet, it will be noted that there are no major or fundamental points of difference among the authors. There is a basic interpretive agreement which was not deliberately sought. It comes as evidence that the Latin American picture is capable of synthesis and simplification without an undue amount of distortion.

The relations between the United States and Latin America are, naturally, a continuing process. The past has shaped the present and we, today, are shaping the future. We can do so with more hope if we have some degree of knowledge and understanding.

Frank Tannenbaum

1

Toward an Appreciation
of Latin America

Don Federico de Onís, for so many years the leading influence in
Hispanic studies in the United States, likes to say that he can always
recognize an American in Paris, but cannot tell whether he comes from
New York or Buenos Aires, from Chicago or Caracas. There is something
about his bearing—the way he holds his head, his swinging arms and long
strides, the innocence and optimism reflected in every gesture—which
marks him as a child of the New World. This is one way of saying that
Americans, North and South, are in some measure interchangeable, that
their history has moulded them in a similar if not identical crucible. For
the familiar list of differences between the United States and Latin America is only partially true and denies the imprint of their experience on this
side of the Atlantic. The conquest and settlement of America have
moulded a recognizable folk. Four centuries of a common heritage have
given all of us "something" recognizable as American rather than European. It is discernible in our prose and poetry, in our politics, in our
attitude toward the outside world, in our popular heroes, folk tales, the
stories we tell our children and in the moral issues that trouble the
grown-up.

FRANK TANNENBAUM, *Professor Emeritus of Latin American History and Director
of University Seminars at Columbia University, has over the years worked and
lectured in Latin America and by one means or another (on mule or afoot, for
example) has traveled the entire region. Dr. Tannenbaum has been a newspaper
correspondent in Mexico, and member of Latin American or North American
governmental or private commissions, survey teams, and associations. For years
the Seminar on Latin American Affairs which he conducts has attracted many of
the distinguished people of Latin America. He has written numerous books and
articles on various phases of life in that area.*

That "something" comes from the universal American experience with the Indian, the Negro, the open spaces and wide horizons, the peculiar use of the horse (the cowboy, the *gaucho*, the *llanero*, the *charro* are brothers under the skin); the American experience with ranching—driving cattle a thousand miles as is still done in Brazil, for instance. Among all of our people there persists the tradition of a culture uprooted in the old world and replanted in the new: the mixture of races from many parts of the globe, the continuing flow of immigrants and their rapid conversion into something different from what they were, the evidence of social and physical mobility, the pride and self-confidence born of a world easily moulded. It derives from the common American belief in progress, from the notion that government belongs to the people, that it is a human and malleable instrument that yields to pressure and is open to change by political "revolt" at the ballot-box or by a "revolution," from the rebellions by which all the nations in this hemisphere achieved their independence, from the fact that all of our great national heroes are "rebels" against a king in the Old World. Our Americanism is evidenced by a belief in democracy even in areas where the *caudillo* and the political "boss" are continuing and sometimes sinister figures; it is evidenced by the fact that most of our political upheavals have been in the name of democracy.

These many influences that we have all shared in their different degrees and varying forms have given the people on this side of the Atlantic a view of the world and a sense of meaning about the ways of man with nature and his fellows, a psychological and spiritual heritage deeper than the obvious differences that separate them. It extends even to our sense of isolation from the rest of the world, the feeling of separation from Europe and Asia. It is no accident that an inter-American system, now the oldest international organization, has survived for over half a century.

All these identities deeply based in our common history have given us our cultural similarities and a large measure of what the anthropologist would call a "similar character structure." But the differences are also marked and frequently commented upon. Despite our common origin in Europe, the conquerors and settlers in Central and South America have had a different history from those of the United States. They have had a harder route to travel from the day they established their first colony to their present position of sovereign nations.

For one thing, the West Indies, Central and South America have proved less propitious to human habitation than the United States. Taken as a whole, Latin America is more isolated from the rest of the world, more tropical, more mountainous and has proportionately less good farming land. South America, more than twice the size of the United States with Alaska thrown in, faces Africa rather than Europe and lies at a greater distance from China, India, the Middle East and Europe than does the United States. Until the opening of the Panama Canal, a ship would have to go around Cape Horn to reach the ports of Valparaiso in Chile or Callao in Peru. And until the airplane became an easy means of travel, business men and diplomats going from Lima, Quito or Bogotá to Europe would travel via New York. Through the centuries, South America and Central America as well lay outside the normal trade routes, and it is still almost impossible to go from Panama to the East Coast of South America by ship.

South America stretches 4,500 miles in length and about 3,000 miles in width. The west coast is blocked off from the rest of the continent by a mountain range that, paralleling the ocean, runs without a break from Venezuela to the very tip of Chile, or the entire 4,500 miles. This mountain chain is like a wall between three and four miles in height.

The passes are few; except for the extreme south they are high, most of them 14,000 feet or over. A pass in the Andes is a narrow winding rift in the edging along some mountain stream rushing down from the heights. The mule trail, railroad and more recent automobile road must all crowd the same steep, narrow and circuitous slit, eroded through the centuries, and compete for a footing against the towering ledge. It is worth emphasizing this point—and anyone who has gone by automobile from Lima to Cerro de Pasco or Tingo María will appreciate its significance. These are not trade routes for extensive and heavy traffic; they are skilled and ingenious engineering performances. They are not, except in a limited sense, means of communication between the west coast of South America and the other side of the mountains; they are certainly not commercial routes between the Pacific and the Atlantic—and are not likely to be.

In the Andes themselves, human life tends to be grouped in large and small pockets, valleys tucked away somewhere between 8,000 and 14,000 feet above sea level and overhung by surrounding peaks. This is the case of Quito, Bogotá, La Paz, Cuzco, and even the less high Caracas, which lies a stone's throw from the coast. These are some of the larger cities. And this is the case with the smaller towns and villages in the Andes. They are each separately a little isolated pocket where men have congregated because there is shelter and warmth provided by the surrounding mountains, and moisture enough to nourish animal and plant life. On the whole, the Andes have insufficient rain, and in many places agriculture depends upon irrigation.

On the other side of the Andes going from the Pacific, once across the divide one looks down into the Amazonian basin many thousands of feet below and runs into unceasing rain. This rain forest, *la montaña* as it is called, stretches along the Amazonian headwater from Colombia to Bolivia. The slope of the mountain is practically uninhabited. Closer to the river where the land flattens out and the rains abate, sparsely settled Indian communities are to be found. Farther south along the Eastern Andes in Santa Cruz de la Sierra, and still farther in the Pilcomayo River basin, rain conditions change materially and groupings of human beings are more frequent.

East of *la montaña* and below it is the Amazonian basin, estimated at 2,000,000 square miles, about as large as the United States. The hamlet of Napo in Ecuador, some 2,600 miles from the Atlantic, stands only 1,600 feet above sea level, and Manaus, 1,000 miles from the mouth of the Amazon, is only 100 feet above sea level. The river falls at about one-eighth of an inch per mile for the last 500 miles of its course to the sea. The river itself is longer than the distance between New York and Liverpool and at least one of its great tributaries, the Mamoré-Madeira, is about 3,000 miles in length, and six others are over 1,000 miles. Here is a vast river system, with an estimated 30,000 to 40,000 miles of navigable waters, that lies but little above sea level and is subject to rains so heavy and floods of such frequency that the organic matter in the soil has been bleached away. Agriculturally it is not a productive area.

It might be added that South America has in addition three other river systems, which, if not as great as the Amazon, are formidable by any standards: the Rio de la Plata that empties into the Atlantic at Buenos Aires, the Orinoco that divides Venezuela in two, and the Rio Magdalena, for centuries the main route from the coast to Bogotá.

As we reach the east coast of South America we find a steep mountain range rising 10,000 feet, with an average height of about 4,000 feet. This escarpment is close to the sea and runs for some 1,700 miles from north to south, almost the entire length of Brazil. Between the Andes on the West, the Brazilian range on the East and the Amazonian rivers and forest on the North, the interior of South America is difficult to penetrate, to cross, or to abide in. The Amazonian forests, stretching endlessly along the rivers and covering the Western mountains, are more difficult to traverse than the Sahara Desert. Only the rivers give access to the interior and so far they have not induced extensive internal settlement.

In southern Brazil we enter a temperate climate, and as we reach Argentina we are in treeless pampas, flat, rich in good soils, with adequate rains and an almost ideal climate. These good lands, however, are comparatively limited, become drier as one goes West and South, and long before one reaches the foothills of the Andes have to be irrigated for agriculture. The continent narrows sharply below the province of Buenos Aires, and Patagonia has to date, like the Amazon basin, remained for most of mankind an unknown world. One need but add as a generalization that if we take the Equatorial zone as 60 degrees—30 degrees north and 30 south—then most of South America is in the Equatorial Zone and most of North America is out of it. South America is like Africa, North America like Europe. Only about 8 per cent of Europe has a mean annual temperature of between 60° and 70° Fahrenheit while 66 per cent of South America has over 70° and 20 per cent over 80° Fahrenheit. The high temperature is compounded by the heavy rains. The Amazonian basin and Central Brazil have between 70 and 80 inches of rain a year. The La Plata area has adequate rain and temperatures that fall below 70°. Southern Chile is rainy and cool, and the coast between Panama and Ecuador is hot, humid and wet, having one of the heaviest annual rainfalls on the globe. Mexico and Central America, like South America, are relatively cool in the mountains, with ideal temperatures but hot and wet on the coast except for northwestern Mexico, which is more like California and Arizona.

LAND AND PEOPLE

This rather long description of South America seems essential if one is to understand the political, economic and social conditions in Latin America. What this teaches is that Latin America is isolated from the world and isolated internally. Before the airplane it was easier to go to the United States from Lima or Rio de Janeiro than to go overland from the capital of Peru to the capital of Brazil. The interior of South America is empty. Whatever the figure means, it is asserted that in the Amazonian basin—an area of 2,000,000 square miles—there is about one person or less per square mile and most of these live in the scattered small towns. In fact one half of the continent has only one person per square mile. The vast majority of the 130,000,000 people in South America live within 200 miles of the coast. All of the really big cities lie at the edge of the Pacific or Atlantic Oceans—Montevideo, Buenos Aires, São Paulo, Rio de Janeiro, Caracas, Lima, Callao, Guayaquil, Valparaiso and Santiago. Bogotá, Quito and La Paz, though away from the coast, are, relatively speaking, coastal cities. The great urban centers face out toward the sea and not toward the interior. There is no St. Louis, Chicago, Minneapolis, Denver or Salt Lake City in the center of South America. In all of the Amazonian basin there is only Belem with 230,000; Manaus, 1,000 miles up the river, with 100,000 people; and another 1,000 miles farther up and serving as the commercial center for the upper Amazon is Iquitos, with about 42,000.

Latin America as a whole has a population of about 185,000,000 people scattered over 7,769,247 square miles, with about 23 persons per square mile as against 57 in the United States. Significantly, only 4 per cent of the area of South America is in tillage or under tree crops as against 24 per cent in the United States. Nearly 50 per cent of Latin American lands are in forest; nearly 30 per cent are unused or unusable, and the rest in pasture and other uses. In some ways South America represents what the United States would have been if its people had not crossed the Appalachian Mountains. This can best be illustrated by some figures. In Brazil 89 per cent of the population and an even higher percentage of the railroads and area under cultivation are in the coastal area. In Argentina one-third of the population is in greater Buenos Aires and is increasing relative to the rest of the nation. Montevideo has more than half of Uruguay's population. It is almost a universal rule in Latin American countries that the vast majority of the population occupies a fraction of the area.

Isolation of the provincial town

The impact of mountain, desert and jungle on the history, politics and social organization has been profound. Almost nowhere in Latin America does one meet with human occupancy that covers the countryside and fills in the space between the towns. Quite the contrary, Latin America consists of cities, towns and villages, with no human habitation in between. This is true almost everywhere. Buenos Aires, Quito, Lima, Caracas, are large cities surrounded by a human vacuum. This is true of Cuzco and Arequipa, of Cuenca and Ibara, of Zacatecas and Chihuahua, and of the thousands of smaller towns and villages. The mountains on the Pacific side of Central and South America, and the broken character of the Mexican *altiplano* have all served the same end—to isolate the community, large or small, and shut it off from the nation.

The large city is impressive and dominating. In Mexico, for example, there are over 100,000 little villages. The vast majority do not have more than 400 inhabitants; 99 per cent of all the towns have fewer than 2,000 people. This is a universal phenomenon.

Brazil and Ecuador differ to the extent that each has two large metropolitan centers, and Colombia has nine cities of relatively equal size. Beyond that, we have thousands of provincial capitals, pueblos, villages, large or small, equally isolated from the rest, surrounded by high, almost impassable mountains, cut off from the nation. It has always been that way.

The typical community is a little town of a few houses grouped about a square, with a church, a municipal building, a jail, a few poorly stocked stores. The rest is probably unpaved streets, houses with doors closed and no windows facing the street, a courtyard where the life of the family goes on, where the few animals are kept and where flowers may be grown. The house, isolated from the community, is shut in on itself. So is the town: it is peaceful, quiet, self-conscious and proud. Its contacts with the outside world are limited; it buys little and sells little. The capital of the state or of the nation is a long way off; there is no reason for going there. Most of the things needed are locally produced. The houses are built of local materials, the shoes and clothing locally made, and even now perhaps they are fashioned from hide tanned and cloth woven locally. In the main, the food is locally grown. If it is a large town of, say,

5,000 people it will have a local band. It may have a 4-page weekly newspaper. The big paper from the capital may be received by a few more
sophisticated people. The important institutions will be the town government, the school, and most important of all, the church. These are the
places where the town as a whole gathers.

But the community we have just described is relatively large. Most
inhabited places are much smaller, perhaps under 400. Of the nation and
its politics this little village knows little—the police, the administrator
appointed by the center, the echoes of the occasional political campaign.
And this little village, or larger community, even the provincial capital
lives in a world a thousand miles away from the big city where the President is located. It is almost as if we were dealing with two different
universes.

The capital city has millions of people—Mexico, 2.5 million for the
city proper and 4.5 million for the metropolitan district; Buenos Aires at
5.6 million for the metropolitan district; the municipality of Rio de
Janeiro with about 3,000,000; Lima, over 1,000,000. But the difference is
not merely in size, though that is important. The case of Lima, the capital
of Peru with its million people, is typical. It is not only the largest city,
it is, one might say, the nation. It dominates all other towns. The next
largest city is Arequipa with a little over a hundred thousand, followed by
Trujillo with fifty thousand, Cuzco with another 50,000 and then Huan-
cayo with 40,000. It is worth putting them all down for the lesson they
teach: Icá—29,000, Piura—27,000, Cajemarca, where Atahualpa was
strangled by Pizarro—21,000, Puno—21,000, the recently expanded Chi-
clayo—45,000, and the Amazonian city of Iquitos—about 42,000. That is
all in a population of some 10,000,000 people. The capital is larger than
all of the other cities combined.

If one takes out Brazil, Colombia and Ecuador, this is the case all over
Latin America. And to leave the capital is to leave the center of power,
wealth, education and the sophistication of the modern world. The gap
between Lima and Cuzco, Trujillo or Cajamarca is very wide. But the
contrast between Lima and the thousands of little isolated towns hidden
in mountain crevices and cut off from contact with the outside world is
so great that Lima, in fact, lives in a distinct universe. We are dealing
with one of the basic dilemmas in Latin America. The little town of 100
or 200 families is the typical community. That is where the people live,
not only in Peru but in all Latin America. If one excepts Argentina, and
Uruguay, 50 to 70 per cent or more of the people live in villages. And
this little village in Peru has almost nothing that identifies it with the
modern world. If "nothing" is too strong a word, it has little—very little.
It has no Spanish, for the people speak Quechua; it has no newspaper for
the people are illiterate; it has no books; it may have no school. The
people are barefooted or wear homemade sandals; they sleep on the floor;
they carry their burdens on their own backs; they have no modern tools;

they have few animals. They have retained many of their ancient family customs, such as trial marriage. They may work their land in common if they have any land. In look, manner, attitude and belief, they are not part of the same world as Lima.

The proverbial wisdom of the peasant and the sophisticated knowledge of the elite operate on two different planes, and it is difficult for them to meet. But this is true not only in Peru; it is true in Brazil, in Colombia, in Guatemala, especially perhaps in Guatemala. For in Guatemala the incomprehension, if not the outright hostility, of the *ladino* (mestizo) toward the Indian and his colorful dress and stubborn unyielding ways is very marked indeed.

Regionalism

There is, however, another side to this story. Isolation has given strength to regionalism, a pride in the locality and its ways. Arequipa is "the mother of revolutions." Presidents of Venezuela come from "Táchira." Sucre is the "real" capital of Bolivia. "Cuzco" is the "heart" of Peru. The region has been the source of vitality, and the Latin American nations, it can be said, have been governed not by political parties, but by regions, regional families and regional *caudillos*. A political change has often meant merely that the people from one region have displaced those of another, that the Venezuelan *llanero* has been substituted by the people from the *sierra*, that Rio Grande do Sul has replaced São Paulo, that Guayaquil rather than Quito is ruling Ecuador.

Regionalism is not only political. It is often social, racial, linguistic and economic. In Brazil, Bahía has many elements of a distinctive culture different from that of Rio Grande do Sul. Almost every part of Brazil is conscious of such differences. The language is filled with local words, meanings and accents. In Mexico, the people of Yucatan, Tabasco, Sonora are equally proud of their own ways and scornful of the rest. The important influence has been the region. And this is understandable enough. A place like Arequipa has been isolated from Lima throughout the centuries. Overland, it took about a month, as there were no roads and the mule paths were not made for speed or for a large army; and by sea, after spending three days to get to Mollendo (before the railroads) it would depend upon the good fortune of a boat going north. In Brazil it was easier to go from Belem, at the mouth of the Amazon, to Europe than to Rio de Janeiro. Before airmail it required a minimum of forty days for a letter to Rio de Janeiro from Porto Velho on the upper Madeira River. The distances between Santa Cruz and La Paz in Bolivia are so great and, with the bad roads, so difficult, that there has long been a current of separatism in Santa Cruz.

From the other side of *la montaña* it seems natural to believe that the

outlet is down the rivers to the Atlantic rather than through the jungle
and difficult trails over the Andes to the Pacific. Really heavy traffic from
the Pacific side until only a few years ago, and perhaps even now, in spite
of the new roads, had to round Cape Horn or go through the Panama
Canal to reach either Iquitos or Santa Cruz. And these are merely extreme
examples of what is a daily occurrence.

These regions are not merely physical but in many instances linguistic,
racial and often economic as well, so that the center, i.e., the world where
the capital is located, is really a different and perhaps a hostile world,
where the leaders of the locality have been killed and exiled, where manners, attitudes and ways are so strange as to seem foreign. If one remembers this, then the significance of regionalism becomes clear.

These are different universes and difficult to contain within a single
political frame, and difficult to forge a nation out of or to develop a party
system in—or even a common idea. *Caciquismo*—local bossism bent on
looking after its own, with all of the possible variations for local tyranny
and injustice—has this virtue, that it is local. The people can identify
with it against the center and follow the local leadership against the national government just because it belongs to the locality, and the local
leader, no matter how repugnant or terrible he may look to the "civilized," sophisticated and educated in Mexico City, Bogotá, Caracas or
Lima, has the support of the locality. I am speaking of the past, not the
distant years of long ago, but of the days before the airplane and radio
communication, when the center was much farther away and much less
well informed, and when the locality and its leadership were not only a
political but a military threat, and socially felt "superior" to the center
and its leaders. But this is not very long ago, and when the regions get
their tempers up—as illustrated by Colombia in recent years and to some
extent still evident—the natural difficulties can still make the region con-
fident and the center fearful and uncertain. All of this merely points to
greater instability on the part of the national government than would
appear even under the best of conditions.

One could, of course, speak of Texas, California, the South and New
England as illustrative of the point—except that one does not see Texas
marching on Washington to place a Texan hero in the presidential chair,
either before or after an election. And that is what has happened a thousand times in Latin America. The national energy and turbulence have
come from the locality, the group, the region, the state—and this region
was often both political, economic, social, and geographic. This, however, is still only part of the story of the meaning of internal isolation.
We must not see Mexico, Peru or Guatemala, as a large capital, with a
number of smaller but comparable cities. It is very much more accurate
to see Mexico as a country of over a hundred thousand neighborhoods,
i.e. *pueblos, caseríos, ranchos,* etc., with an average of fewer than 400
people, with more than 50,000 hamlets having fewer than that, and to

recognize that each of these little pueblos is a self-contained world, separated, if not cut off, from the rest by a thousand elements that isolate them from each other.

I remember on a market day standing in the doorway of a grocery store in one of the larger towns of Chiapas as the Indians were coming into market carrying their burdens on their backs, and the owner of the store remarked as each one passed, "Tlajobal," "Chamula," "Matananguero." "How do you know?" I asked. "Oh, by their hats." That was true. Each one that passed had a different hat. He wore the hat of his community; all the people in the village wore the same kind of hat. All the Indian women in the villages of Guatemala wear a waist specially colored and designed and with a special cut. No such waist is worn by any other woman of any other village, and wherever a woman may be, she is known by her waist as belonging to a certain village.

But most of all, the individual living in one of these communities belongs to a society and is related through an extended family which will include almost every member of the community. For not only are the families large and have intermarried with each other generation after generation, but the system of *compadrazgo* (godfather, godmother relationship) will effectively have tied people together in such a way that in smaller communities (and most of them are small) the individual is part of a beehive where the community acts, feels and thinks as a group. As one man explained the difference between his and a neighboring village, "Say the children, say the women, say the men, says the whole village." The *pueblo* belongs to the individual and he to it.

These villagers have not migrated to other villages, because they would be strangers; they would have neither house nor land, neither family nor friends, and they would find the customs different. In fact, they might not be allowed to stay. I have heard reports of cases within the last years of villages in Guatemala, Colombia and Bolivia where strangers were encouraged to leave before nightfall. The rural community (and in most of the countries under consideration, over 50 per cent of the population lives in little communities) may outnumber the larger cities by a hundred to one. The world we are talking about lacks integration, and not just politically. And this picture of separation, regionalism and localism to be complete has to include the fact that the hacienda, which occupies so large a place in the Latin American scene, is almost completely autochthonous. It not only keeps, if it can, its people from moving from one place to another, but its people stay out of the local and regional market, for the hacienda has its own store, and sometimes its own coinage.

It must be evident to the reader that the centrifugal forces are more active than the centripetal. The capital city with its centralization notwithstanding, the making of a nation has proved more difficult than the proclamation of nationalism as a credo and a policy. This is even true in Argentina.

The Limits of the Conquest

If isolation is one of the keys to an understanding of Latin America, the character of the Spanish conquest is another. The emphasis is upon conquest rather than colonization or settlement. If by conquest we mean total submission to a conqueror, it was never fully accomplished. In Northern Mexico, the war against the Apaches went on into the late nineteenth century; so too the war against Indians in Argentina; and in Chile the Araucanians were not united with the Republic until the middle eighties of the last century. But even today there are numerous Indian groups in the high mountains such as the Huichol, or the Lacandón in the jungle in Mexico, or the Indians on the Upper Magdalena River in Colombia, that are continuously warring against the white man exploring the area for oil, the Auca Indians in Ecuador who recently murdered three white missionaries on the Napo River, the Brazilian Indians who attacked the parties stretching telegraph lines through the interior of the country, and other small groups too numerous to mention who are beyond the reach of the nation.

The point to remember is that conquest did not mean effective occupancy everywhere, and that Spanish colonial government and society had an unincorporated frontier which not even the Jesuit or Franciscan missionaries were always successful in penetrating. Here is an area where Spanish influence is minimal, where neither the Spanish language nor the Spanish nor modern republican government have established themselves. This is also the case with the Church, though the Church has penetrated further than other European institutions brought over by the conqueror.

But more important to the history and development of Latin America has been the failure of the ideal of the Spanish crown to convert the Indian in America to a good European on the Spanish model. The conquest was neither settlement, nor colonization, nor effective occupancy except as military outposts, as gatherers of tribute, as managers of mines, as owners of plantations, as government officials, or as a Church hierarchy. The failure to colonize is understandable, and Spanish achievement is of heroic proportions.

The Indian

The difficulty of terrain was much greater than in the United States. But that was of lesser importance than the presence of millions of human beings already on the land. The surprise of the European at the variety of peoples and cultures and their incredible, almost enchanted forms, as if they were of another world, as if they were especially moulded to serve the devil, as many of the Spaniards believed, could not have been greater than the surprise of the Indians. For to the Indians these were creatures come from Heaven—gods possessed of magical powers. Between these two races no effective means of understanding, no moral basis of accommodation, was found by the Spaniard, or by his Latin American successors. These races met as billiard balls do: they met but did not penetrate. The one exception was the Catholic missions. It was only there that the Indian prospered and multiplied. Everywhere else he was troubled by disease, mistreatment, and most of all perhaps by the strange ways and expectancies of his conquerors. The missions had relatively a marginal role in the total enterprise and an unhappy ending.

For the rest of the story of the relations between the Spaniard, better perhaps between the European, and the Indian has been one of incessant attrition. The Indian proved stubborn and unyielding, and Spanish colonial policies in some measure insulated the Indian from the disintegrating influences of the conquistador and his heirs.

The complicated history of colonial legislation and administration cannot be considered here. Sufficient for the purpose at hand is to say that wherever the Indian managed to retain his land and his own community, he remained an Indian, keeping his language, his customs, his family organization, his religious rituals even if he became a Catholic, using the same tools, working the land much the same way as before the conquest, eating the same food and living in the same kind of house. The Spanish influence was important enough. It deprived the Indian of his leadership, of his learned men, of his old idols and old priests, of his men of science, of his government, of his faith in himself as a man. It imposed on him tribute, services and demands for labor which proved damaging and led to a decline of the Indian population during the colonial period. Letters from the viceroys of Peru are filled with the repeated prognostications that the Indian *"se está acabando,"* is disappearing.

But in those places where he lived in his own community, if he survived at all, he remained an Indian in his ways and attitudes. In some degree, but less so, the Indians incorporated into a hacienda, and retaining some form of community organization and collective responsibilities, also survived as Indians. Only where the natives were drawn into the urban centers, into mining towns, into cities as servants and individual workers, or where they learned European skills, did they cease to be Indians. The Spanish conquest found in the Indian population a barrier which it never fully overcame. A cultural community is more resilient than a forest. The American pioneer could fell his trees and clear his lands, because on the whole the country was empty. In Latin America all of the seemingly occupiable land was already filled, and the people on it continued to till it as they had before, for a European master, or to pay him tribute, but continued Indians in all of their language and ways. They would not learn to be good Europeans, not even if they were beaten or had their ears cut off. They obeyed their new masters because they had no choice. They did his services, but closed in on themselves and became silent, with bowed heads, with no claims on anyone—except, if possible, to be left alone. The result was a nation within a nation, a culture within a culture, two people living in proximity but belonging to two different universes.

A contemporary Ecuadorian historian describes what happened to the Indian in the following words: "The psychological resistance of the Indian to the Spaniard was and remains to this day in his repugnance to the assimilation of the white man's civilization, one of the most extraordinary phenomena in human history. This resistance has lasted for ages . . . and has the frightening implication of collective suicide." (Pareja)

This is not the entire story. There were, as there always are, notable exceptions. But the Spanish conquest did not change the Indian into a good European on the Spanish model nor has he become a good Latin American. Anyone who will take the trouble can see this today easily in Guatemala. The Indian in Chichicastenango, or in San Miguel Acatlan, is not a white man, does not want to be one, and disciplines those of his members who are too friendly or try to ape white men. The few white men govern and collect taxes and exploit the Indians as they can. But there is no friendship between them, no understanding, and in spite of proximity, in spite of the fact that both the Indian and the *ladino* (white man) have taken over from each other certain cultural traits, like the tortilla on one side and the European chicken or sheep on the other, they are not intermingling socially; they are not intermarrying, and the process of amalgamation between the two races has in Indian areas probably declined. And the Indian is in all probability increasing more rapidly than the more urbanized population.

What we have are two nations and two cultures and here, as in Peru, Ecuador and Bolivia, the Indian is in the majority—regardless of what the official statistics say. The statistics, to repeat Luis Alberto Sánchez, are poetry. And this problem of the Indian in varying degrees is well nigh universal. It was eliminated in Argentina in 1879 by what can only be described as extermination under a military campaign by General Julio A. Roca. In Uruguay and Costa Rica it is practically non-existent. But in most of the continental countries there are smaller or larger groups that do not identify with the ruling elements of the nation.

When one asks for an explanation of the difficulties in any one of the Andean countries, or in Central America and Mexico, one of the answers is that they are not homogeneous nations. No one knows how many Indians there are in Latin America. Figures have been given that vary between 14 and 30 million. It depends upon the definition of who is an Indian. If an Indian who learns to say a few words in Spanish is no longer counted an Indian, you get one result. If race rather than language is used, then you get another. The point to remember is that the population in Latin America has doubled in the last thirty years, and the Indian population has also doubled. We can now see that racially the conquest has left the modern countries a heritage which they have found difficult to deal with.

In failing to integrate the Indian, Spain also failed to make the Spanish tongue the universal medium of communication. It was a very great achievement to have spread the Castilian tongue over so vast an area and to have made it possible for the people in Chile to feel at home in the language spoken in Mexico. But this achievement again has fallen short of its ideal aim. The Indian does not speak Spanish, or if he has picked up some Spanish words, he does not use them at home. The women usually know less of the white man's language than do the men; and the farther we get away from the big city, the provincial capital, the county seat, the less is Spanish the language of the people. In Mexico, according to the 1950 census, 30 per cent of the people were Indian who spoke a hundred languages, if one can take the census figures at their face value.

We really have no adequate picture of the effective reach of Spanish and therefore no real understanding of the political, social and cultural difficulties that face these nations. Our preoccupation with the big city and its many ramifications has blinded North and South Americans to the complexity of the culture south of the United States.

That culture is not only Latin but also American. And American means Indian—and Indian means non-European not only in race and language but in a thousand other things as well. That the Latin will ultimately absorb the American has been taken for granted from the beginning, which is more than four centuries ago. And so it may prove in the end, but the end is a long way off, and history has shown itself capable of many an unexpected turn.

The mestizo

This brings us to the mestizo. The mestizo, the child of a European father and an Indian mother, is the most important by-product of the Spanish conquest. For this child of Europe and America has taken over the leadership of Latin America. The president of the country, the member of the Cabinet, the general of the army, the artist like Diego Rivera, the novelist like Ciro Alegría, or Machado de Assis, the politician, business man, university professor, is likely to be a mestizo.

While Argentina, Uruguay and Central Chile are classified as white, the dominant European immigration in these countries is of the middle of the nineteenth century or later. Until then the population was predominantly mestizo, and the mixed strain has not entirely disappeared. And as one goes from Buenos Aires to Tucumán, Salta and Jujuy, the

Indian strain becomes more and more evident. Taking Latin America as a whole, where the Indian has disappeared or declined in numbers, the mestizo, the Negro and mulatto have taken his place. It is, I think, a safe generalization that the mestizo is the dominant influence in Latin America. This is a remarkable achievement. For the mestizo is a new race, non-existent at the time of the discovery and looked upon with suspicion and hostility throughout the three centuries of colonial rule. The colonial governments, the Spaniards and the criollos treated the mestizo as an inferior human being, described him as undependable, as possessing the bad characteristics of the Spaniard and Indian, as lazy, vagabond, unstable and untrustworthy. And in fact more than one Latin American sociologist, as for instance Bunge, in the early part of this century ascribed Latin America's political and social shortcomings to the racial hybrid and saw little hope for the future. They repeated the estimate of the Spanish viceroys who deplored the presence of the mestizo as a disturbing element, as difficult to discipline.

Whatever the objective merits of this judgment, the fact remains that this being who came into the world (usually outside the marriage bond, though in the days of the conquest there were some notable cases of marriage between conquistadors and Incaic "Princesses" in Peru), who was abandoned by his father and raised by his mother, was neither Indian nor Spaniard. He grew up in a world of unstable values, where his mother and father lived in different cultures, had different standards, different notions of good and right, and different basic loyalties. He had no tradition, no invariable rules, no place in the community comparable with his ambitions. For here he differed from the Indian who wished only to be left alone in his little village; the mestizo aspired to the role of his father, the European, the criollo. The wars of independence gave him his first opportunity to play a role on the public stage and gave him a footing on the social and economic ladder. (An exception must be made for Brazil, where the Bandeirantes played an important role in the development of the country.) The mestizo was the soldier, the corporal and sergeant, the subordinate official. It was only after the wars of independence, whose chief leaders were criollos, that the mestizo began to rise from petty official to colonel and general.

The turbulence and the civil wars that tore Latin America apart for a century provided him with the opportunity to assert his leadership. A glance at the figures who played the dominant political roles before 1850 and after the mid-century is revealing. The mestizo had established his dominance in government and politics, had risen in social status, had repudiated his Indian heritage and taken over criollo and European ways and had done it all by the skin of his teeth. The turbulence, the instability, are in one sense the evidence and the means of the change that was taking place in this child of two races which never came to understand or appreciate each other. The mestizo in time replaced both races in the exercise of political power, in wealth and in the practice of the civilizing arts. Where he reached for status and worldly goods, he did so largely at the expense of the Indian and at the price of increasing the gap that separates the two groups. The so-called liberal revolutions in Mexico, Guatemala, Ecuador and generally throughout the area, which ended in the defeat of the criollo oligarchy that had survived the independence and that stripped the Church of its lands, endowed the mestizo with worldly goods.

He became the master of the Indian and the owner of land. He acquired land taken from the Church, and now as general, governor, cacique, president, he married into the older oligarchy and replaced it as the dominant figure, not only in politics but in rural wealth as well. The liberal revolutions in the mid-century and later, as the one in Guatemala in 1871, tended to give the Indian equality before the law but it did not change his social status or increase his economic opportunities, and as in Mexico it weakened his ability to defend his communal lands against the expanding hacienda. Nor did these changes bring the Indian and mestizo closer together. In fact, it increased the distance between them, and the mestizo took over the prejudice of the criollo against the Indian as an inferior being. So that now, as one American anthropologist has said of a certain part of Guatemala, it is "completely improbable" for a marriage between an Indian and a mestizo to take place. And this statement for a particular community in Guatemala can be generalized for the Indian areas as a whole. The Indian, to achieve social status among mestizos, must first shed his language, his clothes, his ways, his occupation, his family and his community—a difficult venture at best.

The Negro

The Negro, like the Indian and mestizo, has a special place and a unique role in the Latin American complex, and is one of the essential keys to an understanding of the area. Of the 12,000,000 or more Negroes transported by slave traders to the Western Hemisphere in the 350 years between 1500 and 1850, a large proportion went to what are now the Latin American nations. In greater or lesser numbers they were to be found in every part of the area from Chile to Cuba. Next to Haiti, the largest proportion probably went to Brazil, though Cuba was a close second. There are certain general features of Negro occupancy in Latin America which have influenced both the economic as well as the social development of Latin America. For one thing, the slave filled in those areas where the Indian disappeared shortly after European arrival, or was so intractable that Negro labor was used instead. As a general rule the Negro did not play an important role in those parts of Latin America where the Indian survived in large numbers, and that was usually in areas of sedentary agriculture. The Negro survived and prospered best in tropical parts of America, and these were largely coastal lowlands. The Negro was mainly used in the cultivation of sugar, cacao and other crops that do well in warm moist climates.

The Negroes were purchased as *individuals* by European masters and were therefore closer to and more dependent on the white man. In fact, they were present in the early Spanish expeditions and, though slaves, were in some ways treated as superior to the Indian and were used occasionally as foremen or overseers where Negro and Indian labor were found together. Unlike the Indian, who proved extremely recalcitrant, the Negro was malleable and culturally receptive. He acquired European language, religion, dress, food and habits with surprising speed, and has in those countries where he is numerically important become a significant influence in the economic, political, and notably in the cultural life of the countries he resides in. He has, as the Indian has not, become culturally a European; and in Brazil, Cuba, Venezuela and Panama, important in literature, music, art, and architecture. Notably so has this been the case in Brazil where some of the greatest figures in the arts, music and literature have been mulattoes and Negroes.

The Indian had no natural and trusted spokesman and interpreter acceptable to the large community, whereas the Negro had many of them. The Negro felt at home in some subtle sense even while he was a slave— as the reading of the literature will reveal. The Indian has never felt at home with the white man and does not do so today. But there are other historical influences which help explain the accommodation of the Negro within the Latin American community in a way that has not happened among us.

The Negro slave brought into the Iberian peninsula as early as 1442 fitted into a society where slavery was still in existence. As a result of the many centuries of warfare with the Moors, if not for other reasons, it had remained a traditional feature of the Spanish society to accept slavery as normal, while it had long since died out in Western Europe. At the time the Negro was brought to Spain, there were Moorish slaves, Jewish slaves and Spaniards as slaves. Prisoners taken in battle could be held for ransom or could be held as slaves, and the laws allowed other reasons for slavery. The important point is that there was a slave law, an elaborate code embodied as part of the *Siete Partidas* going back to Alfonso the Wise (1252-1284) which endowed the slave with a legal personality, with duties and with rights. The slave was known to the law as a human being; he could marry; he could buy his freedom; he could change his master if he found one to purchase him; he could under certain conditions testify in court even against his master. And if a slave became a priest, he had to give his master one slave, but if he became a bishop, he had to give him two slaves.

The Negro brought over from Africa became the beneficiary of this body of law. He was not merely a slave, a chattel under West Indian and American colonial codes, but also a human being with rights enforceable in the king's court. The Negro under Iberian conditions was also converted to the Catholic faith and the master had to see to it that he came to church. While the Catholic doctrine did not oppose slavery as such, it asserted that master and slave were equal in the sight of God; that what mattered was the moral and religious character of man and that the master must treat his slaves as moral beings, as brothers in Christ. It also emphasized the merits of manumission. The Negroes in the Spanish and Portuguese colonies were the inheritors of this legal and religious tradition. It is not suggested that slavery was not cruel; that in Brazil, Cuba, Venezuela or Peru abominable and inhuman acts were not committed against Negro slaves; that they were not chained and beaten. But cruelty was against the law, and unusual punishment could be brought before the court by a recognized legal protector of the slave, and the killing of a slave was treated as murder. The entire atmosphere was different, and manumission was so frequent that there were often more freed Negroes than there were slaves.

The fact that the slave had both a legal personality and a moral status made manumission natural, and the abolition of slavery no great shock. The question of the slave's fitness for freedom never arose, and the freed Negro was a free man, not a freedman. He was legally the equal of all other free men. And when slavery was abolished in Brazil the crowd in the galleries threw flowers upon the members of the Congress, and the people danced all night in the streets of Rio de Janeiro. The question of segregation, so agonizing and so disturbing in our own South, could never have arisen anywhere in Latin America—neither with the Negro nor with the Indian. And this tradition in Latin America makes it most difficult for them to understand our problem or our way of dealing with it.

Racial prejudice

This does not mean there is no racial prejudice in Latin America. It exists against both the Indian and the Negro, but it is a prejudice which has no sanction in the law. It is social and economic and cultural. It is determined more by social status than by a sense that people of color are inferior in nature—though this feeling exists particularly about the Indian. But any Indian, and any mulatto, if he can escape from his poverty, if he can acquire the graces, the language, the manners, the dress, the schooling and the associations that will admit him into the best society, will have no insuperable difficulties socially, especially if he is wealthy, and will, if he has it in him, be elected to Congress, be a member of the Cabinet or become president of the country. The fact that he is an Indian or a mulatto will not bar him—and there are numerous instances of mulattoes and a few of Indians who have risen to the highest or to very high posts politically. In that sense there is no race prejudice. The case is different for the pure black man—in some countries at least, Peru for instance, or Ecuador, or Colombia, or Venezuela—or perhaps even Cuba, and even in Brazil, the pure black man has not, perhaps could not, rise to the highest political post, or really be accepted by the "best" social set. That is the difference between Latin American racial conditions and our own.

There is something else that needs adding. The opportunities for wealth, education, professional advancement as doctors or lawyers, and for active politics (outside of the South) is very much greater among us in the United States than in Latin America. True enough, this advancement economically and professionally takes place mostly, though by no means entirely, within the colored community. But the way to opportunity is not closed—neither in the arts, nor in the professions, nor in education, nor in opportunities to distinction. The road is narrow and steep —but there is a road. In contrast, in Latin America the road does not exist. This is too strong a way to put it. Perhaps it would be more accurate to say that the door is shut but not locked. The gap between the "lower" classes, between not only the Indian and the Negro poor, but between just the poor, just the illiterate, just the children of the little rural hut that I saw in Cundinamarca and the elite in Bogotá, or between the Hauasipongo on a hacienda in Ecuador and the traveled sophisticated literary people in Quito, is so wide that it is almost unbridgeable. That is in part because the countries are poor, the wealthy families fewer and the poor more numerous.

But I think there is something else and that is the hierarchical structure (the aristocratic tradition, the basic authoritarian character of the society, the essentially caste-like form of the way people are grouped and identified, and the paternal concept that the poor must always be poor, that the servant must always remain a servant) has set a division in the culture between the "upper" and the "lower" that is very great indeed. Never in the history of the United States has there been such a distance, such a seemingly impossible distance, between our poorest farmer or immigrant and the wealthiest and most self-conscious of our aristocracy—if that word has any real meaning in our culture. This difference I am noting is obviously not racial, not biological, not the color of skin, nor origin— but it is perhaps even more effective as a dividing line, and perhaps more permanent. It is an ingrained part of the total scheme of things.

But we are fooling ourselves—and Latin Americans who speak as if this were not the case are also fooling themselves—if we or they think that what we call democracy is a thing of formal law and constitutional enactment. It has as a background a feeling of equality, or perhaps egalitarianism, "where a man is a man for all that," where no man rides a high horse, and is not expected to ride one. At this point American and Latin

American society stand wide apart. And the difference socially at this level of discourse between the basic conditions of social equality and opportunity in the United States and Latin America are broad and deep —and not really changeable for a long time to come.

We can at this point turn from race to religion as another key to the culture we are trying to understand.

RELIGION

The American Indian at the time of the discovery was a profoundly religious and mystical human being. A great part of his daily existence was bound up in religious rites, in propitiating his many gods, in finding grace, justification and peace. Every act had its religious significance; every wind, every change in the color of the moon, every appearance of the unexpected had its religious portent. In the highly developed cultures such as the Aztec and the Inca, a large priesthood served to interpret the will of the gods, and a profound mystic philosophy and a questioning of the essence of human existence informed and disciplined their attitude toward life and death.

The Spanish conquest was insensible to the spiritual and moral values that ruled the lives of the American Indians. The conquistador, whatever his virtues of courage and fealty, was no philosopher, no mystic; and he was obtuse—in most cases—to the values inherent in this strange world he found himself in.

The greatest shock to the American Indian civilization was the complete denial of its existence by the soldiers of Spain, a denial manifest in indifference or in brutal destruction of ancient gods, their objects of worship and their temples; pulling the gold off the walls in the Temple to the Sun in Cuzco was merely one of a thousand instances of an irreverence for the spirit of a culture that centered in its religion. And in destroying the religious temples and the religious leaders the soul of Indian civilization was also destroyed. Its values, its beliefs, its pattern of existence and its great art and artists were scattered by the wind that blew across the ocean.

What was left of the Indian as a human being with a belief in God and the burden of the sudden tragedy that had overtaken his world, found refuge in the Christian Church. That is the true meaning of the conversion of millions of Indians in so short a time. The Catholic Church saved what meaning there was left to existence, after all had been taken from him by men he could not understand and whose motives were completely incomprehensible to him. And in the Church the Indian could rebuild a faith in the forces that govern the world, that bring day and night, sunshine and rain, life and death. And the Church wisely built where the old temples were, and the saints in the Church gave the Indian full scope for his attachment to a particular mystery, a special symbol, a unique identity with the forces that lay beyond human reach and were all powerful. The Church did something in addition. It in some way brought the conqueror and the conquered into the same Church. It gave the Indian identity with the European, a sense that they were both mortal, and gave the conquistador a conscience that he was dealing with human beings who had souls and who were inside his Church and children of the same God as himself. It required a papal bull to make that point for the conquistador. For the strangeness of American culture, the ways of the Indians, the bitterness of the conquest, and the belief in the devil working his evil designs through strange beings made it easy to deny to the Indian his claim to human fellowship.

The Church was the Indian's salvation here and now by giving him a place where he could feel free in spirit, and where he could reweave the threads that had always bound him to the world beyond his immediate senses—and that service the Church has continued to perform for the Indian through the centuries that have changed both the original zeal of the early friars and raised problems and difficulties of a political and social nature. But these are secondary to the great spiritual role in the life of the Indian, that of giving a meaning to existence in a world ruled by men who have remained strange and incomprehensible.

It is useful in trying to unravel the mysteries of Latin American culture to remember that during the colonial period the Church ruled while the State governed. While the State in its paternal preoccupation was meddling with the public and material aspects of life, the Church ruled the most intimate and personal needs and preoccupations of the individual, from the cradle to the grave and beyond. The Church in the large city, small town, village, and even on the pathway over the mountains was ever present, for there would be a cross or small chapel at every difficult passage, at the top of every hill one climbed. The Church was everywhere— even when the priest was absent. But so it had been before the conquest and before the white man. Every mountain, every stream, every strange and marvelous thing (and to the unpretentious, the humble and the pious, simple things are marvelous and strange) had its own *huaco* (shrine, holy place) and continued to have it in the new faith by identification with a favorite and miraculous saint.

The Church was everywhere and with every individual all of his life and filled all of his days. The day began with early morning Mass and ended with an Ave Maria, and every occasion, every sorrow, every joy, every holiday had its own special religious symbolism to be acted out in church. During the colonial period the Church was also the school, the university, the hospital, the home of the aged, the sick and the abandoned. It served the individual and the community in many ways. In the absence of newspapers, libraries, museums, theaters, the religious exercise and ritualism in the churches, the orders, the monasteries and the convents filled the role of giving the individual his place in an enchanted and meaningful world. And everything that happened from a bull fight to the arrival of a new Viceroy, an earthquake, or the king's birthday always required public manifestation, processions, prayers, masses and sermons in which the Church was active, perhaps the chief actor in the drama, or better, the chief embodiment of the symbolism that endowed every activity with meaning. It surrounded life at all turns and all times. The church or cathedral bell dominated the community, and daily life was disciplined and ordered to its sound.

In cities like Lima, Quito, Mexico, the church buildings, the monasteries dominated all buildings, and the profession of priest or membership in an order, belonging to a monastery or convent, was a high calling and a privilege. The few diaries that have come down from the colonial period reveal preoccupation with the ever present Church. The daily record is filled with religious processions, with the celebration of the saint's day in this or that monastery, church, convent, or ward, with gossip, scandal and even riot, because of the great popular interest in the election of a prior or prioress in monastery and convent.

The independence movement brought so many difficulties to the Church that it has not to this day fully recovered from them. For one thing the hierarchy being largely Spanish were less friendly to the independence movement than the lower clergy. And as a result the American churches were to considerable extent without bishops during and for a period after the conflict was over. And during the conflict the Papacy sided with Spain against the independence because of the pressure of the powerful Spanish Embassy in Rome. After all, Spain had been the great Defender of the Faith since the Reformation. The ideas of the French Revolution which were not unknown or unspoken in Latin America made the claims of Spanish sovereignty also seem on the side of justice, morality and faith.

The resulting rift between the American leadership and Rome was aggravated by the claim of the new governments to the rights of the patronage which had been exercised by the Spanish Crown and by the insistence of the Church that the patronage had been personal with the king and that now when the king was gone from America the Church was free. This question remains in fact unsettled and variously compromised in different countries.

But more serious perhaps than the above was the struggle that emerged between Church and State when the new governments attempted to pattern themselves on French and American constitutional precepts. It became evident, and quickly, that trouble lay ahead for the Church from the modern State with its claim to the control of education, to the equal enforcement of the same law against all citizens; with its opposition to corporate privileges, i.e., *fueros,* in a special law enforceable in ecclesiastical courts; and with its opposition to exemption from taxation of the

Church for its properties. In fact, the revolutionary lawyers trained in the Roman law and imbued with French anti-clericalism on one side, and the priests traditionally identified with the corporate Church and its claims on the individual on the other, found it most difficult to abide in the same world. The quarrel between the anti-clerical lawyer steeped in concepts of absolute sovereignty and the priest, who looked upon all matters that might touch the soul and affect human salvation as the special responsibility of the Church, ended in a conflict often bitter and bloody. And the lawyer won the battle. The Church in most countries lost its land, its wealth, its monopoly over education, its censorship over the literature and the press, over the hospitals, over public charity, over the universities, over marriage (for civil marriage became legal), over the registration of birth, over the burial grounds and over the right to exclude other faiths from the country. It came out of the struggle much poorer, much less influential, and in most places on the defensive against continuing threats to its remaining power.

A hundred years of conflict have gradually attenuated the bitterness, and the Church has recovered a measure of the prestige it had lost by taking sides in recent years against the dictatorship in Argentina, Colombia, Venezuela and less openly in Cuba. It has also taken a definite position on behalf of land reform and has slowly come to voice the social doctrines expressed in the *Rerum Novarum* of Pope Leo XIII and most recently in the *Mater et Magister* of Pope John XXIII. In some measure the Church's political position is therefore better than it has been since independence. It is more independent of the State and perhaps closer to the social movement sweeping Latin America than it was a few years ago. But these changes vis-à-vis the State and public policy have had little to do with the role of the Church as a religious institution. The people have remained Catholic, and the Latin-American anti-clerical often dies in the faith, is married in church and his children are baptized as if he had never fallen under the influence of French philosophers or the more recent Marxists.

The role of the Church in Latin America is therefore very different from what it is in the United States. There is personal or family identity with the favorite saint which to this day has a quality of intimacy. The city, the town, has its patron or patroness: Santa Rosa in Lima, the Virgin of Guadalupe in Mexico, etc. Every parish in turn has a saint of its own: St. Francis, St. Dominic, St. John. All guilds—the goldsmiths, the seamen, the carpenters—used to have their own saints with their own *corfradia* inside the church, their own chapel in their corner. Every large hacienda had, and mostly still has, a chapel or sometimes a church—which occasionally connects with the main house, so that one goes from one part of the house to the other by passing through the chapel. And this chapel has its own saint that in some intimate way belongs to the family. He is the family patron who looks after its members and protects them. His name is invoked on every occasion. He has a familiar presence in family affairs as if he were a living member of it—and the children are baptized and married inside this family chapel and in the presence of the family patron. And in this chapel the members of the family used to be buried. The patron of the plantation is the patron of the plantation community, and the entire life of the plantation community is lived and in some measure ordered by the sound of the chapel bell. This is true of the smaller towns, the smaller cities and to some extent of the larger ones.

Not so much as a hundred years ago, travelers tell of the cathedral bells in Quito ringing for vespers and the entire city becoming quiet, the people kneeling down in the streets, taking off their hats and saying their prayers. But in essence it is still true—more of the women than of the men, of the unsophisticated, the poor, the illiterate (much more for these than the others), and it is true for the country folk and for the Indians very much indeed.

This personal sense of intimacy with the mysteries is seen in the family in another way. Each member old or young has a patron saint. The big occasion is not the birthday but the saint's day after whom the child was named—St. Francis, St. John, St. Peter, St. Katherine—depending on the name one received when baptized. The day is like Christmas. It begins with going to mass with one's friends, all in their best dresses. There are presents, music, visits. It lasts all day and sometimes with dancing late into the night. As the families are large, there are numerous occasions for such festivities, for each member of the family; for each of the grandparents, the parents, the children, and the grandchildren has his own particular patron saint who when his day arrives is celebrated in a similar fashion. Then there are the numerous first, second, third and fourth cousins, the aunts and uncles, the school friends, the companions and associates in business or the professions and last but not least, the "compadre"—the godfathers and godchildren—and these may literally run into the dozens. The life of the family and of the individual is greatly and continuously involved with the Church.

This is the most continuing influence in the life of the individual, especially as one gets away from the large urban center. It begins at birth and terminates only in the burial ground. One must not exaggerate the implications of this relationship of the individual, the family and the community to the Church. But one need be careful not to underestimate it. It gives life a certain quality and adds something to the meaning of daily activities which is lacking in our community—for going to church is not just a Sunday affair—it is a part of daily life. And the priest and the bishop are present on every important occasion—personal, family or community. There are few gatherings of intellectuals where some member of a religious order does not take an active part. And there are certainly few public affairs where the members of the Church are not active participants. This participation is uneven and varies with the community, but there is added colorfulness and solemnity. And a certain emphasis upon eternal verities on even the least religious occasions is added by the presence of Franciscan or Dominican brothers, or when the Bishop of Ibara takes part in a conference on history and illustrates a point in popular folklore by playing the song on a piano.

THE HACIENDA

The hacienda plays a special role in Latin America. It would be no exaggeration to say that the hacienda, or as it is known in Brazil, the *fazenda,* set the tone and determined the quality of Latin American culture during the nineteenth and early part of the twentieth century, until the First World War and in some instances (as in Ecuador, Chile and Peru, and in spite of appearances in Argentina and other areas) until the present. This is not an argument for unitary causation. There are also the Spanish tradition, the presence of the Indian and the Negro, the broad influence of the Church and the impact of the larger world to consider. But we are dealing with an area where in most places over one half of the population is rural, and until very recently the rural proportion was much larger. We are also dealing with an area where the typical holding is in large units. The United Nations estimated in 1951 that 1½ per cent of the total land holdings in lots of over 15,000 acres are equal to half the agricultural land. Some of these are very extensive indeed. There were plantations in Mexico of a million acres, and there are similar units in Brazil and in other countries. And one family may have a number of agricultural units of large acreage scattered over the country.

It is not the size of the hacienda that is in question, but its organization. Before entering into a discussion of the hacienda as such, it is useful to note that at least in the Andean countries and in Central America and Mexico we are dealing with two distinctive agricultural systems: the hacienda and the village community. In Guatemala, for instance, the hacienda will have the valley, the slopes and rolling hills, the best agricultural lands, while the Indian villages will occupy the steep mountains, the inaccessible areas and the poor soil. This was true in Mexico; it is true in Ecuador and in Peru. In fact, the hacienda has the best agricultural lands, and the Indian or mestizo villages the poorest. The village may be communal, following an older Indian tradition, or it may have adopted every possible variation that lies between collective and individual ownership.

But the village is a community with its own local traditional government, and the closer one gets to an Indian community the truer this is, and this village government is participated in by the entire male population. It looks after the public works, the policing and the roads; it builds a school in common, if there is a school, and cares for the church. Each individual as he grows up has in turn to share in the various tasks that the community requires. In the case of Amatanango in the State of Chiapas, Mexico, as an example, each boy begins as a messenger for the town government, takes his turn in time as one of the policemen, and after satisfying all the required offices in the civil government and in the church, ends up as an *"anciano,"* one of the elders who govern the community as a council. The Indian and the mestizo village is a community, with its own collective personality. Each member has a recognized place of his own and a defined relation to all the others. He is a participant in government and church because he has regular functions to perform in both. This village may be next to a hacienda, and there are instances where the village somehow survived surrounded by a hacienda.

Generally speaking, however, the rural world divides sharply—the hacienda in the valley and the village on the steep mountain sides. Between these two agricultural organizations there has always been friction, the hacienda encroaching upon the village, absorbing its woods, pastures, water supply; and the village every now and then rising in rebellion, protesting, going to court. The story is an old one and goes back to the early days after the conquest when the Indians crowded the offices of the Spanish officials asking for protection against the hacendado who was encroaching upon their lands.

After independence, the Indians were less able to find protection against the neighboring hacienda. The history of rural land holdings since independence is one where in the name of liberalism, equality and individual rights the Indian was increasingly dispossessed of his lands in favor of the hacienda. The struggle against the Church by the new national governments tended to increase the size of the hacienda and the power and prestige of its owner. The little villages during the same period decreased in number, size and significance. Where they expanded—in relatively small number and isolated areas, as in Southern Chile, Southern Brazil, and some places in Argentina—they had little bearing on the general trend in rural organization. The private hacienda had carried everything before it.

The hacienda is not just an agricultural property owned by an individual. It is a society, under private auspices. The hacienda governs the life of those attached to it from the cradle to the grave, and greatly influences all of the rest of the country. It is economics, politics, education, social structure and industrial development. It is a curious fact in Latin American intellectual life that the hacienda, which is so all embracing in its influence is, except for an occasional novel, never written about or seriously studied. It is, or was, so taken for granted that the intellectuals who were mostly the children of a hacienda were not conscious of its existence—like the air we breathe. When the Latin American sociologist looked for something to write about he worried about the unemployed in

London or about the new sugar or banana plantation in foreign hands.
The hacienda, which was the basis of the politics of the country as a
whole, he was hardly aware of.

The hacienda as a society may be described by saying that it was—and
is—an economic and social system that seeks to achieve self-sufficiency or
autarchy on a local scale. It seeks this not as a matter of malice, but in
the logic of a given institution to expand so as to have within its own
borders all that it needs, salt from the sea, *panela* (black sugar) from its
own fields, corn, barley and wheat, coconuts, bananas, apples and pears.
All of this depends upon where the hacienda is located. If it can run from
the seacoast to the mountain top, from the river bottom where sugar cane
will grow to the snow line, then it can raise all of the crops that will grow
in all of the climates. Not all haciendas—not any perhaps—satisfy this
ideal completely, but that is the bent of hacienda organization: buy nothing, raise and make everything within the limits of your own boundaries.
The big house is built from the timbers on the place—and these may be,
as I have seen them, of mahogany. The furniture is made at home; the
cloth is woven on the place from the sheep; the llamas that graze in the
hills, the oxen, the horses, are raised and broken on the place; the saddles,
bridles, harnesses, are made from the hides of the slaughtered animals.
The wooden plow, the wagon, the windmill for the grinding of the corn,
or the water-mill for the grinding of cane are all made on the place. The
table may be loaded at a meal with every kind of meat, grain and fruit—
and all of these, the table itself, the house, and the servants as well, will
all have been raised, contrived, conserved, grown on the place, including
the tablecloth that covers the table, the sandals of the servants, if they are
not barefooted. And perhaps even the Indian musician who sits behind the
screen and plays his old songs on the homemade instrument is also of the
plantation. I am recalling this from personal experience on a plantation
in the Province of Ayacucho in Peru.

The people on the plantation are born there. They cannot leave because they may be in debt, or because there is no place to go, for this is
home and every other place is foreign. And here too their fathers and
grandfathers were born and are buried. If the place changes hands, they
change with it. In 1948 the leading newspaper in La Paz, Bolivia, carried
an advertisement offering for sale on the main highway a half hour from
the capital of the country a hacienda with five hundred acres of land,
fifty sheep, much water and *twenty peons*. And similar advertisements
have appeared even more recently in Ecuador and Chile. (This I have
from others, one a native scholar, the other an American political scientist.) The point is that what we are dealing with is a closed economic,
social, political and cultural institution.

Its administrative organization is an interesting adaptation to an aristocratic agricultural society of a non-commercial economy. For the hacienda
is a way of life rather than a business. It is not an investment. It was

inherited. It is operated with the expenditure of as little cash as possible. If the hacienda is large there may be a couple of hundred or more families residing within its borders. These are scattered in groups of five or ten families in different parts of the hacienda, depending on the kind of land, crops, forest. The laborer usually has a hut which he has built, and a given amount of land, which he works or shares. The hacienda provides the land, the work animals and the seed; and the peon turns over, carrying to the granary by the big house, the share of the crop belonging to the hacendado. The share is determined by the crop, and the tradition of the hacienda. In addition, the Indian also owes the landlord a given number of days' work each week throughout the year. This practice varies. It might be one day's work a week for each hectare of land, or so many days a week for living on the land. The families might also owe a certain amount of service in the big house. The point is that the hacienda has its labor supplied to it without the use of money. If there are two hundred families on the hacienda and if they each owed only one day's work a week for each of two hectares allotted to each family, it would have 400 work days each week.

The labor at its disposal without expenditure of any money for wages is used by the hacienda for working those lands which it tills on its own account. These lands might be in sugar cane, from which it can either with oxen or water power in a small homemade *trapiche,* squeeze out the juice and make *panela,* a dark unrefined sugar, and manufacture rum as well. Or its cash crop may be coffee or cacao, or other products which can be carried to the market on the backs of mules, or on the backs of men, over steep mountain and narrow gorges, to the nearest railroad station, or more recently to the nearest automobile road, or to the nearest town. The cash crop will have been raised, harvested and delivered part or all of the way to the nearest market without the expenditure of any money.

In a curious way, the hacienda is largely beyond the reach of the money economy. Internally it provides, so far as it can, for all of its needs as a going concern as well as a community without recourse to the market. The seed the hacienda supplies to the sharecroppers comes out of the store houses in which it was deposited in the fall; if the laboring population living on the hacienda runs short of food or other supplies they can be purchased in the store—*tienda de raya,* in Mexican parlance, or *company store* in our own economic history. The peon will pay no cash for his purchase for he has no money. It will be written down in a little book by a storekeeper, usually some distant relative or *compadre* of the hacendado. The debt can be liquidated by labor, but it rarely is and serves to tie the laboring population to the hacienda, as they cannot leave without first paying off their debt. This has long been so. It has roots in the colonial system. It persisted all through the nineteenth century, and is still in full vigor wherever the hacienda system survives. It is as hard to kill as was the company store, token coin, or script, in the mining and lumbering camps in the United States. And token coin has its use on the hacienda, for the payment of wages, for the extra labor which may be needed beyond that owed by the peons, or for tasks which for some reason lie outside the traditional work the peons accept as theirs. These token coins, sometimes bearing the name of the hacienda, or a piece of metal stamped with *vale un día de trabajo* (it is worth one day's work) can only be exchanged in the hacienda store.

As the hacienda satisfies its own and its community's needs with as little recourse to the market as possible, it buys little, and it sells little as well. The distances, the poor roads, the primitive means of communication, make the transport of goods from one part of the country to another difficult and expensive. The relatively small income from the hacienda is, so to speak, net profit—taxes on land have always been low, the cost of production is at a minimum in monetary terms.

The hacienda is, however, not merely an economic enterprise. It is also a social, political and cultural institution. Socially it is a closed community living within its borders. Part of the hacienda population will be located near the big house, where the store, the church, the school (if there is one), the repair shops, granaries, the blacksmith, carpenter, harness shop will also be. The grist mill and the *trapiche* (sugar mill) will also, in all likelihood, be near the big house if there is water close by. The stables for the favorite horses, cows and other animals raised for household use or consumption will also be close by. The laborers about the big house tend to all these different functions. This is usually the larger part of the hacienda community. The others are scattered in small groups in different parts of the domain, tending to different duties and raising crops appropriate to the altitude, the climate, moisture and heat. Each little *rancho* hamlet is isolated and far away. It may be anything from one to ten or more miles from the next hamlet, depending upon the size of the hacienda. Their contacts with the outside world are few indeed, and the paths on the hacienda lead to the center where the big house is located, and only one rarely used path goes off to another hacienda, and to still another until the neighboring town is reached, which may be ten, twenty, thirty or more miles away.

Community activity takes place in front of the big house, on Sundays, when the peonage will have come to church, even if there is no priest in regular attendance. All burials, christenings, marriages, when they are solemnized, are social matters involving the church and as large a part of the hacienda community as is aware of the occasion. The important feast days are likely to be the saint's day of the owner, or of some other favorite member of the family. Then the entire community will turn the event into a holiday with decorations, music, dancing and drinking. A similar event is celebrating the patron saint of the church. There may be others, depending on the local Indian, mestizo or Negro traditions. Beyond these festive occasions, the hacienda community has no public functions or responsibilities. It is not a political unit, an organized parish, a government, or a cooperative. If any vestige of the older Indian community survives on the hacienda, it is unrecognized by the hacendado and what functions it retains must of necessity lie outside of the hacienda as a going concern.

There may be and often is a bond between the peons and the hacendado which goes beyond the formal manager-laborer relation. The hacendado may have stood as godfather to many of the children born on the place. He may have a role not as employer primarily, but as the head of a family of which all the laborers consider themselves members. The hacienda laborers' community may have an integration resting on many years of cooperation, interdependence and mutual aid. The hacienda is an old institution. It has usually belonged to the same family over many generations, sometimes for centuries. Isolation from the larger world has tended to bring the hacendados within the same region close to each other. By intermarriage the owner of the hacienda tends to be related to most of the proprietors of the neighboring properties. Time, circumstance, and danger have brought the hacendados of the region close together, and their family connections will have knitted an extended family over a vast area where everyone knows and is related to everyone else.

One or another of these closely knitted families will have, through time, acquired an ascendancy over the others, a kind of traditional leadership in the region. And given the basis of fealty in the extended family and the godfather relation that always exists, you have the basis of political power and regional *caciquismo*. Because of the turbulence and instability that succeeded the independence, *caciquismo* served the important end of protecting its own. The interdependence of the regional hacienda owners became an essential means of self-protection and defense —either military or political. The rule that developed, logically required by the situation, was that the locality and its inhabitants followed their own leader against the national one. The leaders of the localities each had a following which belonged only to them, and the great leader was dependent upon the support of the little leaders each with his own following.

In that situation the power of the great leader tended to be unstable, temporary and subject to many hazards. He really lived on borrowed strength—while the power of the local *cacique* was very great and beyond the effective control of the central government, where the great leader was located. The hacienda thus became the basis of a system of local *caciquismo*, and the local *caciquismo* the major reason for political instability. It must be clear that with the weakening of the central power, the decline in the wealth, prestige and influence of the Church, the only power that remained was that of the locality—and the locality in Latin America has meant the haciendas in the locality. They were substantial; they had a strength which was genuine. The hacienda community's fealty gave the hacendado a power which was immediate and direct. And a group of hacendados, related and interdependent, controlled a region. The *cabildo* which they controlled was for a long time the only effective government.

Before closing this discussion of the hacienda, there are certain other elements which must be brought out. The hacienda both dominated the small neighboring city and prevented it from developing economically or politically. The complaint so often heard in the Latin American smaller town, that it has no "movement" that it is "dead," is true and no great mystery. The haciendas which surround this town for many miles about buy little. Their peons have no money. The town has no important distributing function. The hacienda sells relatively little, considering its size and the number of people living on it; and what it does sell is marketed, usually, on a wholesale basis, by some agent employed by the hacienda, or by a member of the family, and is sent on, if possible to a larger city at a distance, with the result that the smaller neighboring city is bypassed. Even the mule pack carrying the hacienda goods to the city or the nearest railroad belongs to the hacienda.

The better houses in the town usually belong to the neighboring haciendas, and are occupied by some members of the extended family, probably an old mother, or a brother who does not like to live on the hacienda, or who has some professional interest. The children of the hacendado will also be in this house during the school year. The servants in the house will come from the hacienda and will be a permanent part of the household, requiring no specific money wage. In the mountains of Peru, the house will also have the service of one or more *pongos* who come to work in turn for a week, and then go back to the hacienda. This is part of their payment for the few hectares of land they till on the hacienda. In addition the house will be supplied from the hacienda with a large part of its needs—wheat, barley, rice, corn, in the grain or as flour depending on whether the hacienda has a grist mill. It will also get what fruits are raised, and depending on the distance, may be supplied with butter, cheese and whatever else the distance and the climate will allow to be transported. So the big houses in the town are not important participants in the local market.

All of this and much more has kept the town commercially inactive. If the hacienda dominates the town economically, it does so politically as well. The great family will control every local office, from the colonel of the local militia to the rural police. The tax gatherer, the mayor, the judge, the postmaster will be related to or married into or be godfathers to, members of the family. And unless the president of the country feels strong enough to be indifferent to the interest and pride of the local leadership he will not impose "foreigners" on the locality.

If we now summarize the role of the hacienda in the development of Latin America we will see that it has been and has remained, where it still

exists, an isolating and conservative influence. It lived by routine share-cropping methods which prevented the use of improved machinery, methods or seeds. It tied its labor force to the property and kept mobility down to a minimum. It was a dampening influence on commercial development by buying little in the open market and selling relatively little. Its huge areas and internal system of paths leading to the big house discouraged road building. It established and maintained—and still does—a system of dependence between the hacendado and his peons which perpetuated an authoritarian tradition of master and very humble servant (I saw in Bolivia the Indians on a plantation bend their knees and kiss the hands of the hacendado) which leads directly into *caciquismo* and instability. It prevented the accumulation of capital, required no investment, called for no change, did nothing to prevent soil erosion or improve agricultural techniques. The hacienda family controlled the local political scene and set the tone socially. As a dominant influence, the hacienda paid little taxes, and neglected to, or was unable to, put all of its resources to good use.

Perhaps most serious of all is that it fostered and maintained a social ideal in which the hacendado was the representative type—ideally a superior being possessed of broad acres and numerous servants, dominant, domineering, patronizing, and paternal, with nothing between himself and the peon on the plantation. All other elements in society (craftsmen, businessmen, entrepreneurs—in the parlance of the day, the middle class) were looked upon with disdain as a necessary affliction that had at best to be suffered. The hacendado was the master of all he surveyed, and the world looked good to him. It gave him economic stability, social prestige, political power, affluence and leisure. Those of his children who did not remain on the hacienda went off to the capital of the country, attended the university and became lawyers, doctors or literary men. Many of them combined literature with a profession. They might also meddle in politics, especially if the administration was one which their family—always the extended family, always the people who come from the same region, who followed the same local traditional leadership—had helped to bring to office.

Education fitted the ideal. Primary schooling for the mass of the people was a matter of indifference; higher education in the main led to a limited number of professions—medicine, law, and to a much lesser degree civil engineering. In the earlier days, the university also taught theology. The emphasis more recently fell upon philosophy and literature instead.

The hacienda system was thus a major influence in preventing either the democratic or economic development of Latin America. If Latin America has fallen behind the United States and Western Europe in industrial expansion, politically stable and democratic government and in the growth of an educational system adequate for the present time and present need, much of the fault lies with the hacienda system.

The hacienda system has in fact reached an impasse from which it cannot escape. The pressure for economic, political and social change is building up so rapidly that the system cannot avoid the challenge to its traditional ways, and it cannot meet it. *The hacienda has no built-in device that will allow for reform of the system,* that will enable it to transform itself so as to survive and propitiate the new ways that are undermining a traditional and age-old form of social organization. It has no way of meeting the challenge and yet cannot remain indifferent to television, atomic energy—and, if you like, psychoanalysis and Karl Marx as well.

In the two countries where the hacienda has been repudiated, Mexico and Bolivia, it was by revolution. The question of whether there is another way of dealing with impending change remains to be seen. I say "impending," for it would require undue opaqueness to assume that the demands for industrialism and democracy can be met without seriously affecting the total role of the hacienda. What is happening in a small way in Peru is perhaps a suggestion that the government could if it had the energy, vision and political courage attempt a program of agrarian reform that would meet the modern challenge without a previous social convulsion. But who is there to say that the organized forces of government could move fast enough to satisfy the increasing pressure which the government would stimulate by its policies? I am not suggesting that cataclysm is inevitable. What is inevitable, if Latin America is to industrialize effectively and meet the demands for a higher standard of living and a more democratic society, is a wide agrarian reform which is not compatible with the survival of the hacienda system.

All of this discussion does not include the problem raised by the large commercial plantation in sugar, bananas and other crops raised for the international market. The fact that these large plantations may be foreign owned is only a minor complication to a difficult problem. What is involved in any attempt to apply agrarian reform policies to them is that they are efficiently operated, that they require a high degree of scientific and technical skill, that they have a foreign market which they control; or that they have to meet the world price at which the commodity is selling; that they yield a cash income per acre higher than any other crop that could be grown. These are questions of such magnitude, especially where the government gets a large part of its income from the export of a single commodity, that any policy that would price the commodity out of the market, reduce the required investment, and cut down efficiency would not necessarily improve the economic conditions either of the peasantry or of the government. The fact that the properties have to be paid for merely increases the difficulties. But it must be clear that in their modern form these enterprises are relatively new, that they are to a considerable extent foreign owned and foreign managed, and that they are so large that they tend to dwarf all other domestic enterprise.

This raises political questions that may in fact be insoluble. This is a hard thing to recognize and to accept. But politically a certain institution may prove intolerable even if economically it can be shown to be highly beneficial. The large modern plantation is probably more like a factory than a farm, and if it were possible for modern management, the workers and the government to believe that they are involved in an industrial rather than an agricultural enterprise, then issues other than land reform would control whatever controversy might arise and require attention.

The modern sugar and banana plantations are, however, not the major issue in any discussion of the hacienda. These enterprises, except in isolated areas like Cuba, are only a small part of the total agricultural plant. The hacienda is another matter; it has set the tone for a whole society— and while it differs greatly between Argentina and Peru, for instance, it has been the controlling influence in shaping the cultural development of the area and has influenced the educational system in many ways.

EDUCATION

In the kind of world we have been describing, education will take on special forms. It will have given the relatively small group of Europeans and their descendants an education fitting the aristocratic, authoritarian role that tradition and expectancy have demanded of them. It will have given them refinements and interests seemingly natural to "superior" persons in an authoritarian society, while the mass of the people will have received little instruction at public expense and that of poor quality. This whole matter is a delicate and sensitive issue, hard to deal with and hard to evaluate.

We must always begin with remembering that the universities in Lima and Mexico are a century older than Harvard; that the Franciscans carried on a most notable educational enterprise in Mexico within a few years after the conquest, where among other things Indian boys learned to read Latin, and some became good Latinists; we must also remember that the Order of Jesus had a notable career in the field of education among criollos and Indians.

All of this is in the background. But the published figures, whatever their accuracy, record that in mid-twentieth century at least one-half of the people in Latin America could neither read nor write. That would mean something like 70 to 80 million people. Countries like Argentina, Chile, Uruguay and Costa Rica can boast of a literacy rate of 80 per cent or more, while in Bolivia, El Salvador and Guatemala the people counted as literate are somewhere around 30 in a 100, and in Haiti, only about 10 per cent can read and write. These figures are probably somewhat optimistic. It has been estimated that something like four or five years of primary schooling are required before it can be assumed that the child will not fall back into illiteracy. If this is the case, then there are many more people who are functionally illiterate than is indicated by the published figures.

On the whole, the children who enter the primary school do not reach the top grade. This is especially so in rural districts, and we are dealing with a rural area. In the rural schools in Brazil, according to a United Nations study, less than one per cent of those entering reach the fifth grade, whereas urban schools have a record at least nine times as good. In 14 Latin American countries, 1.7 per cent of children of school age reach the highest primary grade.

As we have already seen, the Latin American population is growing fast, faster perhaps than in other parts of the world. This means that the number of children to the total population is relatively great. The children of school age—five to fourteen—are proportionately twice as numerous in comparison with the adults in the Latin American countries as they are in Europe. There are four adults to every child of school age in the more industrialized countries, and only two in Latin America. The relative burden, all other things being equal, of the educational costs to be borne proportionately by each individual would therefore be twice as great in Latin America as in England or Belgium. And this burden falls on people who have a much lower income and on countries where the investment per capita in industry is lower and where productivity per individual is smaller.

This however is only part of the difficulty. In many of the countries in Latin America there is the additional impediment of language other than Spanish spoken by a considerable number—in some cases the majority—of the population. This added task might well discourage even an enthusiast for popular education. How to get the teachers who know the language (Mexico lists a hundred), how to prepare the schoolroom materials so as to make them meaningful, how to persuade the parents to send their children to school, and how to interpret to the children of an entirely different cultural universe the values derived from European antecedents, might well tax the ingenuity and the will even of the idealistic reformer. I always recall the little Chamula child of about seven or eight, who had learned Spanish while his mother had been working in town, acting as an interpreter for his teacher to some dozen other Chamula children of about his own age. It was heroic and pathetic at the same time. Only the greatest devotion would explain the effort to pass on European culture and the ideals of Mexican nationalism through the medium of a little child. But he was the only interpreter available for the task in hand. It was pathetic, for the one or two years schooling to be had in that school would in the end avail but little to the children by the time they came to be full grown men.

At least half of the people in Bolivia, Ecuador, Guatemala and Peru lie outside the Spanish medium as a means of instruction in schools—and Indian children do not know Spanish even in families where the father speaks it. For, at home the mother tongue is Quiche, Aymara, Trique, or whatever the language of the Indian group happens to be. The language barrier is more formidable than enthusiasts for converting the Indians into good nationals like to believe.

This raises another question. How effective is a literacy campaign in a country where there are no books for the mass of the people, no magazines, no newspapers, in fact no reading matter? The literacy campaigns, and there have been a number of them, have accomplished but little. For literacy is not something by itself. It is an expression of a total cultural situation. Where reading and writing are not used because no one writes letters, because there is nothing to read, because even the first-grade primer has disappeared (mouldered away with time if one did once go to school), because newspapers are unknown—then it is difficult to learn to read and easy to forget the alphabet one acquired in the primary grade. It is hard for city dwellers here or in Latin America to visualize the poverty of the ordinary rural school and rural community in literary materials. As everything in the school usually comes from the central ministry of education the school teacher will, with the thousands of other teachers, receive a scant supply of schoolroom writing material, a blackboard and chalk, first and second grade primers. And that may be all. He may in some places receive a magazine published by the Ministry of Education filled with articles on the theory of education, which the teacher will probably not understand. For in most rural schools even the teacher may have scant book learning.

The undertaking to suddenly provide a school system adequate to the needs of a modern nation is a Herculean task. In Latin America the schools are usually maintained, supported or supervised by the national government, which appoints the teachers, builds or rents the schools, plans the program, supplies the classroom materials and orders, regulates, examines by long-range control everything, from the school desk, the blackboard, the final examination and the morals of the teacher.

A bureaucracy, well intentioned, perhaps well trained, that knows exactly what is to be done and how to do it—this bureaucracy, by giving orders in long *reglamentos* to teachers off in the jungle or in some mountain crevice fills the air with sounds of activity which make little difference in fact when one looks at the situation at a distance from the capital where the ministry is located. And in periods of political instability—and political instability is something of a norm in the last quarter of a century—the educational directors at the center change with each government. The old plans are thrown out, new plans devised because they are said to be better; and before these new plans can really take effect, a change in government will bring a new Minister of Education, who will have a newer and better plan that in its turn will fail of fulfillment.

These are pessimistic views—but how can one run away from the facts? Because of the high degree of centralization, the central government must provide for 50 or more per cent of the school population now without schools. It must find, educate, "shanghai" double the number of teachers it now has and place them on the national payroll. It must print twice as many books and notebooks, procure twice as many pencils and blackboards. It must double the school inspectors, bookkeepers, clerks, supervisors and normal schools for the training of teachers. It must do all of this and a great deal more, and it must do it in a hurry, for the population is growing so fast that at the moment the school system is losing ground. From some source the means has to be discovered to double the education budget, which in some countries is already very large. And when the President has done all of this (and no one else can do it) he will have universalized the present situation: a little over one per cent of the children of school age will complete the fifth or sixth grade, and half of the children matriculating will not go beyond the first year. The amount of literacy will have increased but slightly, and the extent of functional illiteracy will probably have doubled.

Centralization demands that the national government do it all and the central government expects to do it all, or leave it undone. But what is required within the national ideal is a school system rural and urban that will give at least a primary grade education of six to eight years for all the children everywhere, and do it soon. And this the government cannot do. Physical impediments of geography, different languages, poverty, insufficient teachers, schools and money make the demand for a universal primary education for all children an ideal that can have no present fulfillment.

To make the project a reasonable one, that is, a possible one, the country would suddenly have to be endowed with an industrial system, an economy, a social structure, a national income sufficiently large and sufficiently well distributed. It would also require the quite sudden appearance of teachers in sufficient numbers and adequately trained as well as administrators willing and able to organize and manage so large an undertaking. These things are not done by sheer exercise of will. They have to grow together. And those who are concerned with education would do well to recognize that the educational system is a function of the total society and cannot be treated in isolation. One could say that a society has the school system its culture can contrive and absorb. The school system changes as the society changes, and there are no miracles to be looked for.

It is interesting to have a look at the remarkable Mexican experience in rural education. The Mexican effort came out of the revolution and had in its initial days the impulse to remake the nation and to bring the rural folk, including the Indian, into closer contact with the modern world. Beginning about 1924 under the leadership of José Vasconcelos and later of Moises Saenz and Rafael Ramirez, the attempt was made to carry the school even to the most isolated villages. Starting with inadequate funds, insufficient teachers and a not-too-clear idea of what could be done, the movement had the advantage of enthusiasm and faith in the beneficence of the revolution and its redeeming qualities, for it was to redeem the rural population from the effects of peonage and to incorporate the Indian into the nation that the school was expected to contribute to.

The important lesson for the future revealed by this undertaking was that the rural community, no matter how poor and abandoned, could become an active participant in a system of rural education. Having neither much money nor trained personnel, the ministry resorted to sending "missionaries" on horseback to the villages in the mountains to preach the gospel of education for the children. The villagers were gathered together and the problem and prospects were discussed in a kind of open assembly. It soon became apparent that the communities would provide the school—build it themselves. The missionary turned architect; and the men, women and children in their spare time, Sundays and holidays, gathered and hewed stones, mixed lime, worked the adobe and built the school on land the community had given. In a short time over six thousand rural schools were built by the villages without any cost to the central government, and having built them they felt as if the schools belonged to them.

As there was no experience, no confining traditions, and as the missionaries and officials in the ministry had the ideal of using the school as an agency of social improvement, they permitted themselves to be influenced by the communities who wanted the school to be useful to the village. Out of this there developed without any initial plan a body of what came to be called "anexos" to the school. The basketball field would be one anexo. A lamp for the school that could be used by the adults in the evenings would be another anexo. A shower bath made of a tin can raised on poles was another.

It soon turned out that the anexos were the important part of the rural school. They included such things as a school garden, a house for the teacher, a plot of school land worked by the adults to provide additional income for the school or the teacher. The school also developed a kitchen where the women could learn to cook. It had a sewing machine, a barber shop where older boys cut the hair of the younger ones, a medical kit, or primitive dispensary where the teacher acted as nurse and applied iodine, bandages, and had some other simple remedies. There was no standardization in these matters. Each school adopted and contrived those anexos most convenient and useful to its particular community.

The rural school came to be judged not primarily by its reading and writing, but by its anexos. One school boasted of 33 separate activities in addition to teaching the three R's. One result was that the school was always open and members of the community participated in its goings on. Another was the formation of "committees" to look after different needs in the school sanitation, the school garden, the school plot, the furniture, the attendance, the night school and so forth. One teacher remarked that the school kept going day and night: "When I get tired I take a rest."

The most important lesson taught by this movement was that there is a latent initiative and enthusiasm in the community that once awakened can be of great help in the development of rural education.

Now, more than three decades after this movement got underway, Mexico has some 20,000 rural schools, and the government prides itself on its large educational budget. But the rural schools in their vast majority do not go beyond the third grade. A large proportion of the children do not attend school beyond the first year. But more significant, half the children in the rural districts have no schools to go to. The population has more than doubled and the number of children has increased more rapidly than the adults. The government has not been able to carry a sufficiently effective campaign for rural schools. And this is the story in Mexico, which justly prides itself on its contribution to education and its efforts to meet the challenge of literacy in the modern world.

For Mexico has made important strides in converting a hacienda-dominated and peon-ridden society into one that is democratic and progressive and full of confidence in its own future. A careful analysis of what has happened in the last 30 years would show that other influences in addition to a rapidly growing population must be reckoned with in explaining the failure of the school system to keep up with the school children clamoring for schools. One of these undoubtedly has been an over-emphasis upon urbanization and a tendency to neglect the needs of the rural community. This is true even in Mexico, where the Revolution of 1910 was primarily a protest against just this kind of neglect. But rural people are on the whole voiceless and fail to bring their needs to the attention of the government immersed in the large city.

More fundamental perhaps is the simple fact that in spite of the great changes which have taken place functionally, literacy in the rural districts remains less important than in the cities. If this is the case in a country like Mexico, where the hacienda system has been destroyed and where the impulse toward a fuller democracy is the outstanding feature of the present day, what can be said of the rest of Latin America? One must be on his guard against generalizations and dogmatic assertions, and no one really knows enough to be absolutely sure of his own position in matters as complex as those we are dealing with. But it seems obvious that a country divided into large haciendas on which a large proportion of the people live, lacks the motivation for organizing, and lacks the income to finance an effective system of rural education. The hacienda is chiefly responsible for the dilemma faced by Latin America in its ambition to adapt to modern ways, not only in the matter of schooling for the mass of the people but also in its efforts to industrialize or for that matter to apply scientific methods to its agriculture. The dilemma lies in the demand for modernization by the very elements who are most insistent in keeping the older social and economic institutions. They are clamoring for progress and at the same time resisting effective change. They would like to retain their hierarchical, authoritarian and centralized social structure on one side, and have the values that only come with an egalitarian, mobile, individualistic society which industrialism both needs and promotes on the other. It is, I think, clear that an effective modern school system would require so many other changes that it can only come into being as the countries develop the resources, the needs and the competencies which make universal literacy an integral part of a modern society.

Higher education in Latin America is going through a profound crisis. The older university which served a small aristocracy has been challenged to meet the seemingly impossible demands of a suddenly expanded urban population. The needs of a growing middle class and an expanding industrial system with its emphasis on science and scientific training are more than the older university with its literary traditions, its emphasis upon the humanities, its specialization in law, medicine, and civil engineering is currently prepared for. The sudden flow of students has turned the relatively small, traditional institutions of higher learning into great centers of discontent. The universities on the whole lack the means, the trained personnel, the physical room, and the scientific equipment required to train the thousands of students clamoring for instruction. In addition, because of inadequate secondary schools, the students are not always well enough prepared for the university. The professors in the majority of cases make their living by practicing a profession or occupying some post in the government. Their teaching is in a sense an honorific exercise for which they receive a modest, almost a symbolic stipend.

With a part-time teaching staff, inadequate finances, overcrowded halls and classrooms, poor or non-existent laboratories, the universities have difficulty enough to meet their obligations without the added perplexities of involvement with the government. There is a tradition of autonomy and freedom from state interference in university matters. The older rule allows no policeman within the precincts of the university. But the ideal of academic inviolability has been frequently disregarded: Venezuela, Cuba and Argentina are only recent instances of the State's indifference to academic pretensions. State intervention on one side and students' demands for administrative and policy-making participation on the other make academic life exciting if not entirely peaceful and make devotion to research and the scholarly life difficult. There are many distinguished scholars and teachers who have somehow managed to find the serenity needed for creative work within this difficult environment, but there are also many teachers and students who find the going hard and the rewards inadequate. A few private, usually Catholic, universities add to the educational opportunities. These are less troubled by politics, but in the broad field of education they differ but little from the nationally supported institutions.

If one is to offer a constructive comment on so sensitive a matter as the university in Latin America, it should be done humbly and with many apologies. But it does seem that it is an error to overemphasize the university in capital cities—Lima, Mexico, Caracas, and to neglect the smaller regional institutions in Cuzco, Morelia and Cuenca. This is but one suggestion. There are many others that an outsider could make, but then an outsider does not understand or have to deal with the ten thousand difficulties that stand in the path of modifying the ways of a tradition-bound university that must continue to live with a centralized, authoritarian and all powerful government.

LEADERSHIP

When Latin Americans say, as they often do in speaking of themselves, "We are a young people," they must have in the back of their mind Bolivar's remark that the inhabitants of the former Spanish colonies were neither Europeans, Africans nor Indians, but Americans. That too was the idea of the "Cosmic Race" popularized by José Vasconcelos a generation ago. These reflections by Latin Americans about their own stage of development is a way of saying that the people of Latin America are still being formed, that the "Cosmic Race" is an aspiration, an ideal to be hoped for but that in the present their character is incomplete. If this means anything—and I think that such intuitive reflections by a people about themselves mean a great deal—it is that the mestizo who is the product of this amalgam between all the races has not as yet become the universal type, the true representative of the "Cosmic Race." They recognize that the character of the Latin American has not yet been integrated. For in spite of their sensitivity about criticism from the outside, they acknowledge the validity of such painful analyses as Carlos Octavio Bunge's "Our America" and Luis Alberto Sánchez's "Does Latin America Exist?" and honor their authors for their frankness as well as their wisdom.

The meaning of the notion that "we are a young people" is that there are still Indians, Negroes and Europeans and that the mestizo, the real American, is an imperfect creature because he is born and reared amid conflicting values and contradictory cultures, compared with an Englishman, a Frenchman or an Italian among whom basic attitudes have sanctions that go back beyond the memory of man, and where notions of right and wrong seem to have universal acceptance. The mestizo, on the other hand, is raised in a world where even the most intimate values are challenged and denied, among Indians and Africans and Europeans who differ in their simplest ideas of the good, and each of whom differs from the mestizo.

The import of all this is unconsciously revealed when we ask about any leader among ourselves. Who is he? Where was he born? Where did he go to school? We ask these questions not because we want to know the man's political opinions, those revealed by his party allegiance, his public statements. The queries go to the heart of the matter. They ask not what the leader thinks, but how he came to be the kind of man he is; his opinions about politics and policy are only part of the question. What kind of a character is he—regardless of his opinions. And this question of character formation in a world of conflicting values, beliefs and ideals has been answered many times and in many places. An unstable and conflicting cultural environment is not conducive to the formation of the "national" type. The contradictory cultures and differing value systems have nurtured refractory characters, especially because the mestizos are "a young people," a people just becoming. Otherwise it would be difficult to explain the turbulence and instability, the passion and the frustration, the alternatives of pride and humility, of arrogant self-assertion one day and sense of inferiority the next, frequently manifested in Latin American history.

The mestizo is a child of conquest, misfortune, denial and contempt. It is a short time between the conquest, when he had not yet appeared, and the independence when he began to emerge as an active participant, at least as a sergeant and sometimes an important leader like Morelos in Mexico. And there has not been time enough, and there will not be until in some way the fusion of the races occurs, for a national culture sufficiently broad to embrace the entire population to emerge. That is the condition of common values, and the basis of that unofficial education in right and good which precedes any schooling in a traditionally pervasive culture.

The difficulty which is widespread is clearly seen in Guatemala. Who in Guatemala speaks for all of the people? Culturally, no one. Certainly not the mestizo (Ladino, as he is called) nor the criollo (who here is also called a Ladino), nor the Indian. The Indian, of course, is voiceless. He does not speak to the public at large. He is confined in a dozen mutually unintelligible tongues, is not really aware of what the Guatemalan nation claims to be. He would prefer to be left alone, to go on with his own ways of worshiping God, ordering his civil affairs, dealing with the complexities of family life and tilling the land as he has always done. How far away and how indifferent to the modern world he can be is illustrated by the active use, among some Indian villages, of the ancient Maya calendar to schedule his religious activities during the year.

The mestizo who does make himself heard and has taken over the leadership of the government is indifferent if not hostile to the Indian and his ways. The mestizo talks in public and to the large world as if the Indian did not matter or did not exist, and General Jorge Ubico, so many years the dictator of Guatemala, attempted to deny the Indian's presence to the outside world. In a motion picture of Ubico's doings as president, for distribution in Central America, the Indian was cut out whenever possible. Wherever Ubico was shown, he managed to be surrounded solely by Ladinos. Only in one flash was the cat let out of the bag. An Indian face and head slipped into one very good shot—too good to be cut. Guatemala was to be shown to the world as a mestizo nation though the Indian is at least one half of the population. The criollo, in Guatemala, has largely lost his identity. There is really no one who can stand above the conflict in cultures, and speak of the body of the nation as one people. If anyone did he would be driven from office by the mestizos because they represent whatever effective power there is.

It ought to be clear that this is not a matter of conservatism, liberalism, democracy, socialism, communism, or whatever other slogan may be in vogue in the next generation. It is the incompatability of two cultures with basically different value systems. The unity that the nationalist aspires to he will have only when the Indian has so completely merged in the mestizo that he is no longer aware of himself. How long it will take no one can tell, but until then there can be no national leadership, because culturally there is no nation. This example is illustrative of other cases. It applies wherever there are very large Indian groups whose presence is looked upon as a burden to the nation.

One can say something very similar about Peru, Ecuador, Mexico before the Revolution of 1910, of Bolivia until 1952 and of other countries in their degree of non-assimilated Indian groups. It is significant that in the midst of the bitterness and violence of the Mexican Revolution, the attitude of thoughtful Mexicans was that they were "making a nation" (*forjando patria*). That is the title Manuel Gamio gave to a book of essays dealing with the Mexican upheaval and published in 1922. It is equally noticeable that after the defeat in the Chaco War the Bolivian intellectuals were obsessed with the idea of making a nation, bringing the Indian into the public arena. That perhaps is as good an explanation of the Bolivian Revolution as can be found. The question of whom the leader speaks for is a baffling matter everywhere and particularly so in Latin America.

There are few places in other regions and none in the Western world where so great a difference can be found among the "citizens" of the same nation. Culturally most of the nations of Latin America are a kaleidoscope of all types of society—from the most primitive to the most complex, from the naked Amazonian being, such as the Auca Indians on the Napo River who recently killed some missionaries because they look upon every white man as an enemy, to the sophisticated intellectual in

Quito, Lima or Mexico who reads Sartre and considers himself an existentialist. And these societies occupying the same territory but standing at the extreme of human experience are more widely scattered across the continent and north of Panama to the American border than is generally assumed. The Tarahuamara in Chihuahua, the Lacandón in Chiapas, and the forest and jungle people in Brazil, Colombia and Venezuela are but the end of a line. They are more significant than their numbers would suggest. For in between the extreme of a primitive group in the jungle that sees all strangers as enemies and the highly cultured intellectuals and artists in the city there is every variety of social organization, family, structure, notions of property ownership and possession.

We have to deal with a society that has well defined groups, who have no notion of property and whose living is acquired within some roughly defined area by hunting and fishing on one hand to the intricacies of the modern corporation registered in Delaware doing business through one or more subsidiaries in Peru, Mexico or Brazil on the other. The communal villages in the highlands with their varied customs and notions, ranging from full collective ownership to the village where the agricultural lands are held by individuals but the pasture lands belong to the community are but another feature of the world we are dealing with. Within these boundaries of collective and private ownership there is every gradation of right. These many different people are as much a part of the nation as the mestizos or the criollos. Statesmanship would require the acceptance of not only the different races, beliefs and language as equally part of the nation, but it would also accept the great variety of customary law by which these peoples regulate the conduct of their members as legitimate elements of the law in the larger unit called the nation. The recognition of unity in variety, of a culture rich in its possibilities because of unique values and meanings carried by each of these groups would be the height of statesmanship. Such leadership is hard to come by. The assertion that all men are equal is an ancient doctrine deeply ingrained in Christian culture. This idea gets itself written into the constitutions of Latin America. But the idea that the various cultures within the nation are equally legitimate, and the local customs and common law by which they arrange their own affairs ought to be protected against violence and abuse has found no Rousseau even in Latin America, where the persistent variable in social structure is so important historically as well as in the present.

It may be asking too much of national leadership to be sensitive and responsive to the needs and difficulties of all the culture groups that make up the nation. But these groups are the body of the nation in a country like Guatemala. They are what leadership ought to be responsive to if it is to be national. One way of looking at the failure of national leadership is to glance at the problem historically.

The Latin American criollo had little part in government during the colonial period and lacked business experience. After the independence and all through the nineteenth century business and industrial affairs fell by default to Spaniards, Italians, Germans, Englishmen, Americans and others. The aristocratic elements who went to the universities either at home or abroad (preferably in France) became doctors and lawyers and dabbled in literature and, if they stayed home, in politics. The tradition of the hacienda opposed preoccupation with the material world, business and industry or even with agriculture. In some sense the upper classes were oriented toward Europe and indifferent to the problems facing their own country. They were after all only a fraction of the total population and because of the prevailing hierarchical society they remained "above the battle," beyond the ability, interest or necessary immersement to take effective hold of the government. They lacked the "esprit de corps" of a governing class. They were not the natural leaders of the populace. They had not risen from them or by their support. They lacked a basis in the loyalty and affections of the populace. They were not only "above the battle" but so high above the people, that the leadership of the nation could not rest in their hands.

By default, the leadership of the nation came to rest with the mestizo. And the mestizo had neither the tradition, the education, nor the experience for the task. Basically the mestizo in the nineteenth century was on the make. The leadership that he took hold of was the means of power, prestige and affluence, and he achieved these with little scruple and no conscience. But he achieved national influence and power as the leader of a faction, a political family, as the caudillo of a region, by a military coup as the "colonel" of the militia or as an ambitious and likeable politically minded officer in the national army. He was not necessarily a philosopher, a political scientist, a man of great vision. These qualities were not excluded but they were not a prerequisite. What he needed was audacity, physical courage, indifference to life, great energy, ambition, friends and a family—a political family, *compadres,* a reputation for loyalty to his friends and the qualities of a demagogue, and an ability to dazzle his followers by an unexpected trait—of some kind. He had to be generous to his immediate followers, offer and exact absolute loyalty from his political family. This leadership was not dependent upon a formal political party, which did not exist.

The leader, however, did not stand alone; he had a personal party bound by ties which could not be broken except in death. For in Latin America there is always in the background a community, a tradition, a church, a family. The individual stands inside and not outside their encompassing influences as he tends to do in the United States. And in instances where these warming and protective relations have been weakened, they are replaced by an informal but compelling association that stems from having been in the same school, lived in the same neighborhood, followed the same leader. These ties have elements of fidelity and identity that will outlast misfortune, poverty, exile and even crime. It would be difficult to find such a group where either family, church or community had not entered in; but even in sophisticated clusters whose main occupation is public service and active participation in politics, there is a tradition of deference to the needs of the members of the Pleiades that takes precedence over every other consideration. To stand by your group, the members of your extended family, your classmates, those raised with you in the same village, the compadre, your companions who followed the same political leader takes precedence over efficiency, public service, budgetary restrictions or formal law.

We call it nepotism, favoritism, political irresponsibility, financial mis-management or peculation. But that is a view of the matter peculiarly unfitting to describe the situation. That assumes that the government is everybody's government rather than that it is our government—the government of those in power for the time being. It assumes that a public official could or should disregard in the name of public service the needs and expectancies of relatives, friends, neighbors and companions, who have lived with us, protected, befriended and perchance housed and fed us. It assumes that the abstract thing called the government should displace in our affection those who have always filled the days of our lives, who came in dozens to see us off when we went on a journey, who gathered and made a festive occasion of our *día de Santo,* who filled the house with laughter and music when we graduate from school, who converted every incident in our life into a symbol of fellowship and identity and will continue to do so long after we are out of the government.

The relations with the group are permanent. Political office is temporary and precarious. And it is expected to be so. The public association, the party, the cause (outside of the Church) to which individuals can be attached does not exist. There are exceptions, of course, such as the Liberals or Conservatives in Colombia, the Colorados and Blancos in Uruguay. But these are isolated instances. The phenomenon so common in the United States of life-long service to a public cause such as the Red Cross, the Civil Liberties Union, the American Prison Association, the Public Library Association, the Federation of Women's Clubs is simply non-existent. The tradition of individualism, the special complex of mestizo society, the sense of insecurity and the preoccupation with the family in its larger sense has confined and circumscribed the individual within his family clan. But inside of that particular association, loyalty and devotion are likely to be life-long and absolute, above both good and evil.

If this does not provide the best of grounds for national leadership, it gives an ideal basis for the perpetuation of local leadership, the survival of the local family, and the persistent influence of regionalism in politics. We have known something of the same sort in our own southern states. But the southern states are one influence in a highly dynamic society, which is not the case in Latin America. There the closely knit regional political family, clan, gang, party or whatever name we choose to give it—and none are adequate—exists in all parts. All of the social and political life has this basis. The region exists in the feelings and the sense of the people whereas the nation is vague and ephemeral. When we talk about leadership this is the ground upon which it stands. Even in Brazil one is a Paulista—that is, from the State of São Paulo—rather than a Brazilian, in a sense that does not exist in the United States, not even among Texans.

In some subtle way these dispersing influences have played an important role in the history of repeated dictatorship. The nation cannot be governed solely in the interest of regional political clans. The national government, however it came to power, has to make its peace with the sectional claimants, with the political gangs—factions, families—that rule the different parts of the country. If the administration, that is the president, will not surrender to the splintering influences, and if he lacks the skill to compose and compromise, then dictatorship has been the means available, if the president had the makings of a dictator in him. This is not a defense of dictatorship; it is an attempt at understanding how the dictator has played so conspicuous a role in this part of the world. This ties in with another aspect of dictatorship.

In one way the army, especially in recent years, is the only secular institution that has a national outlook and interest and can thus stand above party and region. The case of Abramburu in Argentina is illustrative of the point. The government has gone to the army for reasons too numerous to deal with here, but one of these reasons is that the army can see the whole of the nation when other institutionalized forces are only concerned with the particular. We are concerned with the source of the leadership rather than with its quality or character. It is not an accident that the leaders of the nation have so often been soldiers. One of the reasons is that the nation as a nation has a meaning to them, when there is no nationally organized power to challenge the legitimacy of the army's claims to either represent or govern the nation. These are complicated matters that must not be simplified, because they may also be falsified in the process. The leadership of the nation requires a symbol, a vision, a policy and a faith which transcends the particular. But the mestizo to whom the leadership has fallen has on the whole neither the tradition nor the training for national leadership—that is being the leader of all of the people. There are, of course, many individual exceptions that could be mentioned—Lleras Camargo, Lázaro Cárdenas, José Figueres. among others, but these are not typical of the Latin American political leader.

In considering leadership in Latin America, the intellectual plays a special role. Intellectuals come to this role as influential people by the traditional prestige of university training and the high esteem placed on literary production. The recognized poet, novelist, historian, but especially poet, has a distinctive place in the affections and enjoys the regard of his compatriots. The funeral cortege of a well-known literary figure in any of the capitals of Latin America will be followed by thousands of people. Recently something like 30,000 people followed the funeral carriage of a well-known Mexican historian. The literary man is a national figure with an influence independent of government position or party affiliation. This provides him with a base for leadership in the nation which is both admirable and unique. It is admirable because he is independent, and unique because he cannot be deprived of the following that he has, or lose it except by ceasing to write and publish. He has another qualification for national leadership not shared by many of his contemporaries: he more than most is likely to have a vision of the nation as a whole. He can be above party, region, or class. He will, more than others, have had contact with the cultures beyond his own and know something of the complexities and difficulties of the world about him, and understand something of the possibilities and limits of public policy, and be aware of the temper of the age in which he lives.

For reasons that perhaps cannot be adequately explained, the intellectuals, with a few notable exceptions, both past and present, have not become the effective leaders of their nations.

To begin with, the intellectuals, and that includes the better known artists, poets, novelists, historians and literary critics, were oriented toward Europe, preferably France, rather than their own country. This was generally true until the First World War, and only gradually, and perhaps not completely even today, in some countries, have they discovered their own country. It has been remarked, truly enough, that Brazilian intellectual history can be divided into the period before Gilberto Freyre and the period after the publication of *Casa-Grande e Senzala* (translated as "Masters and Slaves"). Until the publication of this remarkable social history of Northeastern Brazil, writers were preoccupied with European subjects and paid little attention to their own country or its problems. And when they did, it was to deprecate its backwardness and reflect in sadness upon the mixture of Negro, Indian and white as something unhealthy if not unnatural, and as condemning their country to inferiority.

Since the publication of "Masters and Slaves" a flood of hundreds of volumes has appeared on Brazilian subjects. That is the great merit of this remarkable book. The Brazilians have discovered themselves. Instead of running away from race mixture as a scandal and a shame they find the vitality and richness of their literature, music, art and architecture in the strength and vigor which a fusion of race and culture has given. They consider Brazil a model for the world to follow and Brazilian culture as a uniquely rich contribution to world civilization.

Something similar has occurred in Mexico following the revolution, and especially after the Cárdenas regime, which greatly increased Mexican self-respect and its feeling of dignity. It was during this period that

Mexico stopped living in constant fear of the United States. Whether this is the immediate cause or not, the Mexicans like the Brazilians have accepted themselves as they are and are proud of it. They are not Europeans or North Americans and do not wish to be. They have a sense of importance and pride in the vast outpouring of energy that has gone into their new art and architecture, their music and poetry, and now their fiction and drama. And all of this is Mexican. It is, I think, admittedly clear that Diego Rivera and Clemente Orozco could only be Mexicans, and no other people could have built the Mexican national University. This too is an acceptance by the Mexicans that their culture is Mexican, as is their race. They are no longer ashamed of having Indian blood in their veins and no longer drive the Indians from the main streets. But in both Brazil and Mexico this facing of the national reality is too recent to have allowed for the growth of a couple of generations to an intellectual maturity free from the sense of being culturally outcast. This self-confidence is an essential for the development of leadership in a nation whether it is drawn from among the intellectuals or not.

Beyond Brazil and Mexico, however, where does one find this kind of intellectual revolution, of a discovery of the national self, as if seeing it for the first time as it really is—and seeing that it is good? The intellectuals have lived for so long immersed in European models that they have in most places barely escaped them. There is obvious danger in overstating this proposition, and I can hear vigorous disclaimers from Argentinians, Colombians, Uruguayans and Costa Ricans, but as an outsider and a friendly one, I can only say that the willingness in gladness to accept oneself and live with oneself that has come as something of a miracle to Brazil and Mexico has not occurred in other countries. Certainly not in Peru, Bolivia, Ecuador, Venezuela or Guatemala, to mention only a few of the nations. And without this acceptance of the nation as it is, effective leadership is impossible.

Intellectuals interested in dealing with the important question of politics and government, of economic growth and business organization, of finance and taxation, unemployment and social security—with any one of the questions that contemporary society has to deal with—had to go to foreign books or foreign universities. And fundamentally, interest in these matters locally did not exist. The intellectual tradition was literary and theoretical. European doctrines in sociology, politics, economics and philosophy were absorbed with avidity. This has happened with positivism, syndicalism, socialism, communism, existentialism, but they were taken over as ideas rather than policies or programs. Traditionally, theory, philosophy, doctrine, intellectual attitude, had little to do with political programs or social policy.

The centralized character of government, the habit of expecting the government to do whatever is to be done, the overwhelming impact of the aristocratic, authoritarian and hierarchical view of life, really meant that ideas were things to argue about, to play with, and not programs or policies. Even when ideas such as democracy or federalism get into constitutions, as the history of the last century and a half will illustrate, they remain ideas rather than norms of conduct. This has occurred more recently with the inclusion of elaborate provisions on human rights and civil liberties into the fundamental document. These too have too often remained just ideas rather than norms of behavior. A theory of democracy, communism, socialism, or what not, has to make its way against a Latin American milieu which is responsive to older and deeper attitudes, attitudes that have no formal doctrinal statement but which are nonetheless very real. For way down deep is the fact that Latin America is humanist rather than materialist. It is compassionate rather than equalitarian; it is authoritarian rather than democratic. It does not understand that authority is divisible, that the president can be defeated by a congress, or flouted by a court and yet remain president. It does not understand that other institutions than the government can exercise important public functions. The attitude is one of acquiescence in the protective power of the mighty one as long as he does not do violence to the basic moral traditions, and, if he does, to destroy his power by revolution and accept a better one in his place.

Basically, Latin Americans would protect the poor, save their dignity, relieve pain and assuage sorrow rather than reform, change, improve or upset status, position, belief or ideals. It is not "progressive," and the reformers are following strange gods and using slogans that stem from other sources. In spite of their many revolutions, the Latin Americans are not either revolutionary or radical. All the revolutions would merely reestablish an older ideal society, hierarchical and authoritarian, compassionate and sensitive to the human dignity even of the least, even of the peon. And the rebellious nationalism so much in evidence is not against authoritarianism or hierarchy but against the materialism and efficiency of modern ways that have no time to be compassionate, that are so preoccupied with success as to take from men what they have most valued— their dignity.

This is perhaps a good place to say a few words about American enterprise in Latin America. The objection to American enterprise is not that it is American. Rather it is disliked because it is efficient, purposeful, direct, single-minded and materialistic. In Latin American culture, business is a part of the total scheme of things; it is part of the family, of the *compadre* relation, of the friendships, of the church. Business is done among friends in a leisurely and understanding way. Material success is at the bottom of the scale. First of all comes the protection of the family, the *compadres,* the friends. Every relation, no matter how unimportant in the business is important on the human side, for each man must be treated with courtesy and dignity, almost as a member of the family. The efficiency and singlemindedness of the American enterprise is unaware of or indifferent to the scheme of ethical and esthetic values by which life is ruled. Its very egalitarianism and familiarity are offensive. It sticks out not because it is American or foreign capital, but because it is not part of the milieu.

It cannot identify with the aristocratic agrarian tradition, or with the growing middle class. To the first it is a threat. To the second it seems a block in their own path, especially as the foreign corporation does not ordinarily (things are changing) offer the young middle class, or the young intellectuals an outlet to their ambitions, and it does not give them, or is not believed to give them, equality of opportunity within the administration. In our own experience a new industry is an opening for new careers. In Latin America a new foreign enterprise has often meant the exclusion of locally competent young people of good families. Neither the business community nor the intellectuals find it congenial. Their life is involved in the total culture, while the American businessman, or manager, stands outside their culture and is somehow beyond their reach. They have no way of bending the new enterprise to their older values and no way of losing themselves within the new venture, or of submerging it within their own system so as to cease to be aware of its irritating presence.

And Americans are not particularly helpful in this. They do not, for the most part, associate with the members of their host community, and if they have to, they often do it in a patronizing way which does not add to their good standing. Mainly Americans live by themselves and do not participate. The rector of the university of an active industrial community in which there were some hundreds of American university-trained specialists in many fields, when asked whether any of this highly select group of Americans took any interest or part in the many interesting activities of this university, replied, "These people do not associate with us."

If one searches into the reason for the hostility shown to Mr. Nixon, here is a key to what happened which has not been explored. And it is the burden of the complaint raised by intellectuals against "American imperialism." The economic arguments and even the political ones, though often used, are of secondary importance. They seem obvious and are part of the contemporary fashion in public debate. The other, the deeper, grievance that Americans are oblivious to and disdainful of Latin American values and sense of personal dignity, is more difficult to express and much too painful to cry in the market place. American business and American policy have often been afflicted by obtuseness and insensitivity. No amount of good will, back-slapping or offers of material aid are adequate substitutes for understanding of and sensitivity to the values that give meaning and direction to life itself. Our efficiency and purposefulness, our "go-getterness," our enthusiasm about success, qualities we greatly prize, prove most irritating and incomprehensible. If only we were less in a hurry, less bent on getting things done quickly; if only we had time for talk and friendliness and courtesy; if only we did not seem to push people around and in our haste forget, or be ignorant of, the amenities essential to friendly relations! As one Latin American expressed it, "Our greatest difficulties are over little, seemingly unimportant, things."

The Latin American intellectual, student, professor, artist, writer, and poet have found American "crudities," as they would call them, so frustrating that on occasion they have been prepared to say "Keep your good will, your material offerings and your bad manners. We will have none of them."

It is important to keep in mind that these feelings and attitudes so frequently voiced, if muted, are not confined to one country. Latin America may be divided into twenty separate nations but intellectually it is very much one community. Many of its most distinguished contemporary writers are almost household words among the literate people in the entire area, particularly in the eighteen Spanish-speaking countries. These include individuals like Alfonso Reyes from Mexico, Germán Arciniegas from Colombia, Picón Salas and Rómulo Gallegos from Venezuela, Luis Alberto Sánchez from Peru, Gilberto Freyre from Brazil, Luis Romero from Argentina, Fernando Ortiz from Cuba.

We are, as a nation, therefore dealing not with single countries even when we are only talking to the minister of Nicaragua or Argentina. Vis-à-vis the United States, there is a community of public opinion which is as wide as the land that includes all of the nations south of the American border. In many things there are sharp differences among these nations and even bitter antagonism. But as against the United States there is wide agreement on many issues and on some there is well nigh unanimity. And to no small degree this is the work of the intellectuals. It could be said that the intellectuals have been the leaders in moulding a Latin American community, at least on the intellectual level, but also indirectly they have had great influence on the political attitudes of their community toward the United States. In some ways the intellectuals have been more influential as leaders of the continental community than of their own particular countries, for the intellectuals, with the exception of Colombia, rarely achieve actual political power.

They are the moderators, the critics, the gadflies, the opponents. They are not the political leaders, though they often have great influence on shaping the opinion that determines the kind of leadership that comes to office and the policies it will pursue. The intellectuals are really caught in a world where their major role is that of critic. The realities of the situation require us to recognize that they are not willing, i.e., able, to face the schizophrenic world they abide in. They greatly value all that a "patronal" and aristocratic society has given them—the ease, the unhurried life, the indifference to great wealth, the presence of many servants to make life easy and secure, the romantic notion of a heroic past, the occasion for friendships and versatility. All of this they would keep. But they also want what the modern world has to offer, or think they want it —modern cities, automobiles, airplanes, factories, the latest products of science, the gadgets of the day. They would have the best of two worlds; the patronal, seignioral society and the egalitarian and industrial one, and will not recognize that they cannot have them both.

There is no way out of the dilemma by a deliberate act of will. They cannot reject either of the two worlds or remain content with one. The schizophrenic world they live in is beyond their control; and we must accept that for the next generation or longer the intellectuals will be possessed by a restless, bitter and turbulent mood. America will be the major target of this inability to square the circle; to make an agrarian feudalism fit in nicely with an industrial egalitarianism, for fortune has cast the United States as the major symbol of their dissatisfaction with both worlds.

K. H. Silvert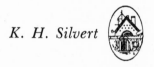

2

Political Change in Latin America

The United States and the Western world as a whole shower Latin America with a persistent stream of cultural stimuli. But even though the West's ideas of industrialization, expanded consumption, and political egalitarianism pour forth equally for all Latin American countries, what is absorbed varies widely from one to another. How and why and toward what immediate ends each nation moves is conditioned by its own traditions and appreciations as well as by the historical course of its particular set of involvements with the technology, ideologies and cultures of the industrially advanced nations. The recurrent crises of most Latin American countries today are of a type symptomatic of a beginning maturity, a ripening understanding of what they want, and of what methods they will use. Thus the recently alerted awareness in the United States of the problems of Latin America is not a simple passage from unthinking Yankee neglect to fatherly notice. It is the direct product of a now purposively and rapidly reacting group of newly synthesizing societies gaining the power to force themselves on world attention.

That the internal dynamics of the Latin American countries are in

K. H. Silvert *has combined an interest in political science and in Latin America since his undergraduate days at the University of Pennsylvania, which awarded him the Ph.D. degree in 1948. At that time he joined the faculty of Tulane University, where he was professor of political science. In 1961 he joined the faculty of Dartmouth, where he is now professor of government. Since 1955, he has also been connected with the American Universities Field Staff as associate first in Central America and then in Argentina and Chile. He has spent over eight years doing research in the field itself and has published extensively on Latin America, as well as within the general discipline of political science.*

part driven by the general cultural stance of the United States as well as by military aid, investments, and loans is obvious. Wittingly or not, then, the United States in the past has had much to do with the social changes which in turn are bringing Latin America new international notice. And indeed, with the inauguration of the Alliance for Progress, the United States has undertaken a cooperative relationship for the conscious social development of Latin America—that is, for the rational attempt to complete the modernization of Latin American life without running any more than necessary the risks of violence and totalitarianism. Whether planned or spontaneous, the growth of national Latin American societies is carrying that region closer to the problem areas and value systems of the European-type states, but what has been occurring is not mere slavish imitation. The many Latin variations on the general themes of underdevelopment and progress toward modernism may well eventually demonstrate to other parts of the world broad and varied possibilities in the decent and dignified adjustment of the individual to national social organization.

To lump the development process of Latin America carelessly in with that of other economically retarded areas is a mistake. Commonly available statistics force one immediate exception of consequence: Argentina, Uruguay, Venezuela, and significant social sectors of Brazil, Colombia, Mexico, Chile, and Cuba must be counted as intermediately developed. Even more important culturally, Latin America has had the longest history of European colonialism in the world. While it may not bear the stamp of Western industrialism, the area has a long and varied experience with a portion of European custom and thought not as a superimposition, but as a deeply internalized aspect of society. Latin America's underdevelopment thus bears a direct lineal relation to idealized Iberian feudalism, and also has the special characteristic of being correlated with under-population, and not with the overpopulation so evident in Asia.

And, lastly, another unusual aspect of Latin America's position is its traditionally close identification with the United States. The intimate relationship has not always been of the most cordial, but it is there and among the reasons for it are proximity, defense considerations, in certain measure shared ideology, and the leverage exerted by the great economic and cultural strength of the United States relative to the Latin American republics. Hemispheric readjustments from paternalism to fraternalism are becoming the order of the day as political change in Latin America mingles with the other social shifts involved in the process of going from systems of necessary authoritarianism to those of possible democracy. These developments should be anticipated by diplomatic policy planners, for the period of one-man, one-family, and one-class government is just about over in a Latin America that is now doing much more than merely copying the standard recipes for democratic government.

POLITICAL LIKENESSES AND DIVERSITIES

The commonwealth notion

The justification for writing about Latin America as a whole is that there are some universal concepts among the symbolic tools used by political leaders within and without the area. *Latin America, Hispano-America, Indo-America,* and *Ibero-America* are more than terms of convenience, for the opinion leaders of the area themselves recognize an emotional commonwealth. They have hardened this awareness in unique international juridical principles, in a regional organization, in their voting in international bodies, in their preferential treatment of their neighbors' nationals, and in their constitutional theories. At this formally legal level, the United States, too, has expressed its recognition of a set of special circumstances through the Monroe Doctrine in its various interpretations, particularized recognition procedures, and participation in regional political and economic as well as jurisprudential arrangements. Special note should also be taken of the strikingly few cases of international warfare in this cartographically Balkanized region, a phenomenon which finds one of its better explanations in the notion of a certain commonwealth identification.

From the historical facts of politics there emerge other likenesses further serving to tie the republics together. If the common experience of colonialism stamped some similar hallmarks, whether the metropolitan power was France, Portugal, or Spain, so did the fact of independence, sweeping through all of Latin America, except for Cuba and Panama, in the same chronological period and under the same ideological banners borrowed from the United States and France. Every country underwent a "time of trouble" after independence, and every one has had at least one great integrating dictator, whether named Díaz, Portales, Rosas, or Carrera. These men are to Latin America as Louis XIV was to France or Ivan the Terrible to Russia: they broke the independent power of the local *caciques* and established centralized control over the territories of their nascent nation-states. Where the integrating centralists could not extend their effective sway to appreciable distances, city-states emerged, as in Central America.

This forced integration almost always was loaded with ideological freight. The *caudillo,* authoritarian leader of a geographically national arena, sought legitimacy in law and authority in party, while he used naked power to break the isolation of the local *caciques.* Although *caudillismo* naturally conduces to the personalistic political parties so widespread in Latin America, conflicting idealisms have also been present. The Conservative-Liberal divisions of the last century, and in some countries even of this century, have echoed true policy and interest clashes as well as mere personality differences. The *caudillo,* then, often has been the personification of ideological disagreement, manipulating the power of the idea as well as the sword.

In contemporary Latin America, the emergence of impersonal political institutions is everywhere clearly visible to one or another degree. Bound into a democratic bundle, economic development, nationalism, institutionalization, and modernism are widely generalized goals. These common aspirations and a common dependence on a common world buttress the fraternal feelings of the commonwealth notion.

Historical range of political difference

A factor weakening feelings of hemispheric identification, however, is that these sentiments are restricted largely to élite leadership groups whose ideas are projected against much political divergence and large sectors of non-participant persons alienated for one or another reason from the mainstream of the nation. In addition, variation among the countries is becoming accentuated as individual national histories become an increasingly strong force pushing the Latin American republics ever further apart into differing political cultures and styles. They are all somewhere along the continuum to democratic nation-state status, but accident, history, and resources combine in differing ways to produce varying results.

Independence sometimes came easily, for example, as in the case of Central America, heir to the greater efforts in Mexico. But in Mexico itself, the independence movement was confounded with social revolution, and the process was painful and relatively protracted. The succeeding times of trouble also varied widely in intensity and duration, from the relatively easy transition of Argentina to the fifty years of convulsion in Mexico. Where the integrating dictatorship came early, as in Chile, national life subsequently has tended to develp with comparative ease; yet other countries, such as Venezuela, show a procession of *caudillos* persisting into yesterday's headlines. The Liberal-Conservative conflicts were usually fairly well resolved everywhere by the turn of the century, the Liberals almost invariably victorious either partially or completely. The major exception is Colombia, where the issue is still not settled. Colombia, in fact, remains the only country in which the two major parties still bear the names *Liberal* and *Conservative.*

National revindication, social justice, economic independence, anti-imperialism, industrialization, and *nationalism* are the words of the current Latin political lexicon everywhere. But they do not have the same tone in every country, nor even within each set of national boundaries does this vocabulary permeate all the population strata. Even though the generalized aspirations of the leadership elements may have ingredients in common, the development of an adequate American policy vis-à-vis the entire area must take into account not only the vast differences of the present, but also the fascinatingly diverse manners in which further development is certain to manifest itself.

Political Values and Types of Polities

Social class

A hobby of Latin Americanists, their hands forced by the variety of their area of study, is to develop sets of social categories within which to squeeze all twenty republics. One of the efficient ways in which to build a distribution is in accordance with social class, a most obvious feature of Latin societies manifested in clothing, speech, occupation, habitation, education, and of course, political power. The allied subjects of social class and social mobility tell us whether a society is open or closed, and thus are essential to predictions concerning stability and the probabilities for democratic processes. Social structural analysis is also indispensable for an understanding of nationalism and potentialities for economic growth.

The simplest societies in Latin America are those popularly called semi-feudal, ruled by a small élite, the holders of major economic power, recipients of the highest social status and prestige, monopolists of the political organism. Under them can be found a shrivelled administrative and professional group charged with the operation of the cities, the public service, and the discharge of the necessary professional functions, especially law and medicine. At the bottom are the peasants, migratory or tenant farmers, sometimes the owners of their own small plots; and in the cities, those persons necessary to the more menial functions. In some countries the lowest agricultural group is divided ethnically into Indians and other persons considered Europeanized, no matter what their physical race, by virtue of their speaking a European language, their wearing of non-Indian dress, and their feeling of being a part of the national life, even though most tenuously.

Guatemala is an excellent case of a structure only slightly more complicated than that described above. Of a total population of about three million, perhaps only 125,000 can be counted as effective actors in the reaching of political decisions at the national level. This figure is arrived at by subtracting the Indian population, those rural *mestizos* who are not truly national in their concepts, the illiterates, persons under eighteen, and a part of the female population.

At the other end of the scale is Argentina. Almost a third of the twenty million Argentines live in Greater Buenos Aires; and in the country as a whole, two-thirds live in towns and cities of over 2,000 population. About a third of the Argentines are in the middle and upper occupational levels. Except for scattered and isolated Indian and mixed rural groups, the population is European. Agricultural labor is not rooted to the soil as in Peruvian and Chilean haciendas; for example, farm workers and ranch hands may and in fact do make use of the channels of social mobility, forming one of the important mass groups supporting ex-dictator Juan Perón and contributing to the huge increase in the city populations of the past fifteen years.

Caste-like racial distinctions and a sharp cultural cut between the city and the country make popular sovereignty and the dispersion of political power at best a very limited possibility in such countries as Guatemala. The homogeneity of Argentina speeds communications, distributes aspirational goals almost universally, and promotes mass participation in politics for good or ill.

The velocity of Latin American social change—and it is in some fundamental respects the fastest moving part of the world—can create very complicated class systems. Mexico and Brazil, to take two examples among various, have what may be called double systems. There is an old and a new upper group, the former generally agrarian and clerical in orientation, the latter urban industrial and secularist. The old service middle class coexists with the new white collar and professional elements, while the industrial blue collar groups find little in common with depressed agrarian persons. Add the racial complication of the Indian populations of Mexico and this somewhat oversimplified picture is complete.

The most important class phenomenon from a political viewpoint is the rapid growth of middle groups. Rooted in the exploding cities and fomented by the complex skills demanded by the new industries, the expanding welfare functions of government, and the extension of the professions, the middle sectors are already the decisive voice in at least half of the Latin American countries. Their presence spells the doom of traditional *caudillismo,* but not necessarily the immediate and automatic stability and democracy which popular myth attributes to them.

Nationalism

An ordinary view of nationalism is that it is a negative sentiment, backward looking, exclusivist, anti-foreign, and at times even insane, as in Nazi Germany. A cooler reaction would be to think of nationalism as a social value elevating loyalty to a state and to the citizenry included therein to a supreme position. In the event of a clash involving, say, religious institutions or even the right of a parent to beat his child, a national society would assume ultimate adherence to the dictates of the state within a broadly prescribed realm rather than of any intervening, buffer institutions. Some of the usual historical manifestations of nationalism are citizens' armies, such symbols as flags and anthems, a public education system, reverence for the past as well as glorification of the future, and so on.

The creation of new middle (as well as upper and lower) economic positions, which occurs in developing countries, forces apart the traditional social structure, introducing the middle classes which are such a dynamic part of the new Latin America. These complications are at the same time rationalized by nationalism, a loyalty pattern to cover not only the geographical areas involved, but now also the new identifications across class lines which build consistency and stability into the higher degree of interdependence that industrial urbanism always implies. Where there are middle groups, there is nationalism, the basic political organizing value of Westernism.

Despite a lack of reliable data, some informed guessing may be done as to the degree to which various Latin American countries have become truly national societies. In point for this subjective evaluation are such criteria as ethnic integration of the population, political history as it may indicate cohesiveness or disorganization, complexity of the city and the occupational range of the economic apparatus, degree of autonomy or dependency of the countryside and the political power of the peasantry, if any, mobility factors, and so on. Closest to nation-state standing in Latin America are Uruguay, Argentina, Cuba, Costa Rica, and Chile, and perhaps in that descending order, although to be so exact as to give rankings within the categories is to open the door to much wrangling. The next category might well include those countries moving rapidly toward nationhood with a solid social consensus approving the trend. Again in questionable descending order, these countries are: Mexico, Colombia, Brazil, Venezuela, and recently the Dominican Republic. The third category includes those in which the upper groups are moving violently toward nationalist objectives, but with sluggish response in the body social. They are Peru, Bolivia, Guatemala, Ecuador, El Salvador, and Panama, once again in dubious order. And lastly, slow rates of movement, with almost all social sectors stagnant, are to be found in Honduras, Paraguay, Nicaragua, and Haiti.

Class, nationalism, and democracy

The social value of nationalism is a necessary condition for democracy, but obviously not a sufficient one. Without it, however, the almost universal acceptance of the rules within which democracy works and the necessary belief in the reciprocating continuity of acquiescence and opposition cannot function.

> Democracy presupposes a toughminded and tenacious acceptance of the nation as deserving a continuing loyalty which transcends loyalty to class. Democracy assumes that the proper adjustments and accommodations among classes, probably accompanied by vigorous debate and pulling and hauling, will be made peacefully within the framework provided. If loyalty to a class, whether a proletariat in the professional sense or an elite group, supersedes the common loyalty then democracy suffers accordingly.[1]

National loyalty identifications, however, are not sufficient to guarantee democracy, since the sentiment may also be employed for the implementation of totalitarian, as contrasted with authoritarian rule. Totalitarianisms are so called precisely because they seek to destroy completely the institutional buffers between the individual and the state, to erase all non-state loyalties, and to void all doctrines propounding governmental self-restraint. When scientific techniques are not well developed, then the full weight of the dictator can fall directly only on the visible élite; others escape for negative reasons, saved by the sheer impossibility of the police task. With IBM machines, radio patrol cars, and modern propaganda techniques, the state gains the power to "finger" anyone, to minimize if not erase the cushioning effects of religious, kin, and class shock absorbers. If technological complication implies middle classes and middle classes imply nationalism, then nationalism in turn also implies possibilities for sterner autocracies as well as fuller democracies. In short, nationalism is a neutral factor, its color a reflection of other choices. It may be argued that full national integration so clearly demands widespread respect for the rule-of-law that all truly mature and self-sustaining nations must be libertarian. However, immature nations sometimes use the power of the almost-national state for anti-democratic purposes.

What we may call "political culture," notions of civic goodness and badness, the attitudes of innovating groups, and the pressures from the international world all contribute to throwing the choice toward more or less freedom. In Latin America, even the harshest dictators customarily attempt to clothe themselves in legal legitimacy and to talk in the name of democracy. This pose is not mere farce; it conditions future action most importantly.

Latin American constitutions are an excellent case in point of the orienting power of expressed traditional goals. Over 200 constitutions have been adopted in the more or less 150 years during which the Latins have been at work on organic law. Most of the changes have been in the

---

[1] Russell H. Fitzgibbon in "Pathology of Democracy in Latin America," *The American Political Science Review*, March, 1950.

hortatory and the distributing clauses as one or another philosophy or this or that administrative gimmick has been experimented with. But the aspirations outlined in these documents have often served to condition the actions of future governments. As a Latin American jurist has said in commenting on the advanced theories contained in constitutional law, "After all, before you embrace a woman, you tell her you love her." Through the schools, law, the writings of impassioned leaders, Latin Americans have been told for almost two centuries that democracy is desirable. The writings of Locke, Bentham, and the two Mills, *The Federalist Papers,* the Constitution of the United States, and the Declaration of the Rights of Man, among many other such expressions of man's dignity, have all been imported to help in solidifying this predisposition. While the economic and social conditions in most of Latin America have not been of a type to support full-blown democracies, these political values have constantly served as a prod for the changing of the opposed root conditions. Small wonder, then, that the 20th century is so often called The Age of Politics in Latin America.

It is thus no accident that included in the list of those countries which are most nearly nation-states are also to be found those usually considered most democratic. A noted American historian, Arthur P. Whitaker, suggests that "the countries which have approximated most closely to the democratic ideal have been—Argentina, Brazil, Chile, Colombia, Costa Rica, and Uruguay." A typology developed by a political sociologist (Seymour Martin Lipset, published in *The American Political Science Review* and subsequently in his book, *Political Man*) posits only two categories, "Democracies and Unstable Dictatorships" and "Stable Dictatorships." He puts in the former Argentina, Brazil, Chile, Colombia, Costa Rica, Mexico, and Uruguay; and in the latter, all the rest of Latin America. While two categories are insufficient to explain all of Latin America, the reappearance of the first seven in high position on all three listings, "The National," "The Democratic," and "Democracies and Unstable Dictatorships," clearly indicates certain factors common to all. Nationalism plus the long belief in the value of democracy may well be in combination as the common denominator.

It should not be expected that such a fundamental change as the transformation of traditional societies into national democracies can occur without great disturbance.

THE USES OF FORCE

A Chilean political figure has written that some Latin Americans want "order even if in despotism," and that others want "liberty even if in anarchy." Before an ordering of liberty is attained, there will probably be much more trouble in Latin America. But the real amount of violence as such should not be overestimated. The number of revolutions in Latin America is accentuated by the North American, who tends to forget that there are twenty different republics all having their own troubles, and who does not understand the patterning of Latin violence, the often reduced number of persons involved, and the built-in limitations of the impact of civil disorder on daily life.

"Unpredictable" and "unstable" are the two adjectives most often applied to Latin American politics. The implications of both pejoratives are partially erroneous. First, to be "unstable" is not necessarily to be "unpredictable." As a matter of fact, one of the easiest things to predict is instability itself. And second, some types of revolutionary disturbance do not indicate instability. If the normal way of rotating the executive in a given country is by revolution, and if there have been a hundred such changes in a century, then it is not being facetious to remark that revolutions are a sign of stability—that events are marching along as they always have. A country can afford such adventures only if they are contained and if there are built-in safeguards against excessive violence. The right of asylum, recognized legally by all Latin American governments, is one of the insurance policies provided to cut down deaths by revolution. Top-level corruption—a kind of saving against a rainy day—is another of these insurance devices. In addition, very strong kinship ties, a sense of class identification, and colleagueship all offer protection against the vicissitudes of politics. Many revolts, then, cost few lives, immediately affect persons only in the élite groups, and do not perturb the normal functioning of society.

In addition we should not forget that some countries have enjoyed very long periods without violence. Mexico has experienced peaceful political transitions for the last thirty years. Of the 105 years between 1839 and 1944, only three presidents in Guatemala occupied 61 years of the time. And yet, not to be too sanguine about the matter, some revolutions have been extraordinarily bloody and deeply disturbing, and there is little doubt that Latin American revolutionary activity is becoming more and more costly. Let us see whether some order can be breathed into this matter.

Types of revolutions and their incidence

There are many different families of violence, and their incidence depends absolutely on the type of society concerned. Here are the more common varieties, past and present:

The Simple Barracks Revolt—More outbreaks have been of this kind than of any other. Highly characteristic of the rudimentary bi-class societies, the army plays out the disposition of force, sometimes in its own name, or in that of a given leader, sometimes with ideological justification, and yet again in various combinations of these three rationalizations. The barracks revolt rarely causes much public commotion, even though at times substantive shifts in policy may emerge from one.

The Peasant Revolt—Only in bi-ethnic countries, or where the rural group is maintained in deep subservience, do peasant revolts occur. They are rarely reported internationally, since by definition they take place in a restricted area and are not of direct significance at the national level. Very few are now seen, although they were quite common in the colonial and early independence periods.

The Regional Revolt—Another type which now almost never occurs, regional uprisings were characteristic of the conflict period attending the rise of the centralizing *caudillos* and the liquidation of their provincial rivals. The history of Argentina, for example, is often written in terms of the "port," Buenos Aires, as opposed to the "interior," or the provinces. Brazil offers many examples, as does Colombia. Regional rivalries are now often played out in party politics through the activities of local bosses, who in many places have inherited the name *"cacique."*

The Complicated Barracks Revolt—The commonest of all at present, this kind of insurrection involves civilian as well as military groups. The immediate events are largely in terms of military action, but the issues are clearly ideological and involve political parties and interest groups. The fall of Perón is a case in point, as well as the defeats of Pérez Jiménez in Venezuela in 1958, Rojas Pinilla in Colombia in 1957, of Argentina's Frondizi and Peru's Prado in 1962. This type can be somewhat costly in lives, although there are many examples (such as Guatemala in 1944) in which almost no one is killed. The issues may be entirely political, or the civilian participation may be so heated and widespread as to involve the attitudes and aspirations of social revolution, as was the case in Cuba with the overthrow of Batista in 1959. The Cuban example is on the borderline, for although Havana fell and Batista fled as the direct result of an army defection, civilian opposition had previously so eroded the Batista government's ability to impose itself as to leave the military with little or no choice.

The Civilian Political Revolt—Because of the active role of the military in politics, there is no abundance of this type of action. Chile, in its 1932 year of revolutions, saw the military discredited and many examples of entirely civilian action in forcing governmental changes. But this kind of undertaking becomes more difficult when the military are equipped with jet planes and tanks. The establishment of irregular armies and the practice of civilian terrorism were easier in the days when the rifle was the common arbiter. The general strike is the contemporary civilian phenomenon most closely allied to this category of revolt.

The Social Revolution—The Mexican Revolution, at its most heated between 1910 and 1917, was the only relatively complete example of social revolution in Latin America before the installation of Cuba's revolutionary socialist Marxist regime. The Mexican experience combined all the other types, involving as it did simple and complex barracks revolts, a large measure of peasant protest and action, civilian participation at all levels, and regional disturbances. The result was to change the nature of the social hierarchy and partially to reorder it, thus, during its frankly violent phase, fitting the classical definition of social revolution. The Cuban Revolution, ostensibly fought in the name of the politics of Social Democracy, involved much less immediate violence than the Mexican case. But because of the more complex technology available to the Cubans, their extended communications network and relatively high degree of general economic development, and their susceptibility to Communist ideology, the social consequences promise to be much more immediately widespread and less evolutionary than in Mexico, and the tension of even longer duration.

Because of their failure to resolve many of the basic problems of even growth, all the intermediately developed countries of Latin America to one or another degree harbor the possibilities of social revolution, the most sanguinary and least predictable and thus potentially most dangerous of all forms of civil disorder.

Unstructured Violence—(1) The Street Riot: *Manifestaciones,* as they are often called in Spanish, usually take place to protest particular governmental actions, such as a rise in bus fares or the arrest of political or labor leaders. University students are very prone to this kind of disturbance; for example, the student riots in Mexico in 1958 and those in Chile in 1957 were both sparked by an increase in bus fares. Deaths are not uncommon in these incidents. (2) The *Bogotazo:* This phenomenon takes its name from the mob violence in Bogota in 1948, when the assassination of the leader of the Liberal Party touched off mass rioting resulting in wholesale looting, burning and killing. These occurrences are undirected, a kind of explosive social vomiting. They indicate that the normal channels of access to the decision making areas have been closed off for too long to bleed off protest pressures. The *bogotazo* is rare, but there are sufficient cases in history—and, dangerously, enough street riots which have had all the preliminary elements of the *bogotazo*—to make this category worth including.

Complicated barracks revolts, civilian political revolts, social revolutions, and unstructured violence are all characteristic of periods in which the middle class is growing and seeking an adjustment. Those countries denominated as quite national (Chile, Uruguay, Argentina, Cuba, and Costa Rica) as well as those on the verge (Mexico, Colombia, Brazil, Venezuela, and The Dominican Republic) are susceptible to these types of disturbance, or already have partially outgrown them. Since these nations have either large, complicated industrial cities or the self-conscious and cohesive landed peasantry of Costa Rica, civil strife is inevitably vastly punishing to major parts of the population, or at best a very grave threat. Bloodless strife is impossible to these countries; the best they can hope for, should they have recourse to revolution, is the stylized combination street fighting and barracks revolts of Argentina, an arrangement which may not hold even for that country should their troubles become more galling.

The more underdeveloped republics will tend to stick to the spread ranging from simple barracks revolts to complicated ones, probably with some peasant and regional difficulties thrown in, particularly in the cases of Peru and Bolivia. But no guarantees against a build-up to social revolution can be given even for the least developed countries, although the probabilities are against it. The uncontrollable factor here is the nature of international ideological and economic stimuli and the intensity of local reactions to them.

The prognosis must be for continued revolutionary activity in many of the countries as they shake their way further into this century. If Europe drew itself from mercantilism to capitalism by way of the French Revolution, Latin America is doing it by way of all those revolutionary conflicts in which so much valor, idealism, and youth are spent.

The role of the military

The military overthrows of the constitutional regimes of Argentina and Peru in the first seven months of 1962, as well as very public military pressure on the governments of Ecuador, El Salvador, and Venezuela in the same period, the role of the military in the resignation of Brazilian President Janio Quadros and the subsequent change of the governmental structure in mid-1961, and hints of similar incidents in other lands—all have once again raised major international policy problems in the attempt to adjust defense requirements to the internal aspects of military organization.

The continuing intervention of the military in the politics of certain Latin American countries is a normal concomitant of oligarchical regimes, or of what may be called political underdevelopment. When government is the creature of only a part of the body social, the employment of overt force cannot be contained by a responsibly acting citizenry operating through the many institutions open to a participant and plural society. Even so, it would be erroneous to presume that politicized military groups in Latin America move in an entirely simplistic and uninhibited fashion. In carrying out their internal political policing functions, the military interact with their peer groups or with those to which they aspire. There is no divorce, then, between the armed forces and the social elements comprising the most effective civilian political groups; on the contrary, often the identification is all too close.

The patterns of the military-civilian interaction change with the nature of the society and the development of the political value system. The historically first and simplest relationship is that described by the traditional caudillistic form, as in contemporary Paraguay, in which the leader is almost always an officer in the armed forces and uses this power position to cement himself into political office. Second, the modern variant of this practice appears when the military pretend to rule in trustee fashion, but yet seek to sustain institutional forms and maintain a degree of impersonalism and aloofness from party politics, so that a *caudillo* does not emerge. This more complicated form of interventionism is what has recently become so popular, as the military assume the role of defenders of constitutionalism and democracy. The governments which succeeded Perón in Argentina and Pérez Jiménez in Venezuela were of this type, and both prided themselves on their mission of preparing the country for the return to constitutional and civilian government which actually occurred. But Argentina has already witnessed another military coup against the person allowed to become president, and Venezuela continues to be perturbed by military elements from both the right and left who aspire to the destruction of the government of President Romulo Betancourt.

A third variant is the military acting as the general orienters of policy. The Mexican situation is thus viewed by some specialists; that is, that the military defines the outside limits within which the constituted authorities may work, thus taking into its own hands only the ultimate tutelary role in partial control of the civil functionaries. The Argentine armed forces played this role in limiting the actions of President Arturo Frondizi from 1958 to 1962 with respect to the unions, communism, *peronismo,* and the Church. Closely allied to this category is the fourth variant, the situation in which no government can exist without at least the tacit consent of the military. Brazil and Guatemala are examples, at least for the moment. Any one of these first four situations is unstable, for slipping from one to another relationship is always a possibility unless social inhibitions against military interventionism have grown strong, as in Mexico.

Fifth, we find the military acting as a veto group only in so far as their own interests are concerned, but otherwise quite powerless politically. It may be that Chile fits this classification, or it may even fall into the sixth, in which the armed forces are professional and apolitical. Uruguay is in this last fortunate position. The ultimate possibility is that the military should be nonexistent. Costa Rica is the lone example, the only country in Latin America which has simply abolished its armed services on the dual grounds that the good citizen himself is enough to defend the country against any neighboring enemies, and that no one is able to defend it against the mighty nuclear weapons of the world powers.

Military intervention in political affairs is a long-standing impediment to the development of responsible government, a constant invitation to the dissatisfied to seek adjudication by bullet. Even though the military, armed with their World War II weapons, have not always been on the side of the devil, by and large they are a hindrance to the development of experience in the peaceful transfer of power. They can be hemmed in effectively only by the development of a complex of parties and pressure groups to orient the collective power of the citizenry. Certainly the growing complication of Latin American governments makes it ever riskier to entrust public administration to untrained and *ad hoc* military governors.

PARTIES AND PRESSURE GROUPS

Party systems

The double class system already discussed also describes the dimensions of a profound clash between traditionalists and modernists which determines the basic nature of party ideologies in Latin America. In traditional societies individual behavior is prescribed for every situation, change is discouraged, and rigid hierarchy is adhered to in the stamping of all action with a moral as well as a secular sanction. Modern persons, on the contrary, encourage the making of deliberate decisions based in good measure on pragmatic considerations; they also seek to order and control change by institutionalizing it, and they strive for a pluralism and an eclecticism in social organization which tends to open society in answer to the demands for specialization and interdependence imposed by industrialization. The traditional-modern schism in Latin America is no less than the chasm between feudal and modern values, two dramatically opposed sets of world views.

The most important reflection of this strife in party politics is that consequently there are two different scales of Left, Right, and Center to match the two different class and value systems. The Right wing of the traditionalists is found in the classical Conservative parties; but there is also a little recognized traditional left, composed of syndicalist and falangist elements who seek to contain the social and political effects of economic development by a corporativist ordering of man, imprisoning him within rigidly hierarchical institutions and denying him the kind of pragmatic individualism associated with liberal capitalistic societies. Thus traditionalists both of the Left and Right denounce liberalism as well as Marxism, and capitalism as well as communism, holding both the United States and Soviet Russia to be anti-religious and materialistic societies. On the other hand, the *modern* Right is normally composed of persons in the Liberal parties and in the Right wings of the Radical parties and other similar groups. And then the spread through Center to Left flows along the usual distribution of Radicals to Christian Democrats to Socialists and Communists. This distinction between the traditional and modern concepts of Right and Left is of great importance in understanding the politics of such countries as Mexico, Argentina, and Colombia, which in certain characteristics of administrative organization as well as in the ideological constellation of important élite groups demonstrate the continuing appeal of corporativist solutions for the entire Latin world. Mexico's official party, for example, is a case in point of neo-syndicalist organization, as are parts of the Colombian labor movement.

What the parties espouse in terms of specific programs is also considerably varied. There are the well known "somebodyisms," the personalistic parties which identify with a charismatic individual. Thus arise such labels as *peronismo, batllismo, porfirismo,* and so on, referring to the conglomeration of attitudes, ideas, and loyalties surrounding Perón in Argentina, Batlle in Uruguay, and Porfirio Díaz in Mexico, to take only three of numerous examples. An ideational tone accompanies these personalistic designations: a kind of Black Populism in the case of Perón; secularist, middle class reform politics identified with Batlle; and the classical marriage of Liberal Positivism and *caudillismo* associated with Díaz.

Aside from propounding ideology and urging programs, political parties have many other functions, of course. They organize the electorate for their periodic interventions in decision making, if they operate within a democratic content. They serve to carry ideas back and forth between the government and the populace when campaigns and elections are not in process. That they also act as employment agencies is well known.

Not every Latin American group bearing the title *"partido"* is really a political party by these criteria. When what is called a party merely performs policing functions for a dictatorial government and serves as a housekeeping agency for the imposition of views from the top, then we are not dealing with a functional party. Of this one-way control type are the single party "systems" of such a country as was the Dominican Republic under Trujillo, or as Paraguay is today. The party is so closely identified with the administration that to be of an opposition group is to be subversive or even treasonous. Venez uela has also operated so in the recent past, as have other Latin countries in their periods of harsher caudillistic authoritarianism.

Mexico, however, offers the case of a single dominant party playing out its role without crudely repressive practices. There are opposition parties, the most important of which are the clerical PAN (National Action Party) on the right, and the Communist Party on the left. Membership in these opposition groups is no crime, and they legitimately serve to organize dissident opinions. But they have no ability to win an election, even though they may campaign, publish, meet, and speak without interference. The PRI (Institutional Revolutionary Party), the official entity, embraces everyone from the industrialist to the government employee to the trade unionist. Sometimes it is argued that the PRI is analogous to the Democratic Party of the American South, in truth representative of many factions, with the real decisions among opposing views made in the primary elections. In Mexico, the arguments take place among the leaders representing their rank and file supporters, and then the party makes known its official position. PRI is not monolithic; it is part of the trust arrangement in which Mexico's development is held by the military, the intellectuals, the new economic élites, the trade unions, and the middle class groups. Labor difficulties offer some hint that the PRI may eventually break into its component interest parts, but it would be a rash man indeed who would presume to predict when this split will occur.

Aside from the false and the real one-party systems named above, there are also a few two-party structures to be counted. Traditionally political development, as has been said, revolved about Conservatives and Liberals. In Colombia, where this division still exists, we have the most consistent case of bi-party politics. Uruguay, with its *Colorados* and *Blancos* ("Reds" and "Whites") has been considered by many political scientists as not a true example of a two-party structure, for the *Colorados* had won office uninterruptedly for almost a century. But in 1958 the Whites finally won a national election, and so we may presume Uruguay to be in the two-party class.

There are also mixed cases, in which two major parties contend at the national level, but a multiplicity argue over the municipal and provincial posts. Argentina is the most complicated case of this kind, for since 1945 only two major parties have presented themselves for the presidential elections. Unhappily for simplicity, they have not always been the same two parties. In 1945, there was the Peronista Party, with virtually all the opposition in a single coalition. The traditional Radical Party led the opposition in the hopeless elections of 1951, but later, in 1958, the Radicals split into their two historic blocs, the Intransigent Radicals and the Radicals of the People, they being the only two serious contenders. The Conservatives, Socialists, Christian Democrats, Peronists, and Communists continue to be forces of some consequence, however, so that Argentina is on the borderline between a two-party and a multi-party system.

The electoral laws of Argentina, modeled as they were after those of the United States, including an electoral college, favored a two-party system even though social practice and the diversity of new interest groups favored a multi-party structure. Chile's laws, however, provide for proportional representation within the neo-parliamentary governmental organization established in the Constitution of 1925. The result has been one of the most stable multi-party systems in Latin America, running from Right to Left, from Conservatives through Liberals to Radicals in the center, and on left to Christian Democrats, various branches of the Socialists, and the Communists. The close similarity both in Chile and Argentina to the political spread of France and Italy is clear, and is no accident, for both countries are deeply influenced by those two European idea sources.

The multi-party system of Brazil, however, is more indigenous in origin and orientation, and also includes phenomena peculiar to the size and population of that huge country. The ideological distribution is strongly influenced by entirely internal considerations and is only peripherally liable to influence from abroad, while the extent and diversity of the country has been propitious for the development of sectional parties. Although these regional groups, or what are sometimes called "particularistic" parties, have died out almost everywhere in Latin America, including Brazil, the regional origins of a political party have much to do with setting present day attitudes. The Province of São Paulo has been particularly noteworthy in its influence on national politics through party mechanisms.

There is little meaningful relationship between formal party system and the social order, except in the most backward authoritarianisms. In those cases, it is only by classificatory generosity that one can speak of parties at all. A better clue to political development is derived from party programs and approaches, rather than from counting the number of parties and relating them systematically. A reasonable hypothesis is that the more national a country, the less personalistic will be the parties, the more they will adjust conflicting interests within their own mechanisms, the greater will be their concern with institutional self-preservation and the winning of elections as a good in itself. As is to be expected, then, Argentina, Chile, Uruguay, and Costa Rica all have long histories of impersonal party politics, even though complicated by the traditional-modern value split. Castro Cuba rapidly succeeded in building a highly professional single party of authoritarian stamp, manipulating the charisma of Fidel as a symbol, but otherwise quite impersonal for the Latin American ambience.

Professional parties coexist with single-interest and personalistic parties in Brazil and Venezuela; these nations are among those in the second level of adjustment to nation-state status. Mexico and Colombia, heading the list of countries in the second level of adjustment, have unique structures for Latin America, but their parties may with confidence be called impersonal, and broadly based in the interests they represent, regardless of their ideologies. In Peru, Guatemala, Ecuador, El Salvador and Panama, the parties tend to be narrowly based, many are shortlived, and in numerous cases little difference can be observed between a party and the single interest it represents.

A preliminary non-public mediation of interest disputes is necessary so that the electorate may choose among alternatives not at the level of detail, but of policy. Without an impersonal political party structure aiding in the day-to-day mediation of disagreement, substantively good voting is difficult if not impossible in anything more than a town situation. The weeding out of issues to simplify national politics is a major party function which also has international effects. The introduction of debate at the party level may slow down the process of diplomatic negotiation but is necessary when a national consensus, rather than a mere executive opinion, is required for lasting agreement on substantive issues. In brief, it is intrinsically more difficult to negotiate truly important matters with democratic nation-states than with dictatorships. It is only good sense to make the effort, however, especially when we recognize that the age of *caudillismo* is drawing to a troubled close, as surely it is in Latin America.

Marxism and Communism as special cases

Marxist thought and Communist ideology, as products of Western philosophy attractive to the partially developed, have no market in pre-industrial and non-national cultures. Naturally, then, the general social and economic development of Latin America opens up possibilities for the growth of communism as for the evolution of middle classes. Communists notoriously gain advantage in periods of turmoil, but especially so in those upheavals connected with rapidly developing nationalism, or in cases in which social balance is denied by fanatical opposition to the full implications of the changes of development. Robert Alexander, in his *Communism in Latin America,* for example, argues that wherever a democratic trade union movement is allowed to flourish, the Communists lose their major source of mass support and are driven back in upon their own professional core. He cites Mexico as the most pertinent example, adding that in a period of national construction Communists may play a very important role, but thereafter they can be "withered away," to turn their phrase against them, by the open play of normal democratic politics. In formally organizational terms at least, the Mexican case seems most appropriate, for the Communist Party, although legal, has lately been unable to muster enough votes to get itself on the ballot.

But the play of Marxist politics in Latin America can no longer be effectively analyzed by an almost exclusive attention to persons formally members of the Communist parties and their fellow-travelers. The emergence of the "Marxist-Leninist" school of revolutionary socialism in Cuba has enlarged the scope of the revolutionary left by providing a living Latin example of a Marxist government, a training ground, and a factory of ideology. The effect has been to frighten less extremist individuals away from the revolutionary Socialist and Communist parties, but also to force a sometimes uneasy alliance between Socialists and Communists who previously had followed distinct policies and practices. The example of Cuba has also sharpened an awareness and recognition of the immediate necessity for a viable opposition to Marxist solutions, especially in the ranks of the democratic Left and Center. While the polarization has undoubtedly increased objective Marxist strength in Latin America, the greater awareness of danger among opposition groups may have decreased their relative strength by and large. The measure of the success of the Latin American role in the Alliance for Progress will be their ability to translate a recognition of danger into effectively affirmative policies of democratic development.

Statistically, the Communist role outside of Cuba seems small at first glance. Active membership in Communist parties is estimated at about a quarter of a million throughout Latin America; the U.S.S.R. maintains diplomatic relations with only five countries (Argentina, Cuba, Brazil, Mexico, and Uruguay), and Communist bloc countries account for only about 2 per cent of the combined imports and exports of Latin America. But figures of this type are increasingly misleading in assessing possible Marxist strength in Latin America. The fact that Communists *acting by themselves* have not the widespread popular support necessary to seize full political power anywhere in Latin America does not mean that rather more broadly defined Marxist revolutionary socialist regimes are not a possibility, as the case of Cuba has so clearly demonstrated. To quote from a prescient report released by a Senate investigating committee in 1959, and even more valid now than then:

> From the evidence at hand, the Latin American Communist parties are not, under normal circumstances, in any position to assume political power in any Latin American country. The exception to this general conclusion arises whenever there is a situation of political economic confusion following the collapse of a dictatorial regime, with the new government in the hands of inexperienced and politically unsophisticated people. In such a situation, the Communists came close to seizing power in Guatemala in 1954. At present, Cuba may be following a similar pattern. . . . This situation holds danger— it can become a touch-and-go matter. Dictators may, and usually do, suppress the Communists—and the democratic political forces, too, as a rule. But dictators are no long run solution to the Communist threat. When the regime changes, and if democratic forces and traditions are weakened meanwhile, then the underground Communist group emerges as a potentially powerful force.

The Cuban example is all the more dangerous because it is not identified only with Communist parties; the Marxism-Leninism ideological tag was adopted by the present Cuban regime to indicate something native, something special to the Latin American experience and somewhat independent of the slavish devotion to Moscow which so long has characterized the policies of the Communist parties themselves. The Cuban line adjusts itself to the political configuration which often develops in times of nationalist revolution, when there is a tendency for all political groups of a nationalistic stripe to join for the attainment of their common national ends. This kind of alliance almost invariably takes place in times of acute political crisis involving all-embracing issues when polarization is the natural result of the utter massiveness of the issues involved. A similar coalition occurred in Mexico during the decade of the thirties, but the period of subsequent consolidation drastically reduced the advantages of alliance with the far left, with the results we have already noted. To broaden the base of the Marxist left inside the nationalist movements obviously increases their chances for consolidating the post-revolutionary regimes themselves, as we are witnessing in Cuba. A distinction must then be drawn between Russian-oriented Communists and Cuban-type Marxist-Leninists to appreciate fully the new strength of this part of the Left in Latin America and thus the new task of the anti-Marxist opposition.

A third Marxist influence must also be noted—the vulgar Marxism, so-called, of that widespread and unsophisticated brand of economic determinism so common among educated Latin Americans. In areas where economic necessities loom large, where the example of the external world continuously pushes toward expanded consumption, to put primary attention on economic factors as the key to social change is only natural. The United States has also contributed to this kind of easy analysis by its past accent on only economic development and its ingenuous insistence that people with full bellies don't become Communists. It is not only Communists, Trotskyists, and left Socialists who have narrowly materialistic ideas; in an amorphous way, anyone who subscribes to the absolute premise that "Money Talks" contributes to a dime-store variety of economic determinism.

Pressure groups

Interest or pressure groups are few in Latin America. Where caudillistic one-party rule holds sway, there is insufficient complication to give much room to variegated pressure groups. And where multi-party systems operate, except in the most developed countries, the parties represent small middle and upper groups and speak in the name of the economic interests themselves.

But still, there remain some extremely important associations which can be called pressure groups. Foremost in rank is the Church, although some analysts go so far as to presume the religious institution almost an integral part of government. The intellectual ground here is very treacherous. Probably nowhere is the Church less than a veto group; i.e., it may not be able to innovate policy, but it can make action against it very costly if not impossible. In Ecuador, where the Church is at its strongest, it probably transcends veto status and can institute action, as it probably also can in Colombia. In other lands where the Church has great strength, such as El Salvador and Peru, it cannot act somewhat in the nature of a party as it does in Ecuador and Colombia.

Legal separation of Church and State exists in Brazil, Chile, Cuba, Ecuador, El Salvador, Guatemala, Honduras, Mexico, Nicaragua, Panama, and Uruguay. The Church is established in Argentina, Bolivia, Colombia, Costa Rica, the Dominican Republic, Haiti, Paraguay, Peru, and Venezuela. But this legal categorization tells us little, for while almost all the established churches have this legal status as a holdover from the rights of the Spanish monarchy and while the purpose of establishment is to make the religious institution subservient to the state, the degree of control varies widely. There has, for instance, been active persecution of the Church in Venezuela, in contrast to the impressively strong Church of Colombia. And where legal separation exists, the same range of attitude is also to be found, from the past bitter attacks on the Church in Mexico, to the comfortable adjustment in Chile, to Church ascendency in Ecuador.

Another variable is the Church itself, which is by no means the same in its politics everywhere. The Gallican-influenced Churches of Brazil and Chile have very different political traits from the Spanish and Italian Church of Argentina. Most of the Chilean clergy now favor Christian Democracy; in the main, the Argentine clergy backed Perón for all but the last years of his regime, and still support many of the ideas of *justicialismo*. The long-range trend everywhere is for the Church to throw in with the rising middle groups, to oppose *caudillismo,* gently to support labor, and to drift slowly toward the official support of Christian Democratic parties. There is much opposition within the Church itself to certain of these temporal decisions, of course, and it would be highly incorrect to indicate that there is a general Latin political consensus in the Church.

The students, notorious political actors that they are, also constitute a pressure group. Latin American universities, organized on the European system, introduce their students immediately to subprofessional life; the social class gulf between student and professor is also minimal, for almost all students in Latin American universities are of middle and upper occupational group parents; their chances to participate at reasonably high levels in the national life after graduation are thus high to begin with. University elections are often good indicators of public elections, a kind of academic Maine and Vermont. Political division among the students parallels that of the major political parties, and student political activities train youngsters for active life outside. There are few Church universities of high prestige in those Latin American countries where they are allowed to exist. Although students in religious universities are also political activists, the incidents about which one reads in the newspapers almost invariably are initiated in the state universities, citadels of the new, rising, nationalistic middle youth.

Other pressure groups are what one might expect: associations of landowners, mine operators, industrialists, chambers of commerce, and prestige social clubs edging into the political sphere. Then there are union groups, invariably politically militant if they are not subservient arms of the state. At times, they are both. Where labor is fairly free of governmental supervision, it tends to group in Socialist, Communist, and Radical camps; and in three countries—Argentina, Chile, and Uruguay —unionism also has had its Anarchist contingents. The union movement of Mexico has been closely allied to the growth of the single party, whatever its name may have been at any particular period. In the most retarded countries, unions are *de facto* or even sometimes *de jure* illegal. Honduras, for example, legalized labor organization only as recently as 1954.

Another kind of occupational pressure group is the professional association, often intimately tied in with the universities from which they depend in many countries.

Groups-in-interest are another crucial index of impersonalism and maturity in the political process. To the extent to which they exist, a polity of countervailing powers becomes a possibility, assuring the operation of lateral controls in the political system and making possible government by decisions as the result of compromise through bargaining instead of by fiat through uncontrolled self-interest.

INTERNATIONAL ECHOES OF INTERNAL POLITICS

As we have seen, the wide variation in the political development of the Latin American republics precludes the application of overly narrow rules to the processes of interpretative analysis and policy making. But even this simple homily is difficult to apply in practice, for not only are Latin American countries broadly dispersed on almost any scale of social measurement, but also, in many short-run, operational respects, they are almost exactly what the United States is not, a fact which makes for difficulties in cross-cultural recommendations. The modernizing elements in Latin America in general want revolutionary changes, whether with violence or without; the United States is moderate in its views and skeptical of wrenching change. Latin American countries are in the early, romantic stages of nationalism; the United States is emerging into a cautious but firm commitment to internationalism. The Latin university student enjoys high social prestige and excellent changes for political power; his American counterpart is career-oriented and drawn from a very broad social spectrum. Latin American labor leaders are devoted to political unionism; American union officials are convinced of the advantages of economic unionism.

Most Latin Americans see the state as a legitimate agency for directing capital accumulation and investment; avowed American ideology is *laissez-faire,* despite the mixed economy of the United States. Latin Americans are more worried about their internal Communist parties than about the Soviet Union, and only as a result of Cuba have generated some relatively direct emotional involvement in the Cold War; the United States views the international clash with Soviet Russia as a struggle for survival in the deepest sense. Latin America wants steel mills and the other monuments of industrialization against a background of the technical full employment of underdevelopment; the United States is dealing with problems of automation and unemployment. Latin American governments are frankly tutelary; the American government is charged with the opposite task of reconciling numerous conflicting issues among laterally competing interests. The Latin American culture includes many Catholic as well as generically Mediterranean notions of collectivism and syndicalism; the United States is generally Protestant and individualistic in its approach to matters metaphysical. This list of divergences could be extended almost indefinitely. The major point is that North American groups cannot talk on the same attitudinal grounds with their Latin American peers, for the immediate aspirations and methods of each are not the same.

It is only in terms of broader and more long-range objectives that the community of interests becomes apparent. The ultimate dedication of the United States to democratic process is clearly reflected in Latin America. Unhappily, discord invariably appears over means to that common end, and the daily decisions of diplomacy suffer accordingly. The United States has often demonstrated itself insensitive to the currents of internal Latin American politics as well as to the variety of solutions possible to those countries. Too often have we defined private ownership as equal to capitalism without taking into account the importance to the maintenance of our system of competition and countervailing powers; we have viewed expropriation as equal to socialism, and nationalism as the same as supernationalism; the governmental authority of dictators has been treated as an honorable equivalent of legitimacy, and rote anti-communism as full partnership in the community of free nations.

Many Latin American countries, for their part, have dedicated themselves to a maintenance of the privileges of the old semi-feudalism at the same time as they seek the revolutionary advantages of modernism. Between the transcendental ideal and the grubbiness of daily administrative practice there is often a yawning gulf filled with ineptitude and corruption. Latin Americans have a long way to go to translate their notions of dignity and the good life into the reality after which they yearn. But, of course, that point is what this chapter concerns. The exciting variety of response being developed in Latin America is a most encouraging sign, and at the same time a challenge to the scholar, the businessman, and the policy-maker. This variety cannot be understood by narrow ideologists thinking in bromides.

Many roads lead to democratic salvation.

Reynold E. Carlson

3

The Economic Picture

The central feature of the Latin American economy in the postwar period has been a broad drive toward economic development. Almost without exception, every government has taken the position that its policies in the economic area will be to direct the available resources and to create the conditions necessary to achieve a substantial increase in the national production of goods and services.

There are several reasons for placing economic development as the top priority. In the first place, the population growth in Latin America is one of the highest in the world, increasing at an average rate of 2.5 per cent annually since the war, which means the total population will double in 25 to 30 years from its present level of 180,000,000 to 360,000,000.

A second source of pressure may be found in the revolution of aspirations that has been evident since the war. The Latin American countries have been subjected for some time to what economists call the "demonstration effect," in which people's wants and tastes have been sharply stimulated through easy access to such media as the Hollywood movies and American magazines, as well as direct exposure through travel to the higher standards of living in the United States and Western Europe. To be sure, this demonstration has been under way for many years, but somehow it seems to have caught hold in the postwar period. Even the rank and file of the population feel they should have a larger share of the economic goods which other countries and, indeed, some groups in their own countries seem to possess. Prior to World War II, these aspira-

REYNOLD E. CARLSON *is a Ford Foundation Representative in Brazil, and formerly was Professor of Economics at Vanderbilt University. He has also directed the Institute of Brazilian Studies and taught at Johns Hopkins University. He has served as an economist and consultant on Latin America for the United States government and the United Nations; he has been senior economist in Latin America for the World Bank.*

tions took the form of widespread legislation in social security and welfare, in some cases virtually copying the legislation of the more advanced countries. However, the aspirations have been largely disappointed because, almost without exception, no country possessed the resources necessary to implement the elaborate legislation. The cost of social welfare benefits has been a heavy addition to the wage bill which, in most cases, was not compensated by increases in productivity. In other cases the competition for the limited resources between social welfare on the one hand and the need for capital formation on the other has been a potent factor in the inflationary pressures plaguing many of the countries. It is precisely because social welfare ends have consistently lost out in the competition that the Alliance for Progress was conceived to channel resources in this direction.

A third factor behind the drive for economic development is the structural problem existing in most of the countries, especially in the area of foreign trade. It is well known that the exports of Latin America consist largely of primary products, such as foodstuffs and raw materials, the prices of which are subject to wide fluctuations in the world market. These fluctuations have served alternately as accelerator and brake to the rate of growth. Out of this situation has grown a whole school of thought that the only solution is industrialization in order to reduce the vulnerability of the economies to changes in their terms of trade.

Another factor of a structural character is the state of agriculture, which still provides the means of employment for 50 per cent of the population in most countries. Yet agriculture has generally lagged behind other sectors with respect to the adoption of known techniques, and has been less successful in attracting capital than industry and commerce. As a result, agricultural productivity has either declined or stagnated. Total output in physical terms has, of course, increased and has generally kept pace with population growth, but this increase has been achieved almost entirely by continual additions to the labor force, working with the same primitive techniques that characterized agricultural production fifty years ago. The fact that the agricultural sector is overloaded with population is, for the most part, the real reason for the low statistical per capita income. As with foreign trade, so with agriculture: there is a strong feeling that economic development cannot be achieved without massive industrialization in order to take people from the farms and to increase the productivity per man of those who remain.

Some notice must also be taken of the growing disposition toward nationalism and the increasing role of the national government in seeking to accelerate the rate of economic development. Two aggressive elements are abroad in the economy of Latin America. One is found in the private sector where powerful industrial and commercial groups are emphasizing the advantages of a nationalistic policy designed to reserve the exploitation of domestic resources for nationals and generally to discourage the foreign investor or businessman. The other aggressive element makes itself felt through the government sector. It actively seeks to expand the role of the government in the economic field as a supplier of capital, as an entrepreneur of new industrial undertakings, and as the architect who designs and influences the economic structure by means of various measures, channeling the forces of economic development in one direction or another according to some judgment as to what is "best" for the economy. In this connection, the position of the military in many of these governments ranges from the relatively quiet role of domestic police force to the other extreme where decisions on the allocation of scarce resources can be made and implemented only with the sufferance of the military group. To be sure, this is an old story in Latin American history, but it is singularly out of place in a region which has "officially" committed itself to promoting economic development while at the same time trying to support a military establishment that absorbs 30 to 40 per cent of the national budget.

DIVERSITIES AND GROWTH RATES

It must be made clear at the outset that the region known as "Latin America" is not a single entity with uniform characteristics about which easy generalizations can be made. It will be useful, therefore, to spell out some of the broad differences found among the twenty Latin American countries. In the first place, the obvious differences are in the size and population of the countries. The Latin American countries range from Brazil at one extreme, with a population of 71,000,000 and a geographic size greater than continental United States, to Panama and Costa Rica with populations of barely 1,000,000 and of equal size with West Virginia or South Carolina. The rates of growth of these populations also vary from a high annual increase of 4.2 per cent in Costa Rica to a low of 1.2 per cent in Haiti and Bolivia.

Next, with respect to the structure of the economy, the range is again very great. At one extreme is Venezuela with a per capita income of $750 and, at the other extreme, Haiti with a per capita income of only $70, which places it on a par with some of the poorest countries of Southeast Asia. Illiteracy varies from 13 per cent in Argentina to 89 per cent in Honduras (ten years of age and over). The productive sectors are marked by the fraction of the population gaining a livelihood from agriculture, i.e., rural population, which is 38 per cent in Argentina and 75 per cent in the Dominican Republic. Dependence upon foreign trade (measured by exports as a percentage of national income) ranges from a low of 13 per cent in Argentina to a high of 49 per cent in Venezuela and 41 per cent in Costa Rica. Four countries have a single export commodity accounting for 80 per cent or more of total exports. An important distinction arises between those which export minerals (Chile and Bolivia), those which rely upon exports of foodstuffs (Argentina and Ecuador), and those with exports of fiber (Uruguay and Paraguay).

In terms of financial stability, the range is again very great. Some countries have been on the brink of runaway inflation, such as Chile and Bolivia, in contrast to other countries enjoying a price level even more stable than that of the United States, such as Haiti, Panama, and the Dominican Republic.

There is no point in laboring the obvious fact that diversity does exist in Latin America, but this fact needs to be remembered in the discussion to follow. The problems of Latin America are no different from those of the other underedeveloped countries of the world, and a more meaningful analysis might be based upon some classification other than mere geographical location. Thus, the mineral exporting countries of Latin America have some problems probably closer to those of Africa and Asia than to the semi-industrialized countries of Argentina, Brazil, and Mexico, that are operating at a level far removed from the poorer agricultural countries like Paraguay and Haiti. In short, the Latin American countries are a heterogeneous group. They are lumped together because of their long historical association through such institutions as the Pan-American Union and the special interest which the region has for the United States on grounds of mutual security, foreign trade, and investment.

In real terms, production in the Latin American region increased at an annual rate of about 4.5 per cent over the decade. With a population growth of approximately 2.5 per cent annually, this means an annual net advance per capita of about two per cent. If Venezuela were excluded from the calculations, the growth of production would still be about four per cent, or a per capita increase of 1.5 per cent annually.

This rate of growth may be contrasted with that of other regions. Gross national production of the United States in the postwar period increased 4.2 per cent annually, or 2.5 per cent per capita. In Europe, taking the countries of the Organization for European Economic Cooperation, the postwar growth was 5.2 per cent, which is a per capita rate of 4.4 per cent. In Asia postwar growth ranged from 8.5 per cent (7 per cent per capita) in Japan to 2.5 per cent (1 per cent per capita) in Pakistan. The sharp difference between the growth in total production and the per capita growth figure in Latin America draws attention to its high rate of population increase in comparison with other regions of the world.

The principal factor in the growth rate is the volume of investment. Thus, in the period 1950-1960, 16 to 17 per cent of total national income was invested in plant and equipment, construction, and inventories. In absolute terms, the increase has been substantial because production has risen by one-third. It remains to be seen whether this rate can be maintained in the next decade. It must be remembered that sharp increases in commodity prices have taken place during the last seven years, in part because of the Korean War which drove mineral prices to new highs, and in part because of the sharp reversal in the world coffee situation which caused prices to double in 1949-1950 and to increase again in 1953. In view of the role of minerals and coffee in the balance of payments of the Latin American countries, these gains greatly increased the capacity of the countries to invest and thus contributed to the high growth rate achieved. The prospect for these commodities in, say, the next five years, is much more pessimistic. Coffee prices have already declined drastically because of the huge increase in world production now coming on the market from the new plantings stimulated by the high prices of 1953-1955.

The rate of investment may also be analyzed in terms of the amounts needed to maintain the capital stock and to provide for new population growth. Although gross investment was 16 to 17 per cent of the total output, roughly one-third of this comes from meeting the depreciation of existing plant and equipment and goes to maintain—but not to increase —the existing stock of capital goods. Another one-third is required just to maintain the per capita stock of capital, that is, to provide the housing and tools needed to equip the annual increase in population and simply to maintain them at the existing low level. Finally, the last one-third of the investment serves to increase the production level of the country. When viewed in this fashion, it appears that even a high investment rate of 16 to 17 per cent results in a net increment of growth which is fairly small. If, as noted above, per capita income increased by two per cent, it would be necessary to maintain this level of investment for a period of thirty-five years in order to double the present standard of living. This is a sobering thought which is likely to be overlooked by the more zealous advocates of economic development.

The second element to be stressed is the origin of the investment in these countries. In general, it may be said that well over 90 per cent of the capital growth comes from domestic resources, such as depreciation reserves, undistributed profits, collective savings from social security institutions and personal savings, while only 10 per cent represents foreign capital entering the country. Evidently, the region's rate of growth has been achieved with its own resources, which fact raises additional problems. The increasing pressure to expand consumption is in direct competition with the need for capital formation. In view of the low levels prevailing in some countries, the pressure to consume is formidable, and many popularly elected governments have come to power on a platform promising to expand consumption or to improve welfare. Nevertheless, if sustained economic growth is to be achieved, it will be necessary to syphon off substantial fractions of the new increments in production in the direction of capital formation.

One of the characteristics of economic development is the changing structure of the economy and the emergence of particular sectors to positions of importance. As noted earlier, gross national production expanded

55 per cent in real terms between 1950-1960. It remains to note the growth rates in particular sectors over this same period.

In agriculture, production increased 26 per cent, or somewhat less than the rate of total production. Per capita, the increase was only 8 per cent, which over the seven-year period means an improvement of barely one per cent per year in living standards. With particular reference to row crops and cereals, the increase was 31 per cent in the period 1950-1957, or a gross increase of 10 per cent over the seven-year period; livestock and meat production increased 18 per cent in this period, but with zero increase on a per capita basis.

Output in mining increased 70 per cent in these years, reflecting the substantial developments in Chilean copper, Brazilian iron ore and manganese, and Venezuelan iron ore.

In the manufacturing sector, the increase over the same period was 37 per cent. This rate is not much greater than that in agriculture, considering the pressures for industrialization in many countries and the forced draft measures taken to promote industrial projects for purposes of import substitution, often with little or no reference to factors of comparative advantage. The process of industrialization in countries like Argentina, Brazil, and Chile has been accelerated by a variety of measures and incentives. Since all three countries maintain exchange controls and have supported over-valued exchange rates for varying periods of time, the incentives to import capital equipment for industrial purposes have been very strong. The same incentives have been applied to imports of raw materials, fuels, and spare parts needed to operate these industrial plants. Protective devices are not lacking and often prove more effective than the tariff, the classical device for protecting national production from the foreign imports. Exchange controls have been administered for the purpose of protecting established industry from the competition, not only of foreign imports, but also of foreign factories which would otherwise be attracted to a country because of growing markets and earnings prospects.

Nationalism has reached one of its more virulent forms in the industrial sector. It is possible for industrialists, already entrenched in an economy, effectively to close the door to new enterprises from abroad which would probably compete for the growing market. Many of the so-called industrialization laws purporting to invite expansion are so designed as to exclude entrants to an industry on various grounds. In some cases existing firms can demonstrate that their capacity or their plans for expansion of capacity are adequate to meet the domestic market at existing prices. In other cases it is considered "unfair competition" for a foreign firm to enter a country with modern equipment and make use of the latest technologies in order to produce at substantially lower costs and therefore lower consumer prices.

In short, the rate of industrial expansion is inhibited by the defensive tactics of existing producers who hope to reserve the expanding market for themselves without being under pressure to rationalize their techniques of production or to meet price competition.

Another element tending to retard the expansion of industries is the absence of the necessary investment in economic overhead capital, particularly in electric power and transportation. These continue to be bottlenecks in the rate of industrial growth. Surveys that have been made in cities like Rio de Janeiro or São Paulo indicate a substantial waiting list of industrial firms unable to get into production or to expand existing facilities until new generating capacity will permit an increase in the connected load. Similarly in transportation, existing firms find that their rate of expansion depends upon widening the domestic market, which can be achieved only by substantial investment in railways, highways, and auxiliary services. In fact, the growing realization of industrialists that power and transportation are essential to their own growth is probably a major reason for the pressures now being placed upon governments to invest heavily in such overhead capital. Not many years ago these same industrialists were indifferent to such developments and begrudged the allocation of resources to those sectors. Private power companies in Brazil, for example, have been able to capitalize on this new awareness and to absorb a substantial amount of new capital in the form of domestic equity participation from the very industrialists who have now come to recognize the critical importance of electric power in their own plans for expanding operations.

Services are also a sector showing considerable expansion (20 per cent in the period under review), and in terms of employment their role is actually increasing relative to agriculture and manufacturing. In 1948, for example, agriculture accounted for 54 per cent of the labor force; by the late 1950's, the employment created by agriculture was down to 50 per cent. Manufacturing and construction remained relatively unchanged, accounting for 18 per cent of the employment over the entire period. Services, on the other hand, have shown a steady increase from 26 per cent of the labor force in 1948 to 30 per cent in the late 1950's.

This suggests the interesting hypothesis that the manpower being released from agriculture is not going into industry as is frequently alleged, but into services. It is possible, therefore, that the familiar phenomenon of disguised unemployment known to exist in agriculture is simply being shifted to the service sector. Anyone visiting Latin America must be impressed by the large number of domestic servants, restaurant waiters, parking lot attendants, and the like, who almost certainly represent some degree of disguised unemployment. Their productivity, for an urban area, is probably not much higher than if they had stayed on the farms. Industry, meanwhile, does not appear to be absorbing increasing fractions of the population but is barely holding its own as a source of employment.

One must hasten to add that these inferences are based upon over-all statistics for the entire region. It is undoubtedly true that in certain countries, like Mexico or Brazil, where industrialization is moving rapidly ahead, industry is increasing its relative position as an employer of labor. Even in such countries, however, it is likely that the services are also absorbing substantial amounts of the labor being released from agriculture. The problems of urbanization, therefore, should not be viewed as a by-product of industrialization alone. They are generated in part by the substantial increase in the number employed in services. These people earn incomes substantially less than industrial labor. They make up the bulk of those miserable souls who occupy the hills around Caracas, the *callampas* outside Santiago, the hillside *favelas* in Rio de Janeiro, and the *villas miserias* of Buenos Aires.

The distribution of the labor force changes very slowly, principally because of lack of mobility (for geographical or educational reasons) and population pressures registering more in one sector than another. The concentration of the labor force in low productivity agriculture and in disguised unemployment services is obviously a major drag on the prospects of increasing per capita output. This is demonstrated by a comparison of gross product per worker at the beginning and the end of the decade.

Gross Product Per Worker
(Dollars at 1950 Prices)

	1950	1959	Per Cent Labor Force
Agriculture	$ 360	$ 430	50
Industry	900	1,060	15
Mining and Petroleum	2,800	3,600	1
Construction	950	960	4
Commerce, Government and Services	1,260	1,380	30
			100%

With 50 per cent of the labor force in agriculture, a decade of development has little effect in remedying the mass poverty in Latin America, although the annual gross rate is almost 2 per cent per worker over the decade. Similarly, in the case of services, where another 30 per cent of the labor force is concentrated, the absolute level in gross product per worker is three times that of agriculture but the gain over the decade is not impressive—barely one per cent a year. The dramatic gain in mining and petroleum affects a very narrow sector with only one per cent of the labor force benefited. When one remembers that approximately 45 per cent of the population in Latin America is outside the labor force (under fifteen or over sixty-five years), the gains per worker, small as they are, are cut at least in half on a per capita basis, with each worker supporting two other people.

Latin American Trade and the United States

The countries of Latin America find their closest ties with the United States economy in the two broad areas of foreign trade and foreign investment. The United States received one-third of all its imports from Latin America and shipped 20 to 25 per cent of its exports to this region during the last few years. Early in the postwar period the fractions were even larger for the obvious reason that other sources of supply in the world were not in a position to resume trade with Latin America until they had gradually recovered from the effects of the war. With respect to particular countries, the United States' role as trade partner shows considerable variation. In countries like Colombia, Guatemala, and Mexico, the United States accounts for 70 to 75 per cent of their total exports. The only countries where foreign trade is oriented toward Europe are Argentina and Uruguay. Here the United States accounts for only 10 to 12 per cent of their exports.

The fact that fifteen countries ship 40 per cent or more of their exports to the United States makes them peculiarly vulnerable to conditions in the American economy. These countries often feel that their economic dependence upon the United States is excessive. Whenever difficulties arise with respect to prices received for their exports, the tendency is to put the entire onus upon the United States rather than upon the world market. The notion that the price of coffee is "set" in New York is widespread.

The composition of Latin American exports to the United States has been fairly stable over recent years:

	Billions
Petroleum	$ .8
Foodstuffs	1.9
Minerals and other raw materials	.8
Total	$3.5

The elimination of Cuban exports to the United States will reduce the above figures by some $500 millions in the foodstuff category. Partial reallocation of the sugar quota to other Latin American producers will, of course, restore some of this cut.

Although all these major commodities are produced in various parts of the world outside Latin America, and world market prices obviously reflect total world production, the question of stability in most raw material prices, including foodstuffs, is one of the topics most frequently spotlighted by the Latin American countries. No international conference of an economic character can take place without putting the issue of price stability for raw materials high on the agenda. The belief that the United States should assume responsibility for organizing and implementing some scheme to achieve greater price stability is widespread through the region.

United States policy has, until recently, been adamant against any institutional arrangements to support international prices of raw materials, but this traditional view is now being re-examined. Numerous illustrations can be found in the period since the Korean War wherein prices of certain principal commodities have fallen drastically in the world market, crippling the exchange position of the exporting country, compelling it to cut back sharply on imports, and casting doubt upon its ability to maintain payments on its foreign obligations. In these circumstances the United States has taken steps to ameliorate the situation, partly to maintain the flow of its own exports in competition with Western Europe and partly to prevent a default on contractual obligations abroad. Thus, when the price of copper or coffee plummets to low levels, the United States feels constrained to compensate, at least in part, for the loss in foreign exchange. Large Export-Import Bank loans, sometimes called "bailing-out loans," are made to the countries having difficulties. When, for example, the price of copper dropped from thirty-six cents a pound to about twenty cents in a period of a little over one year, Chile received loans from the Eximbank, plus standby credits with the International Monetary Fund which, in the aggregate, were practically equal to the amount of foreign exchange lost through the decline in copper prices. While these operations made it unnecessary for Chile to cut back on imports of American goods, it left the economy with a heavy debt burden of relatively short-term maturity. If the price decline persists beyond a year, these short-term obligations tend to be renegotiated, rolled over, or stretched out; and in the final analysis, one discovers that a substantial amount of United States or international resources has been committed. It may well be that some institutional arrangements to dampen the fluctuations in international prices of raw materials and foodstuffs would be "cheaper" than the present measures to shore up sagging economies.

On the other hand, it is perhaps fair to observe that many Latin American producers seek "stability" in world market prices without enforcing upon themselves the firm measures needed to achieve such a result. The history of international cartel and buffer stock schemes over the years does not engender confidence. The prospects are further complicated by the fact that new producer nations are emerging in Africa and Southeast Asia, bursting with nationalism and determined to bid for a growing share of the world market. Meanwhile, the "older" producers seem more concerned about protecting their existing shares in the market by various devices hopefully to be enforced by agreements with the nations that consume these products, and perhaps shifting the onus of enforcement to the consumer nations through quotas and other import controls. Popular opinion notwithstanding, Latin America is no longer a "young" country, with respect to production of primary products, in comparison with the emerging countries of Africa and Asia. Chilean and Peruvian copper, for example, faces the competition of United States and Canadian aluminum for as much as 40 per cent of the technical uses for copper; Brazilian and Colombian coffee seems to be losing ground relative to the Africans; Latin American cotton has already been battered by synthetic fibers. The solution, of course, for a group of primary producers facing the melancholy prospect of "middle age", is to invest the resources required to rationalize production by introducing new techniques and adopting modern marketing practices in order to survive the perennial gale of the world market place.

Intra-regional trade continues to be fairly small with approximately 10 per cent of Latin American exports absorbed within the area. Historically, trade among the Latin American countries has been complicated by geographic conditions, lack of transportation, and, perhaps most importantly, by the fact that principal export products are competitive rather than complementary. Moreover, as long as currencies continue to be inconvertible, triangular trade of the classical variety cannot be achieved. The area's import needs are largely for capital goods and semifinished as well as finished manufactures, and these are not available at competitive prices except from industrialized countries.

Latin American free trade area

One of the by-product results of the creation of the European Common Market was a lively interest in several groups in Latin America to consider the feasibility of a common market arrangement in this hemisphere. Two institutional arrangements have emerged as a result of this interest. The first of these involves a common market area in the five Central American countries where it has long been recognized that each of these countries, by itself, offers a very limited market for the output of any industrial enterprise. Accordingly, the scale of new enterprises would necessarily be so small as to be uneconomic, and the country might be indefinitely burdened with a high-cost operation. The movement for economic integration had several objectives: to stabilize regional prices for basic foodstuffs, rice, beans, and corn; secondly, a common market would provide certain incentives to industrial development by widening the market area in which new industrial products could be sold; next, a Central American Development Bank was conceived as a mechanism for allocating resources to new enterprises which had regional significance. An Industrial Development Center has been developed to give some stimulus to new enterprises, particularly import-substitution projects.

The second institutional arrangement is known as the Latin American Free Trade Association (LAFTA), which was created by treaty in Montevideo in 1960 and was eventually ratified to become effective in 1961. Since the organization was created, negotiations have been under way to establish new tariff rates for a wide variety of commodities which, by agreement, may move between the eight member countries: Argentina, Brazil, Chile, Uruguay, Paraguay, Peru, Colombia, and Mexico. The principle of the plan is to reduce tariffs over a series of twelve years, at last 8 per cent each year, reciprocally, but with a most favored nation clause applicable within the group. Thus, in some twelve years of gradual downward adjustments, the articles on the agreed list of goods may be eventually moved within the area without import duties levied upon them.

The wide range in the level of economic development that has been achieved in the eight countries has caused some apprehension lest the more industrialized members of the group, Brazil, Argentina, or Mexico, capture the growing market for industrial commodities in the other member countries. Consequently, most import rate concessions apply to agricultural products and raw materials, although a few industrial commodities have also qualified. The system is hedged about with various safeguards to offset, whenever desired, the competitive advantages of another member country operating within LAFTA.

At best, the economic impact of LAFTA will be small. In the first place, intra-regional trade is less than 10 per cent of Latin America's total trade and of this fraction 40-50 per cent is agricultural and primary products, 20-25 per cent is petroleum (largely Venezuela, a non-member country), and only 3 per cent is manufactured goods. On the other hand, seven of the member countries account for 80 per cent of the total regional trade; Mexico, in contrast, does less than 1 per cent. Apart from the limited volume, the lack of transportation and especially the deplorable condition and high cost of coastal shipping which handles 90 per cent of the regional trade, is a major bottleneck to any prospect for development of trade. Finally, there is a strong disposition among Latin American entrepreneurs, long conditioned to hyper-protection, to view LAFTA as useful to pushing their own products to other countries, while resisting any incursions by lower-cost producers into their own domains.

In the postwar period numerous attempts have been made to use bilateral trade agreements between countries within the region to expand trade, but generally speaking this device has proved ineffective. A country will usually put its marginal export items on the bilateral list in an attempt to push them into trade channels, while commodities with a normal world market are usually kept off. Thus, on the bilateral list, Chile tries to push the sale of nitrate, but not copper. Brazil will push lumber and fruit, but will omit coffee, and so on.

Bilateral agreements are inevitably inefficient and costly to both exporter and importer. They are usually associated with systems of exchange control, import and export licensing, and multiple exchange rates. In general, the consumer of the commodity traded through bilateral agreements tends to pay more than if the same commodity were available through regular trade channels. This is the real economic cost of such arrangements.

The pattern of foreign trade is important to the extent that its volume and composition reflect the varying rates of growth in the Latin American countries. Gross national product—as already noted—increased in the years 1955-1960 by 23 per cent from $50 billion to $62 billion in terms of 1955 prices. Gross capital formation (fixed capital, excluding inventories) increased 15 per cent from $8.4 billion to $9.7 billion in constant prices.

The value of foreign trade in real terms since 1950 increased 26 per cent in imports and only 4 per cent in exports. The fact that imports are increasing more rapidly than gross production in real terms runs counter to expectations and suggests that the Latin American economies are becoming increasingly vulnerable to balance of payments difficulties in spite of considerable progress that has been made in import substitution.

Notice may be taken of the changing composition of the imports over the last decade as given below in constant prices:

Imports in 1955 Prices
(Millions of Dollars)

	1950		1955		1959		Percentage Increase
	Amount	Per cent	Amount	Per cent	Amount	Per cent	1950-59
Consumer Goods	$1,426	23	$1,541	21	$1,663	21	17
Fuels	508	8	787	10	838	11	65
Raw Materials	2,098	34	2,568	35	2,837	35	35
Capital Goods	2,158	35	2,499	34	2,665	33	23
Total	$6,190	100	$7,395	100	$8,003	100	26

It is surprising to note that total consumer goods imports have increased 17 per cent. It is true, of course, that a substantial part of this increase represents foodstuffs, the importation of which has been steadily going up in the period under review. Import substitution in agricultural commodities is evidently going very slowly. Even in durable consumer goods, the one area in which the pressure to industrialize is supposed to be most effective, imports appeared to have risen 16 per cent. Fuels and raw materials together have maintained their same relative position, but there has been a marked increase in the quantity over this decade. As the above table shows, fuel imports increased 65 per cent, or twice the rate in gross production. This can be explained by referring to such countries as Brazil and, until recently, Argentina, where imports of petroleum products have jumped and efforts at developing domestic resources have lagged behind.

With respect to raw materials, the direction of development is toward firmer ground in comparison with five or ten years ago. At that time, much of the industrialization was based upon imported raw materials, which created an element of vulnerability. Now, with the development of local materials, the industrialization process can proceed on a sound basis.

Capital goods average about one-third of total imports in any given year while, over the decade, the volume of capital goods imports has increased 23 per cent. It could also be noted that, over the decade, capital goods imports averaged 30 per cent of gross capital formation, the remaining 70 per cent consisting of construction, inventory accumulation, and growing output of heavy industries in countries like Mexico, Brazil, and Argentina.

The analysis serves to emphasize once more the important connection between a country's balance of payments position and its rate of economic growth. If export earnings decline for any reason, the country must, barring financial help from abroad, cut back. Since fuels and raw materials cannot be cut back, and much of the consumer goods category consists of foodstuffs, the full impact of balance of payments adjustments must fall upon the capital goods sector. In these circumstances, the economic growth in the next decade may be considerably more irregular than in the past when, in balance of payments crises, it was possible to cut back at various points. Now, however, the axe must fall on capital goods whenever trouble emerges unless, of course, foreign sources of capital—private or official—can be induced to close the gap.

INFLATION

For a number of Latin American countries, inflation has become a major economic problem, although the causes have varied between countries over the last ten years, and the rate has varied from virtual stability to galloping inflation.

There was a short period during World War II and briefly thereafter when export surpluses were a cause of inflationary pressures, but as the world moved into the decade of expansion during the 1950's, this problem ceased to exist. In Latin America, as elsewhere, there are basically three sources of inflationary pressure: the private sector through pressures on the banking system, the public sector through deficits in the budget of the government and operating entities, and third, the cost-push pressures generated by forcing wage levels beyond productivity. In some countries, an active entrepreneurial group, by repeated demands upon the domestic banking system, has brought about increases in the money supply for investment purposes. Inflation generated by these private pressures to invest becomes particularly acute when a government embarks upon a development program, while placing no restraints upon expansion in the private sector. Inflation from private investment pressure is apt to be found in those countries with overvalued exchange rates and with extensive direct controls used to maintain some semblance of equilibrium in their balance of payments. In these circumstances, importation of capital goods and equipment at an overvalued exchange rate is an enormous incentive to construct industrial plants with relatively cheap equipment. This seems to have been the pattern in the countries with the most virulent inflation—Argentina, Brazil, Paraguay, Chile, and Bolivia.

Fluctuation in the balance of payments has, under some circumstances, also been a contributing cause of inflationary pressure, partly in the private sector and partly in the public sector. When terms of trade turn favorable for a particular country, there is a disposition to expand on all fronts, rather than to accumulate exchange reserves. A new level of investment is somehow built into the expectations of the entrepreneurs, both government and private. Then, when a downturn comes and exchange earnings drop back to previous levels, or lower, a country may turn to inflation in an effort to maintain its rate of investment and overall growth at a level higher than can be sustained by the reduced availability of resources. When the terms of trade turn against the country, it frequently happens that unemployment appears in sectors that had previously been booming. Thus, pressure for public works projects is generated to alleviate the unemployment. A sharp decline in the price of copper, for example, will close down marginal mines in Chile, and the government seeks, by all measures including inflation, to soften the blow by make-work projects.

The second major cause of inflation is found in the fiscal deficits, especially of national governments which are monetized through recourse to central bank borrowing. One source of such deficits is the dependence of the national government upon certain taxes, the yields of which may rise or fall with changes in the terms of trade. The pattern tends to be repeated when a sudden windfall of revenue is used, not to retire debt, but to finance new projects. In fact, each upsurge in export prices seems to raise government expenditures to a new high. When the downturn comes, these expenditures, for political or other reasons, cannot be cut back, and a government finds itself resorting to inflation.

Governments may operate public services, such as railroads, below cost, whereby enormous operating deficits are incurred. At times, in countries like Brazil and Chile, deficits on government railroads alone have accounted for one-third to one-half of the total fiscal deficit of the national government.

Still another source of inflation in the fiscal sector is found in the social security legislation of a country seeking to maintain pensions and other welfare payments at levels beyond its capacity. Welfare payments of this type soon bulk large in a government's budget. In Chile, for example, government employees may retire on the basis of years of service regardless of age at full pay, and their pension benefits are automatically raised every time active government employees receive a wage increase.

Finally, a new source of inflation has recently emerged with the stockpiling of products, such as coffee, in an effort to arrest the decline in the world prices. Unless a government is strong enough to shift the financial burden of stockpiling backward to the producers, the cumulative effect of monetizing an annual increase in coffee stockpiles creates enormous pressure for inflation.

The third basic source of inflationary pressure, wages above the level warranted by productivity, is a new phenomenon in Latin America. For many years in Chile the *salario vital* was automatically adjusted each year to a cost of living index and the consequent adjustments through the whole range of salary and wage payments exerted persistent pressure upon the level of prices. More recently, in Brazil, the disposition to adjust minimum wages at least once every year to offset the rapid inflation is bringing about increases in excess of those needed to compensate for the rise in prices. This is due, in part, to the absence of any reliable price index with the result that, for political purposes, the executive branch of the government will decree a level of minimum wage which, when adjusted through the entire range, is resulting in payments beyond that necessary to compensate for price increases and beyond that which would be warranted by increases in productivity. Moreover, since a large fraction of the government budget goes for wages and salaries, increases of this type create very large and "unexpected" deficits in the fiscal sector which are again financed by recourse to the banking system.*

The effect of inflation upon the rate of economic growth is a topic that attracts wide attention and there are different schools of thought. One point of view suggests that a moderate rate of inflation, say 3 to 5 per cent annually, facilitates the structural changes that are a necessary feature of economic growth. Others feel that inflation tends to force savings upon the wage earning group which normally has a high propensity to consume and which is difficult to reach by taxation. According to this argument, inflation tends to reduce real wages and thus increase the entrepreneur's profits and incentives to expand. In those countries where wage increases are brought about by decree, without reference to productivity, the attitude of the leaders in the business community is that inflation is necessary because it is the only way in which they can defend themselves against these wage increases imposed by the government. Evidently a year or more will elapse between such wage decrees and, in the meantime, the upward adjustment of prices by the business community rapidly erodes any gains which might have been achieved by the labor groups as

---

* There are two views or schools of thought on inflation in Latin America and the reader may wish to explore the subject. Reference is made to *Latin American Issues*, New York, Twentieth Century Fund, 1961, especially chapters by Roberto Campos, "Two Views on Inflation in Latin America," David Felix, "An Alternative View of the Monetarist-Structuralist Controversy," and Joseph Grunwald, "The Structuralist School on Price Stability and Development: The Chile Case."

a result of the initial wage adjustment. This, of course, is one aspect of the income redistribution effect of inflation on forced savings.

It will be instructive to examine the record of inflation of various countries for the period, 1950-1959. The table below gives the increase in prices as measured by the cost-of-living index for each of the countries.

Rate of Inflation: 1950-1959

	Cost-of-living Index: 1961 (1953 = 100)	Annual Growth Rate Real Terms (%) 1950-1959
Guatemala	105	5.9
Ecuador	106	5.8
Venezuela	108	8.2
Honduras	109	3.1
United States	112	3.5
Mexico	166	6.3
Colombia	172	4.7
Peru	174	5.3
Brazil	696	5.2
Argentina	741	1.3
Chile	1,022	2.2
Bolivia	2,570	1.3

It appears that in cases of extreme inflation (Argentina, Chile, and Bolivia), the growth rate over the decade is the lowest in the region. The case of Brazil is unusual because the rate of inflation has not, apparently, inhibited the growth rate. A number of reasons might be suggested, but suffice to mention two. There has been a sizeable inflow of official and private capital over the decade in spite of the inflationary climate. Secondly, the price level has until recently been running ahead of wage increases, thereby redistributing income away from the wage group in favor of the entrepreneurial group, and creating attractive incentives to expand production. In short, Brazil's growth has been in spite of, and not because of, inflation. Mexico, for example, has maintained a relatively "stable" economy—with an annual inflation rate of 6%—in recent years and yet its growth rate is appreciably higher than that of Brazil. Suffice to say that no obvious correlation exists between economic growth and inflation except in the extreme cases noted above.

FOREIGN CAPITAL

The importance of capital investment, both private and public from foreign sources, must be stressed even though it represents less than 10% of the total capital formation in the region. In the period 1950-1958, Latin America absorbed $6.2 billion from private sources, of which two-thirds were direct investment and one-third, in the form of suppliers credits from exporters and foreign manufacturers. From public and official sources another $4 billion was provided, mostly in long-term loans. Such loans, however, must be amortized, thereby reducing the net inflow of official capital to about $1 billion for the period, or one-fourth of the capital committed in private direct investment.

At the beginning of the decade 1950-1959, Latin America ranked in first place, representing 38% of U.S. direct investment abroad. In the course of the decade, however, the rapid recovery of Europe, and especially the investment opportunities in Canada, presented formidable competition for the direct investment dollar. Consequently, by 1960, the end of the decade, the amount of private investment in Latin America had increased 90% but, relative to the rest of the world, the Latin American share had declined to about 25% of the world total, while Canada displaced Latin America in first place with 34% of the total U.S. private investment abroad.

The change in distribution in the decade may be seen from the table below:

U.S. Private Direct Investment Abroad
(Millions of dollars)

	1950	1960
Total World	$11.788	$32.744
Latin America	4.445	8.365
Mining & Smelting	628	1.155
Petroleum	1.233	2.882
Manufacturing	780	1.610
Public Utilities	927	1.131
Trade	242	718
Agriculture	520	} 870
Others	116	
Canada	3.579	11.198
Europe	1.733	6.645
Rest World	2.031	6.536

The rising tide of nationalism in Latin America is fostering, in part deliberately and in part through misunderstanding, an erroneous image of the role which foreign private capital performs in the underdeveloped countries. It is not always recognized that in foreign participation in a country's development the capital goods are only one part of the contribution. Other parts of the global contribution include the introduction of new technologies, institutional changes, and the provision of scarce human resources, especially in the field of management.

The inadequacy of the human resources in most of the Latin American countries constitutes a major obstacle to the rate of economic development. One normally thinks of the large population which roams about the continent, but most of these individuals are completely without training or formal education of any type. The best one can say about the population is that it is plentiful and growing at a rapid rate. The bottle-neck associated with the lack of human resources is most conspicuous in the area of managerial and professional skills, which are of the utmost importance in the process of economic growth. A traditional role of for-eign private capital entering a new country is a provision of such mana-gerial and professional personnel which are lacking in the country and which are essential to the operation of a new enterprise. The transfer of skills over a period of time between a cadre of foreign professionals and a number of talented nationals is a familiar story in almost every coun-try. Many Latin Americans, however, have not yet understood that the management of an industrial enterprise is, in itself, a skill of high order and is not to be confused with the role of the technician, or technologi-cally trained individuals who carry out specific operations. There are, of course, many successful and long established business firms in the Latin American area, but most of these have grown slowly over the years as markets gradually expanded; ownership and management have tradition-ally been closely held within a family or small group. In many types of modern industry, such as chemicals, steel, cement, paper and pulp, it is no longer economically feasible to begin on a small scale. Thus, a major bottleneck emerges in the need for executive management capable of handling the complex problems of a sizeable enterprise.

Turning next to the specific role of capital which is introduced into a country, attention may be drawn to a publication of the United Nations* which produced a somewhat distorted view by looking only at the balance of payments effect, namely the inflow and outflow of capital. Since the balance of payments is only one aspect of the problem, it seriously under-states the total impact on the domestic economy. Frequent attempts are made in Latin America to compare the volume of annual remittances of profits and dividends with the annual inflow of new capital funds. There is, of course, no connection between the two factors. Nevertheless, the inference that United States private investment is "decapitalizing" Latin America continues to receive widespread publicity in the newspapers and economic journals of the region. The "decapitalization" argument al-leged that in the period 1946-1951, United States income received from direct investments in Latin America was $3.1 billion, whereas net outflow of capital from the United States was $1.6 billion, suggesting that United States direct investment was taking out approximately twice as much as it was putting into Latin America. The amount of annual remittances must be compared to the total investment in the country and not to the move-ment, purely coincidental, of new capital funds into the country. It would seem obvious—although many Latin Americans fail to see it—that the annual remittance on a capital investment (book value of $8.4 billion)

---

* FOREIGN CAPITAL IN LATIN AMERICA, New York, United Nations, 1955.

would have no relation to new increments of capital coming in annually from abroad. One is an income factor and the other is a capital factor.

It is true, of course, that the total balance of payments includes interest and remittance of earnings "above the line" and amortization of loans or repatriation of capital "below the line." Most private direct investment, however, does not anticipate repatriation of capital or it would not enter the country in the first place. The heavy outflow on capital account is due to the amortization of long-term loans and the total burden on the balance of payments tends to be larger when the economic development is financed by foreign loans instead of by foreign direct investment. The contrary argument is often heard that, after a long-term loan is fully paid off, the balance of payments is relieved of any further charges. But this overlooks the fact that most equipment installed under a long-term loan, say for twenty years, will have its useful life largely depreciated and a new loan must be contracted to bring in new equipment to replace that which is worn out or obsolete. Thus, a whole new series of amortization and interest charges begins to burden the balance of payments.

In estimating the total impact of foreign investment, recent studies have been made on Latin America which place the problem in perspective, and the balance of payments effect emerges as only one part of the whole. The total operation may be seen, by way of illustration, from the table below for the year 1957:

Operations of Private Direct Investment: 1957
(Millions of Dollars)

Sales:		
Domestic Sales		$4,345
Exports		3,028
	Total	$7,373
Costs:		
Materials:		
Local		$2,641
Imported		778
Fees Abroad		62
Wages		1,179
Taxation:		
Income Tax		540
Indirect Tax		483
Depreciation and Depletion		409
Miscellaneous		300
	Total	$6,392
Net Income:		
Retained		$ 176
Remitted		806
	Total	$ 982

From the above data,* certain interesting inferences may be drawn. The total income generated by export and domestic sales is derived from the domestic market, 59 per cent, and the foreign market, 41 per cent. One notes that total taxes ($1.0 billion) paid are almost exactly equal to total net income ($982) available for distribution; remitted earnings ($806) are less than total taxes paid ($1,023). In addition, of course, there is the substantial market created by the purchase of local raw materials and the payment of local wages.

With further reference to the balance of payments aspect, one should note that the entire operation, with the possible exception of marketing and financial services, falls in the category of export promotion or import substitution. One cannot conclude that the total amount of import substitution should be credited to foreign private capital because some part of it would probably have occurred, even without the entry of foreign capital.

The rate of return on investments is one of the important factors which is usually overlooked by those who argue that foreign capital constitutes a drain on the economy due to the high, not to say excessive, profits that are remitted. Taking 1960 as a recent year, total earnings by United States private direct investment in Latin America amounted to $829 million, which is a return of 10.3 per cent on the total capital investment, $8.1 billion, at the beginning of that year. However, only three-fourths of the earnings were transferred in 1960 ($614 million), which is the equivalent of 7.6 per cent on the total capital invested. The situation is even more striking if petroleum investment and earnings are omitted. In this case, total earnings are $484 million, or 9 per cent on capital invested. Again, some three-fourths of these earnings were transferred ($303 million), which represents a return of only 6 per cent to the United States stockholders.

Incentives to foreign capital

The prospect for attracting foreign private capital to the Latin American countries has received much attention in recent years, and two general points of view may be identified. On the side of the United States investor, emphasis is usually given to the investment climate, which is a composite of various elements, including freedom of entry and exit, equal treatment before the law, prospects for earnings, absence of discrimination, and so on. The other point of view, which might be called the Latin American, is inclined to underplay the investment climate and to substitute a series of so-called incentives designed to attract private capital. Many of the countries have enacted special legislation in the postwar

* The table above includes total operations but the breakdown by sectors (e.g., mining, petroleum, and manufacturing) is available in UNITED STATES BUSINESS INVESTMENTS IN FOREIGN COUNTRIES, Washington GPO, 1960, page 147.

period designed to give special treatment to foreign capital in matters of foreign exchange or taxation. Nine countries offer some form of foreign exchange incentives designed to create certain exemptions under exchange control regulations, while seventeen countries have enacted special tax privileges to attract foreign capital. Most of the latter relate to exemption from customs duties on capital goods entering the country, which in some cases is extended to include raw materials, fuels, and spare parts. Three countries (Venezuela, Uruguay, and Peru) have refrained from enacting specific legislation of an incentive character.

In general, the effect of such incentive legislation has been minimal and many of the so-called "incentives" are nothing more than a relaxation of impediments to investment which were created in earlier periods. The Latin American countries are also inclined to argue that United States taxation of earnings from foreign investments is an inhibiting factor and that special concessions should be made in United States income tax laws beyond the provisions which already exist for enterprises qualifying as "Western Hemisphere corporations." These receive a reduction of 14 points on corporate income tax, reducing the effective rate from 52 per cent to 38 per cent. The United States Treasury takes a negative view of additional concessions of this type. The case of Canada may be cited as a good example of what private capital will do when the investment climate is attractive irrespective of corporation tax rates.

It is instructive in connection with this question of taxation incentives to note some of the effective tax rates on locally incorporated subsidiaries of United States corporations. The Canadian rate of 43 per cent compares with 42 per cent in Brazil, 44 per cent in Chile and Mexico, 45 per cent in Peru and Colombia, and 48 per cent in Argentina. These are total effective rates based on generally applicable rules and do not account for special incentives such as initial tax exemptions or accelerated depreciation allowances.

The United States government did, however, move in the direction of incentives by offering a plan for the guarantee of private direct investments against risks of exchange convertibility and expropriation. Investment guarantee agreements have been negotiated with 15 countries in Latin America. It is interesting to know, however, that some of the most important countries (Mexico and Venezuela) have not seen fit to participate. Evidently the flow of private direct investment into these countries has been unimpaired by the risks of convertibility and expropriation, or else the private investor calculates that the cost of such insurance may be excessive, considering the risks that it covers.

Portfolio

Private investors in the United States hold approximately $1 billion in portfolio investments in Latin American countries. These represent, for the most part, the old bonded debt which went into default at the time of the great depression. Over the last decade, however, one country after another has negotiated agreements with its bond holders and has resumed service on the portfolio debt. Bolivia, in 1958, was the last of the Latin American countries to resume service on the old bonded debt.* Notwithstanding this attempt to re-establish their credit, none of the Latin American countries has yet been able to borrow new funds through the issue of securities in the capital markets of the United States or Western Europe. The record of financial management in many of the Latin American countries over the past decade has not inspired confidence in world capital markets. Resumption of service on the old debt thus proves to have been a necessary, but not sufficient, condition to gain access to foreign capital markets where nations may borrow with no other security than the full faith and credit of their governments. Since this condition is likely to continue for some years, the emphasis has shifted to the use of official or international capital for purposes of economic development.

The Export-Import Bank

The Export-Import Bank, an agency of the United States government, has been active since 1934 in providing capital for public and private projects in Latin America. Over the life of the Eximbank, Latin America has received 37% of the total resources made available. For present purposes, attention will be directed principally to the lending activities in the last years, 1954-1961, in order to gauge the net investment which these lending institutions have made possible in Latin America. Moreover, the significant data refer to disbursements rather than authorized credits; years may sometimes elapse between the authorization of a credit and its disbursement, and it is the latter which measures the actual inflow of capital.

Export-Import Bank
(Millions of Dollars)

	1954	1955	1956	1957	1958	1959	1960	1961
Outstanding Balance:								
Year's End	897	897	849	963	1,314	1,471	1,474	1,822
Loans Disbursed	109	118	70	234	485	310	163	488
Repayments	70	119	117	120	134	153	160	140
Net Annual Investment	40	0	−48	114	351	157	3	348

Over the eight-year period, disbursements were $1.977 million, while repayments, that is, amortizations of previous loans, amounted to $1.013 million, leaving a net increment of $964 million. Examination of the above table also reveals the interesting fact that for a period of three years, from December 1953 to December 1956, the Eximbank not only failed to provide any net capital investment for Latin America but actu-

---

* In 1961 Cuba, for political reasons, declined to honor its external debt obligations.

ally slightly reduced its stake in the region. This stagnation was the result of a policy decision by the new United States administration that declared the World Bank to be the lender of first recourse for development capital; the Eximbank was left to operate in the limited area outside the range of World Bank operations. This policy was evidently reversed in 1957 with the reorganization of the Eximbank and a rapid acceleration in the net capital for Latin America.

The principal borrowers from the Eximbank were five countries which together absorbed 75% of the net credits authorized ($3.9 billion) as of December 31, 1961. Of these countries, Brazil accounted for $1.4 billion, or 36%; Argentina $460 million, or 12%; and Mexico $694 million, or 18%. The principal purposes of Eximbank operations over the period were as follows:

Balance of Payments	31%
Transportation	24
Industry	21
Electric Power & Water	12
Agricultural Equipment	5
Others	7
	100%

The fact that balance of payments loans are the largest single item in Eximbank lending in recent years corroborates the hypothesis noted in an earlier section that the United States government, while refusing to be a partner to commodity stabilization schemes, apparently stands ready to provide the resources and to compensate, in some sizable fraction, for the short-fall in exchange earnings occasioned by drastic swings in the prices of principal exports. To be sure, the earlier balance of payments lending to Argentina, Brazil, and Chile had no direct connection with export commodity price fluctuations, but the last year's balance of payments loans to Brazil, Colombia, and Chile, for example, are directly associated with the decline in exchange earnings in those countries as a result of declining coffee and copper prices.

In connection with these balance of payments credits, the Eximbank endeavors to use its lending capacity as leverage to induce monetary and fiscal reforms that will correct the fundamental problem, and, hopefully, prevent a repetition. The borrowing countries, however, tend to resist proposed corrective measures and the record of the last few years is not an impressive one. In the last year or so, this leverage function has been delegated to the International Monetary Fund, as will be discussed presently.

The World Bank

The operations of the International Bank for Reconstruction and Development (World Bank) in Latin America represent total loans of $1,307 million at the end of 1961, of which Brazil alone received $267 million, or 20 per cent of the total; Mexico received $226 million, or 17 per cent and Colombia $220 million, or 17 per cent. The rate of disbursement over the last years is set forth in the table below:

The World Bank
(Millions of Dollars)

	1953	1954	1955	1956	1957	1958	1959	1960	1961
Outstanding Balance:									
Year's End	244	309	368	445	506	547	565	594	650
Loans Disbursed		69	77	95	82	72	53	67	97
Repayments		4	18	18	21	31	35	38	41
Net Annual Investment		65	59	77	61	41	18	29	56

The purposes for which World Bank loans were made in Latin America were as follows:

Electric Power	52%
Transportation	36
Agriculture	6
Industry & Communications	6
	100%

The role of the World Bank in financing economic overhead capital is conspicuous in comparison with the Eximbank. Thus, electric power and transportation account for 88 per cent of loans for Latin America, as against 36 per cent for the Eximbank. Moreover, the World Bank does not lend for balance of payment purposes, which is a second reason for the difference in loan composition of the two institutions. Although the World Bank does not engage in balance of payments lending as such, it endeavors to use its lending capacity, like the Eximbank, as leverage to induce borrowing governments to adopt monetary and fiscal policies which will promote development and, particularly, to create the conditions under which private enterprise may take up its role in the development process.

International Monetary Fund

The resources of the International Monetary Fund are to be distinguished from the Eximbank and the World Bank, because they are not drawn directly for development purposes or specific projects, but rather to assist countries having balance of payment difficulties. Nevertheless, the use of Fund resources through the mechanism of drawings or through standby arrangements does provide foreign exchange exactly like the balance of payments loans of the Eximbank. Drawings from the Fund may be repaid over a period of three to five years. Since the Latin American countries have been experiencing chronic difficulties over the last five to ten years, access to the Fund is an additional source of capital, and drawings may be "rolled over" if the need can be demonstrated.

The volume of Fund resources being used by Latin American countries is substantial and has been increasing over the last ten years. Thus in the first 5 years, 1952-1956, total Fund resources used were only $29 million dollars net, while in the second 5 years 1957-61 total net drawings aggregated $453 million. The principal recipients in the last 5 years were: Argentina, $227 million, Brazil, $143 million, and Chile, $76 million. These substantial drawings are an important supplement to lending from the two banks, and they play an important role in the growth rates of these countries. Having access to Fund resources of this magnitude, the borrowing countries are able to maintain a level of imports, including capital goods, higher than they could otherwise afford. Moreover, development programs need not be discarded or sharply cut back for lack of foreign exchange. Thus, the Fund resources permit some continuity in development plans and avoid costly interruptions in the construction of development projects into which considerable capital may already have been committed.

The Fund has come to occupy a position of increasing importance in the last year or so by virtue of the leverage which it employs upon would-be borrowers to take the fiscal and monetary measures needed to correct the conditions causing chronic balance of payments deficits. In recent years this leverage has not been very effective, because the would-be borrower could go to the United States government and get financial aid from the Eximbank for balance of payments purposes. Now, however, a significant change may be noted. Both the United States government and the World Bank have increasingly adopted the line that a borrower must first make his peace with the Fund before he can hope to qualify for loans from either of the Banks. This position enormously increases the leverage which the Fund now exercises. At the same time, it suits the purpose of the United States to delegate the bargaining function to the Fund, because, as an international organization, it is perhaps in a better political position to mobilize a consensus of world financial opinion and to bring the weight of such pressures upon a country reluctant to undertake the necessary reforms. The United States is always limited by political considerations in the amount of pressure which it can bring to bear upon Latin American countries, but the Fund, as an international organization with 75 members, does not necessarily suffer from the same inhibitions. In short, therefore, the significance of the Fund in Latin American economic development is much greater than the resources which it can supply for relatively short periods of time.

Development Loan Fund

The volume of hard currency lending by the Eximbank and the World Bank, over the last decade, to Latin America has reached a point in a number of countries where the service on these loans, including amortization and interest, is producing a burden on the balance of payments. The capacity of a country to absorb external debt is known as its "credit worthiness" and this depends largely upon its balance of payments prospects, which in turn is influenced by a variety of circumstances, including the outlook for production and cost from monetary and fiscal factors, the investment climate, and so on. Nevertheless, at any one time there is a calculable limit to the service obligations which a country may assume with prudence. When this limit is approached the country is said to be "loaned up" and further long-term financing will be suspended until amortization makes room for new debt obligations. Meanwhile, such countries often have many attractive development projects which will not be financed unless foreign private capital can be induced to come in.

Toward the end of the decade 1950-1960, it was realized that Latin America would not be able to support much more in dollar obligations from the traditional hard currency lending agencies, e.g., Eximbank and the World Bank. Accordingly a number of new lending agencies were created to lend dollars repayable in local currency, or to provide resources in local currency through sales of surplus agricultural commodities, thereby continuing to finance the development prospects. The first of these agencies was the Development Loan Fund, created in 1957. At the time of its termination in 1961 a total of $337 million was authorized in credits to Latin America (15% of the world's total). These credits to Latin America were made in dollars but repayments were, on the average, scheduled one-third in dollars, two-thirds in local currency.

In addition to the innovation of accepting loan payments "in soft currency," the DLF devoted a large part of its resources to social development. Projects, such as housing, were hitherto considered improvements in "welfare" but not directly linked to production and, therefore, not bankable. Latin America was destined to receive only a small fraction (15%) of DLF resources which were largely committed to other areas of the world, especially to the Middle East, South Asia, and the Far East for reasons that are more or less self evident.

Public Law No. 480 agreements

Another important source from which Latin American countries are receiving resources for economic development is from U.S. surplus agricultural commodities under Public Law No. 480 agreements. The program for disposal of surplus commodities was begun in 1954 and provided for sales under three titles, or three kinds of programs. Title I is specifically for economic development purposes, Title II, for disaster relief, and Title III, for donations. Since the inception of the program in 1954 to the end of 1962, Latin America received a total of $801 million, which is the market value of the commodities purchased under sales agreements (Title I), together with disaster relief and donations. With special reference to the economic development prospects under Title I, Latin America received $530 million which is 8% of Title I sales in the world; within Latin America, Brazil alone accounts for 48% of the purchases.

The first step in the transaction is a sales agreement whereby the United States delivers certain tonnages of specified foodstuffs and is paid in local currency. The second step involves the negotiation of a loan agreement whereby the United States lends to the government the local currency it received for the sale of the commodities, after reserving some 15-20% of these currencies for its own use within the country. The local currency generated by the sale of the commodities is the property of the United States and is either spent by United States agencies in that country, or loaned as stated above. These are long-term loans, perhaps 20 or as long as 40 years, with interest rates of 1 or 2%. In most cases there is no requirement to maintain the value of the loan in local currency so that, under inflationary conditions, a loan in local currency is soon wiped out. In these countries such loans are becoming, in effect, grants.

These funds are being used to finance the local currency cost of various development projects since both the Eximbank and the World Bank lend only the foreign exchange components. These resources make it possible to finance additional projects without creating inflationary pressures on the economy. In the case of Brazil, for example, virtually all of the loan proceeds are allotted to the National Bank for Economic Development, which carefully allocates the amounts to development projects of high priority, principally for the expansion of electric power, which the Brazilian government has accepted as a top priority item in its current development program. In Chile, for example, some portion of the loan proceeds were allocated directly to private projects where the foreign exchange components were supplied by the World Bank (coal mining) and the Eximbank (nitrate mining). Since one of the major limitations on the capacity of a country to absorb foreign loan capital is its ability to mobilize the necessary domestic capital for local expenditures, these P.L. 480 funds may provide the means for accelerating economic growth. The evidence suggests that they are being wisely used in the countries of Latin America where they are available.

The Inter-American Development Bank

In 1959, a new development banking institution was created to assist in the development of Latin America. All twenty countries joined the Bank with substantial paid-in capital; Cuba subsequently withdrew from the Bank for political reasons.

The principal capital of the Bank was paid by the subscribing countries, one-half in dollars and one-half in local currency; the share of the United States in the total capital structure is nominally 41 per cent of the ordinary capital and 66 per cent of the Fund for Special Operations. The latter fund was conceived to meet the growing number of social development projects which might be financed on more favorable terms, both in interest rates and in maturities. In addition to the regular paid-in capital, the subscribing countries committed themselves to provide additional capital when called by the Bank to meet its obligations and especially to serve as a guarantee fund or security on borrowings the Bank might obtain in the open capital market.

The total capital structure of the Bank may be summarized as follows:

		Millions of Dollars
Regular Paid-In Capital		$382
Callable Capital		432
	Total	$814
Fund for Special Operations Paid-In Capital		146
	Total	$960

A third department in the Bank, known as the Trust Fund, received an allotment under the Bogotá Fund for Progress in the amount of $394 million. These resources are considered to be a part of the Alliance for Progress program and the Inter-American Bank was chosen to administer this sum in financing social development projects, such as education, public health, housing and land settlement.

The maturity of loans in the regular department and in the Special Fund for Operations ranges from ten to twenty years; interest rates for ordinary loans run at the same rate as the World Bank and the Export-Import Bank charge for their loans, currently 5¾ per cent (1962). In the Fund for Special Operations, the interest rate is the same except for loans to other development banking institutions for relending to private enterprises, in which case the rate is 4 per cent. Finally, in the Trust Fund —part of the Alliance for Progress financing—maturities are much longer, ranging from twenty to thirty years with interest rates from 2 per cent to 3½ per cent.

The year 1961 was the first year of loan operations for the new Bank and its results may be briefly summarized. In the ordinary department, total loans amounted to $130 million. These loans covered a wide range of projects in the private and public sector and particularly loans to development banks in the Latin American countries to be reloaned to enterprises in that country. In this first year, loans to private enterprises, directly or indirectly, represented 56 per cent of the total loans, while credits to governments and government entities represented the remaining 44 per cent.

In the Fund for Special Operations, total loans in 1961 were $48 million and in credits from the Social Trust Fund, loans in the amount of $116 million were provided. The activities may be summarized as follows:

	Millions of Dollars
Ordinary Department	$130
Fund for Special Operations	48
Social Trust Fund	116
Total	$294

On the basis of disbursements made, approximately 20 per cent of the loans will be repaid in local currency and the remainder will be repaid in dollars. This fraction comes close to that which was observed in the Development Loan Fund before it was terminated and incorporated in the new Agency for International Development.

The future role of the Inter-American Bank will depend almost entirely on its ability to raise funds in the open capital market, either in the United States or Western Europe. The first of these participations has been in connection with individual loans, aggregating approximately $4 million in 1961. A second and even more important development was the ability of the Inter-American Bank to sell its own bonds to a consortium of banks in Italy.* There is, of course, a price to be paid for getting access to the open capital market and this is the continuing scrutiny that these capital exporter countries will subject the Bank's loan operations in Latin America. To date, the Bank has demonstrated strong management and it has begun to earn the respect of other capital exporting institutions. In short, as long as it may maintain its present high standards and the quality of the loans which it is making, it will undoubtedly continue to receive the confidence and the increasing participation of the world capital market. Without this support, however, the Bank will exhaust its present capital resources within another year or two, if the rate of loans made continues as in 1961.

Finally, with respect to the role which the Bank occupies in the overall structure of the Alliance for Progress, the scrutiny to be made by the United States Congress, will surely be as critical and probably more exasperating than the scrutiny the Bank will receive from the European and

---

* $24 million equivalent (in lire fully convertible into dollars or other currency) were obtained at 5% on a twenty-year bond issue.

American capital markets. If the operations carried out to date under the Trust Fund can pass the Congressional scrutiny, it seems probable that additional appropriations will be made and allocated to the Bank for its administration. The idea of entrusting a portion of the Alliance for Progress program to the administration of a bank whose management is largely Latin American represents a useful innovation in United States foreign aid techniques. Evidently, the Latin American governments must, through their appointed directors to the Bank, decide among themselves how a given sum is to be allocated and agree upon priorities. In the past, all these decisions were made by a United States government agency and subject to the innumerable pressures of the individual Latin American governments, each striving for a larger share in the total sum, with resultant strains upon relationships between the United States and single governments.

INCOME DISTRIBUTION

One of the important aspects of the development process is the effect on the distribution of income within a particular economy. Most of the literature which deals with aggregates usually suffices to point out changes in gross product, national income, and per capita incomes, but the all-important question of the distribution of income under the impact of development has been virtually ignored. A recent study on the changing distribution of personal income in Mexico produces such interesting— not to say disturbing—questions that the study may be cited in its possible relevance to the over-all situation for Latin America.*

The study compares family incomes, in constant prices, at two points of time, 1950 and 1957. The average family income per month rose in the 7-year period from 916 pesos to 1,128 pesos in real terms (1957 prices), an increase of 23 per cent. Nevertheless, the lowest 20 per cent of the families (the two lowest deciles in the statistical distribution) received less real income in 1957, while the third decile income was approximately the same. In relative terms, the share of this lowest 30 per cent of the families declined from 9.9 per cent of family income in 1950 to 7.5 per cent in 1957. It is in the upper two deciles that a sharp concentration of income begins to appear. Thus the ninth decile share rose from 10.8 per cent (1950) to 14.7 per cent (1957). The concentration in the tenth and highest decile was largely unchanged, accounting for 49 per cent of family income in 1950 and 47 per cent of total income in 1957.

* Navarrete, I. M. *"La Distribucion del Ingreso y el Desarrollo Economico de Mexico"* Mexico: Instituto de Investigaciones Economicas, Escuela Nacional de Economia—1960.

In short, the inference is suggested that the lower third of the population is worse off after seven years of development, both in absolute income and relative to the total number of families. These figures, which include imputed income, are before income taxation, but the effectiveness of income taxation in Mexico, as in many Latin American countries, is such that the redistributive effect must be minimal.

A second bit of evidence that the process of economic development is widening the personal income gap within a country may be seen by comparing incomes in an earlier period, 1940 to 1950, in Mexico.

Changes in Personal Income Distribution: Mexico

		Labor Force			Individual Income	
		(Thousands)		Per Cent	(1950 Prices)	
		1940	1950	Change	1940 (Pesos)	1950
Wage Earners	Agric.	1.913	1.431	−25	820	734
	Non-Agric.	1.156	2.400	108	4.753	4.465
Entrepreneurial	Agric.	1.726	2.536	47	1.209	3.131
Earners	Non-Agric.	685	931	36	12.353	15.798
Labor Force		5.480	7.298			

The above table summarizes the changing position of salary and wage earners and the entrepreneurial earners, which include farm operators, managers of business enterprises, and so on. The labor force increased by one-third in the decade.

In agriculture the independent farm operator increased his average real income from 1,209 pesos to 3,131 pesos per year, an increase of 159 per cent, while the agricultural wage earner's real income actually declined 10 per cent, 820 pesos to 734 pesos, despite the reduction (25%) in number. In the non-agricultural sector, a similar gap emerges in the decade under consideration. Entrepreneurial average real income—independent farmers, operators of industrial and commercial establishments—rose from 12,353 pesos to 15,798 pesos, an increase of 28 per cent, whereas wage earner income in this same sector decreased from 4,753 pesos to 4,465 pesos, a decline of 6 per cent in the decade.

These sobering conclusions provide the basis for one of the elements or preconditions stressed in the Alliance for Progress which calls for some modification of the tax structure. If the Mexican experience is indicative of other countries in Latin America, the problem is compounded. The poorer sectors seem to be getting poorer and richer sectors seem to be getting richer; at the same time, the over-all incidence of taxation in Latin America tends to be regressive so that the poorer sections not only receive less income but also support a higher burden in the tax structure.

ALLIANCE FOR PROGRESS

In the years following World War II an increasing dissatisfaction has developed with the magnitude and direction of United States economic assistance in Latin America. The dissatisfaction was deepened by the realization that the United States was giving priority to other regions of the world and not to its "friends" in Latin America. No sooner had the massive investments in Europe under the Marshall Plan begun to phase out when the Korean War launched a second massive program of military and economic aid to the countries of Southeast Asia. Meanwhile, assisttance to Latin America was restricted to technical assistance, plus loans from the official lending agencies. At the same time, the terms of trade for many Latin American countries were unstable, if not declining, and the great expectations which followed the coffee boom beginning in 1953 were short-lived.

An attempt was first made in 1958, in "Operation Pan-America," to mobilize the Latin American countries and to present the United States with a series of targets designed to overcome economic and social underdevelopment. "Operation Pan-America," however, seemed to be wholly occupied in drawing up targets and paper plans, but no resources were being mobilized.

It was not until the Economic Conference of the Organization of the American States at Bogotá in September, 1960, that concrete measures were developed to include social objectives as well as economic ones. The Bogotá proposal recognized that economic development was a slow process at best and meanwhile social tensions were accumulating. A "Fund for Progress" was authorized by Congress following the Bogotá meeting and by October 1961—one year later—a sum of $600 million was appropriated. This sum provided for $100 million to Chile for earthquake relief, $100 million as additional funds to accelerate Point IV operations in the region; the remaining $400 million was divided in two parts, $394 million was transferred to the newly organized Inter-American Bank, under a trust fund agreement, and the residual sum of $6 million was alloted to the OAS. Because of the delay in voting funds, this "Fund for Progress" did not come into being until after the Alliance for Progress had been conceived in March 1961.

The second step in orienting the new policy took place at Punta del Este in August 1961. The Punta del Este Charter promulgated the principle that aid for social development and welfare projects, together with investment in social infra-structure, should be provided *pari passu* with aid for economic development. Great emphasis was placed upon self help on the part of the Latin American countries. This self help was partly to provide local resources but especially to adopt a planned approach to development and to include far reaching structural changes in such items as agrarian reform and a more equitable and effective tax structure.

One year after Punta del Este, it was already evident that a number of Latin American governments were encountering resistance and were either unwilling or unable to undertake seriously the reforms that they had accepted—albeit with tongue in check—at Punta del Este. Meanwhile the United States continues to urge the Latin American governments along the agreed path and, by offering to finance some $20 billion in social and economic development projects over the next 10-year period, it hopes to mobilize a much larger sum in local resources and to coax them into channels such as education and housing that have hitherto received minimal support.

There appear to be two or three points at which the designers of the Punta del Este program allowed their enthusiasm to gloss over certain hard realities. In the first place, the emphasis placed upon closing the development gap between the Latin American countries and the industrialized nations creates illusory expectations. The discussion of the economic gap usually fails to recognize that the developed countries enjoy a higher rate of net savings applied to a much larger stock of capital; the stock of capital has come about, in considerable degree, by the cumulative adaptation of scientific technology. Finally, there is a disturbing possibility that the population growth in the Latin American countries may largely nullify their best efforts to raise per capita income 2.5% yearly.

A second miscalculation may be implied in the assumption that existing governments in Latin America will, or can, bring about changes in their basic institutions. Meanwhile, there is a great show of activity as the countries hasten to organize national planning councils and introduce innumerable bills for agrarian reform in order to qualify for Alliance for Progress assistance. But serious resistance is being encountered from the "vested interests," which command political power in these countries.

Finally, perhaps the most serious miscalculation is in failing to recognize that the present social, economic, and political structure in the Latin American countries is based upon a natural aristocracy, coupled with illiteracy, and a set of social relationships that are founded upon paternalism rather than equality; in fact, the inequality of the existing taxation systems exacerbates the over-all situation and serves to consolidate the existing order.

The question which remains to be explored is the extent to which the United States can insist that reluctant governments implement their reform programs as a precondition of Alliance aid. The probability is that such conditions will soon be relaxed, not to say abandoned; otherwise, the Alliance will grind to a halt.

Meanwhile, as the fragments of evidence begin to show (e.g., the Mexico study on income distribution cited above), economic development by itself is no panacea. There are new and virulent forces at work; stresses and strains are accumulating in many sectors, often exacerbated by inflation. In short, unless some frontal attack on the social and economic structure can be successfully mounted, Latin America will reap the whirlwind. This, then, is the importance of the Alliance for Progress.

4

Diplomatic Relations

We need not be too precise in defining United States diplomatic relations with Latin America. Geography put us in one hemisphere, and history followed as a matter of course. Our destinies have gradually been woven together until there is now an interlocking pattern of politics, trade, strategy and culture. Our relationships today are a mixture of what the past has contributed and forced upon us, what we judge to be the possible and desirable objectives today, and what actions we are taking to achieve these aims.

But it takes two to make a relationship as well as a quarrel. We must not get so involved in United States relations with Latin America as to forget that there is such a thing as Latin American relations with the United States. The two influences work upon each other, sometimes hostile, sometimes friendly, clashing or coinciding, adamant or yielding, and often failing to meet for lack of understanding.

The dominant feature is best realized in the Latin label for the United States: the Colossus of the North. Our power and wealth and their weakness and poverty form the background against which the hemispheric drama has to be played. The adjustment and conciliation of these two inequalities in the midst of the global struggle of democracy and totalitarianism is the major problem. The gap between us has been growing

HERBERT L. MATTHEWS *has been on the editorial board of* The New York Times *since 1949. Before that he was war correspondent and foreign correspondent for nineteen years in Europe, Africa, and Asia for* The Times. *For the last thirteen years Mr. Matthews has specialized in Latin American affairs for* The Times *as editor and on occasion as correspondent. He won the Maria Moors Cabot Award in 1956. He is the author of the following books:* Eyewitness in Abyssinia, Two Wars and More to Come, The Fruits of Fascism, The Education of a Correspondent, Assignment to Austerity *(co-author with Mrs. Matthews),* The Yoke and the Arrows, *and* The Cuban Story.

as we get richer and the Latin American countries, with some exceptions, stagnate or even get poorer.

Underdeveloped agrarian nations demanding industrialization, the great mass of the poor demanding social justice, the emotional thrust of nationalism, the pressure of the greatest population explosion on earth, the paradox of "rising expectations," the wave of anti-dictatorial revolutions followed by the threat of violent, Leftist social revolutions or another wave of Rightist military reaction—such are the forces working in Latin America and therefore working on us.

Twenty different countries are heaving and thrusting under the compulsive drive of these forces, each at a different stage of progress, each demanding and needing different things or more or less of the same things. We on our part have global responsibilities, domestic needs and our security and way of life to defend.

To fashion an ideal "Latin American policy" out of these diverse and conflicting forces and aims would be a superhuman task. Diplomacy, like politics, is an art not a science. United States relations with Latin America have never been neat or precise and never will be. We muddle along, doing well and badly, rightly and wrongly, all at the same time. History tells us that; so does contemporary study, and so, no doubt, will the story of the future.

THE MONROE DOCTRINE

United States relations with Latin America are generally considered by historians to have begun with the No-Transfer Resolution of 1811. Samuel Flagg Bemis in his "Latin American Policy of the United States" calls this "the first significant landmark in the evolution of United States-Latin American policy." It was a Congressional resolution concerned with Florida, then under the weak control of Spain. The key phrase held that the United States "cannot without serious inquietude see any part of the said territory pass into the hands of any foreign power."

What we said then, we still say, and the Latin American republics say it with us, although most of them would confine the "no-transfer" principle to teritorial conquest while we (as Guatemala and Cuba have shown) would extend it to ideological subversion by international communism as well. The possibility of a victorious Nazi Germany taking over the French and Dutch possessions in the Caribbean at the time of the Second World War showed that the "no-transfer" policy could still be challenged.

Our attitude toward the Latin American countries as they struggled for and won their independence in the years from 1810 to 1824 has left a generally pleasant legacy. The picture of a young United States stoutly championing the brave efforts of the other American nations to win freedom from Spain, France and Portugal is true enough, especially at the beginning and the end of the period of conflict. In between, we had our war with Britain, starting in 1812, while our successful negotiations to purchase Florida from Spain, which did not end until 1821, made it impolitic to offend the Spaniards.

We were the first outside nation to recognize the new Latin American states, and that was a great service. There were, of course, hard-headed reasons both of trade and strategy to want to see the European powers weakened or driven out of the Western hemisphere. It happened also to be in England's interest to keep the European continental powers out of the hemisphere. England herself, then going through the Industrial Revolution, was interested in trade and investments, not conquest. She wanted a balance of power on the European continent and as part of such a policy "called the New World into existence to redress the balance of the Old" in George Canning's immortal and somewhat exaggerated phrase. Thus it was that American policy was made feasible because of British control of the high seas.

The Monroe Doctine was part of President James Monroe's message to Congress on December 2, 1823, and in form it was a purely American statement of policy, as Secretary of State John Quincy Adams wanted it to be. The key sentence comes in the middle:

> We owe it, therefore, to candor, and to the amicable relations existing between the United States and those [European] powers, to declare that we should consider any attempt on their part to extend their system to any portion of this hemisphere as dangerous to our peace and safety.

The Doctrine was not, at the time, an incentive to closer relations between the United States and Latin America. Three years before, in his famous conversation with Speaker of the House Henry Clay, Secretary Adams said pessimistically: "I have little expectation of any beneficial result to this country from any future connection with them [the Latin American countries], political or commercial."

At first the Doctrine was little heeded on either side. As Professor Dexter Perkins wrote, "There can be no doubt at all . . . that Monroe's message of 1823 was directed against an illusory danger. There never was any fixed purpose to reconquer the Spanish colonies."

Moreover, when it came to minor infractions of hemispheric territory, the United States did not consider that the Monroe Doctrine obligated us to employ military force. The British and French were especially active— in Mexico, Brazil, Argentina, Uruguay and Chile—with no reaction from the United States. So long as the Latin American states maintained their sovereignty and independence from Spain, France and England, we paid little heed. In any event, Britons ruled the waves, not Americans.

The Doctrine, of course, was never intended to prevent the United

States from getting more territory. "Manifest Destiny" was leading us to covet and acquire the land stretching West to the Pacific Ocean.

It was President James K. Polk (1844-1848), with an eye on Texas, who revived the somewhat neglected Doctrine. It also proved useful later in restraining England's activities in Central America, in forcing the Emperor Maximilian and the French out of Mexico, and in blocking Spain's efforts to regain Santo Domingo and Peru.

The greatest mark left on hemispheric relations by the Monroe Doctrine stretches over a period from 1875 to 1921. Our Good Neighbors will never let us forget those years.

In 1875, Great Britain and Venezuela started a controversy over the Venezuelan-Guiana boundary. Venezuela tried in vain for two decades to appeal to the Monroe Doctrine. A good public relations man, former American Minister William L. Scruggs, is credited with finally stirring up United States opinion. Congress passed a resolution urging arbitration, and Secretary of State Richard Olney sent a fiery note to Lord Salisbury, the British Foreign Secretary, on July 20, 1895. Lord Salisbury replied that the Monroe Doctrine had nothing to do with the dispute.

"The Government of the United States," he wrote, "is not entitled to affirm as a universal proposition with reference to a number of independent states for whose conduct it assumes no responsibility, that its interests are necessarily concerned in whatever may befall those States simply because they are situated in the Western Hemisphere."

This was cruelly logical and doubtless right in international law, and it is the interpretation now accepted by the Latin American countries. But in practice it can be argued that we have never accepted it, and in 1895 we were starting our one and only burst of genuine imperialism.

President Grover Cleveland replied vigorously to Lord Salisbury, and the British, no doubt with an eye to their great and lucrative investments in the United States, yielded gracefully. The boundary was settled by arbitration as the United States had asked.

The dispute was interesting in many ways. In reality, as Lord Salisbury unkindly wrote, the Monroe Doctrine had nothing to do with it, but it was invoked by the Americans; it was an example of defending a Latin American republic against a European power, and it did stir up American nationalism to a point that made intervention in Cuba less than three years later a natural sequel. We were, in effect, proclaiming a hemispheric hegemony.

Moreover, the realization that we were threatening to fight with a navy containing one modern battleship against much the greatest naval force in the world, started the United States on a rearmament program that was to make us a world power in reality.

Aside from the natural rejoicing in Venezuela, the Latin American reaction was mixed. Any display of power by the United States was always calculated to arouse fear and jealousy. The specter of intervention was only too visible to Latin American eyes. And as some commentators pointed out, the danger of a European attempt to conquer hemispheric territories had long since passed. The peril, decades later, was to become one of political and ideological subversion by totalitarian powers and their doctrines, not one of forceful conquest.

In the brief imperialistic phase of our history it was natural that the meaning of the Monroe Doctrine should be stretched to include an American exercise of "police power." This was done in the so-called Roosevelt Corollary to the Doctrine. It followed a ruling of the Hague Court in 1904 on a Venezuelan claims controversy of the previous year. This gave Great Britain, Germany and Italy priority over the claims of other foreigners because these three countries had resorted to military operations to force Venezuela to pay claims of their citizens residing in Venezuela.

This confirmation of accepted international law—that armed force could be used to collect debts—seemingly opened the road to much European intervention. The political instability of Latin American countries often led to defaulted loans or to seizure of alien property so that there was a constant temptation to the European powers to intervene.

For President Theodore Roosevelt this meant that "in the Western Hemisphere the adherence of the United States to the Monroe Doctrine may force the United States, however reluctantly, in flagrant cases of such wrong-doing or impotence, to the exercise of an international police power." This was the "Roosevelt Corollary."

We were at the time imposing an American customs control on Santo Domingo to forestall action by European continental creditors, and Germany, incidentally, was also showing undue interest in Venezuela at the beginning of the century.

To "Teddy" Roosevelt our response was "part of that international duty which is necessarily involved in the assertion of the Monroe Doctrine." Even President Woodrow Wilson, the spiritual father of the Organization of American States as well as of the League of Nations and the United Nations, could argue that "chronic wrong-doing, or an impotence which results in a general loosening of the ties of civilized society, may in America as elsewhere ultimately require intervention by some civilized nation."

THE ERA OF IMPERIALISM

Roosevelt, as stated, felt this was "part of that international duty which is necessarily involved in the assertion of the Monroe Doctrine." In reality, the Roosevelt Corollary was a complete departure from the spirit of the Doctrine, and it came to be so regarded. The whole system of "protective imperialism," as Bemis called it, had to go—control of customs, Marines, the right to intervene unilaterally, "dollar diplomacy."

The focus of our brief imperialist fling was not unreasonable—the Isthmus of Panama and its role in the defense of our continental Republic. By any concept of strategy, the United States either had control of the Isthmus (and the Canal when it was built) or our Atlantic and Pacific coasts were going to be endangered. As a corollary, the approaches to the Canal had to be ours or in friendly hands. This principle was appealed to in the case of Guatemala in 1954, and earlier it was a factor that led us to fight Spain over Cuba and Puerto Rico.

The value of the Panama Canal today is greatly reduced, especially militarily. The fact that we now have navies on both the Atlantic and Pacific, the growth and importance of air power and the vulnerability to atomic or nuclear bombs, all reduce the Canal essentially to its commercial value. In a limited war, in which nuclear weapons were not used, it would still be of great value. And the convenience of getting the strategic raw materials of the West Coast of South America up to the East Coast of the United States by a direct route is also something to consider.

In general, there was one simple, basic factor—which seemed obvious, natural and necessary—behind the Monroe Doctrine, the imperialist fling, and, indeed, every aspect of our Latin American policies. This was the security of continental United States.

Our five Caribbean interventions (Cuba, Haiti, Dominican Republic, Nicaragua and Panama) had in each case a two-fold objective—to restore order to the finances of the country involved and to build up or train military forces in each case in order to maintain political stability. In all five cases the immediate results were beneficial, and in all five the long-range results were nil, or worse. We put political power in the hands of the military and made them invincible. Since the bases on which to build democracies were still not present in these countries, and since the traditional concept of politics as a spoils system still prevailed, our well-meant efforts led inevitably to results like Trujillo in the Dominican Republic and Somoza in Nicaragua.

Every one of our interventions—Mexico included—left a legacy whose effects are still operative. The most obvious is the case of Panama, for the very creation of that country was a result of American intervention.

The French, it will be recalled, began digging a canal under a concession from Colombia, to whom the territory then belonged. The activities of the Panama Canal Company, organized by Ferdinand de Lesseps, aroused fears in the United States and much talk of the Monroe Doctrine, but the venture failed before anything could or had to be done about it.

Our manipulation of the diplomatic, legal and financial aspects is something that most Americans wish they could forget—without losing the Canal. Nicaragua was the better site, but some shady lobbying by the clever Frenchman, Philippe Bunau-Varilla, and tricky legal work, switched the locality to Panama. Then some more highly dubious machinations by President Theodore Roosevelt, and the men who were financially concerned, led to the desired solution. Bunau-Varilla managed and financed the revolution of the Department of Panama, then part of Colombia, but Teddy Roosevelt could rightly boast later: "I took the Isthmus." Morally speaking, it was one of the most shameless incidents in United States history; practically and strategically it was a valuable thing to have done.

The first intervention in Santo Domingo (1904) was to force that country to meet its debt obligations to all foreign nationals, including Americans. The alternative would have been European intervention. The reason was justifiable, especially as Santo Domingo was in a state of anarchy and chaos. There was no thought of annexation.

This was the occasion when Roosevelt put forward his novel thesis (the "Corollary") that the Monroe Doctrine not only forbade intervention from Europe but sanctioned intervention from the United States in order to prevent such intervention. It was also called the policy of the "Big Stick," and we have spent generations trying to live it down. Actually, the Roosevelt interventions were missionary in intent, not aggressions, and there was never any idea of endangering the liberty or sovereignty of these nations.

The "dollar diplomacy" of his successor, William Howard Taft, was more directly intervention by and for the United States, not deliberately for private business interests. It led to outright military interventions.

In 1909 we landed Marines in Nicaragua to protect American nationals and mining property at Bluefields during a revolution against the dictator, General José Santos Zelaya. Zelaya was overthrown. Again in 1912 we intervened to bolster the regime of Adolfo Díaz. The Marines stayed until 1933, preventing revolution, not uprisings, supervising elections, training the Nicaraguan police force. However, we were ineffective in other respects and earned much criticism in Latin America. Nicaragua is generally considered as the classic type of military intervention to protect American investments—or "Wall Street"—which is an exaggeration, for the intent was basically neither mercenary nor aggressive. Actually, we had few investments in Nicaragua, Santo Domingo, Panama and Haiti, and it was not business interests who favored intervention in Cuba and Mexico.

The worst result of the Nicaraguan interventions was to turn the country over to a Marine-trained officer named Anastasio Somoza, who maintained a tight dictatorship until his assassination in 1956, when his power and wealth were assumed by his two sons.

There was another revolution followed by chaos in Santo Domingo in 1912, and Taft intervened with 750 Marines to restore order and supervise the collection of customs duties. The disorder continued, and the next time it was Wilson who intervened. American troops occupied the capital in 1916 and remained until 1924.

Haiti fell into a state of anarchy that became complete in 1915. The next year Wilson felt impelled to land Marines. The alternative, as in other cases, would have been to see Britain, France or Germany—or all three—intervene. American financial advisers, customs officials, health experts and officers to train a native constabulary were sent in, and the United States was given the same powers of intervention as in Cuba. By any long range view, our intervention was a complete failure, for Haiti in the 1960's is still in a state of utter poverty, corruption, mismanagement and tyranny.

These interventions are still used as sticks by Latin Americans to beat "Tío Sam," but it has to be said in their favor that the policies followed did protect these countries from an intervention that might have been permanent by European powers, and also that the United States certainly proved it had no desire of its own to establish permanent protectorates in Latin America.

The best example of this was Cuba, which many influential Americans in the nineteenth century thought we should annex, and which we could have annexed after the Spanish American War.

True, the Cubans have nothing to thank us for in their long decades of agony, or when they fought a cruel war against the Spanish in 1868-1878, or when horrors were heaped upon them in the years that followed while Grant and Cleveland thought in feeble terms of meditation or worried about the rights of American citizens in Cuba and did their best to prevent hostile expeditions of exiles from the United States to Cuba. Meanwhile, Spain was able to acquire what arms it needed in the United States to suppress the Cuban rebels. This was the pattern that repeated itself under General Batista, although in the latter case we had the excuse of the non-intervention policy. In 1898 we did intervene, and one of the ironies of history is that it seemed probable that Cuba could have had her independence at the time, and the United States whatever we demanded, without armed intervention. Certainly, the Cubans think so.

At least the joint Congressional resolution of April 20, 1898, for intervention in Cuba did contain a self-denying amendment:

> That the United States hereby disclaims any disposition or intention to exercise sovereignty, jurisdiction, or control over the said island except for the pacification thereof, and asserts its determination, when that is accomplished, to leave the government and control of the island to its people.

We were not entirely self-denying because we insisted on adding the so-called Platt Amendment to the Cuban Constitution. Its main purpose was not intervention, although it led to a number of interventions; it was to keep any foreign power out of Cuba by being sure it had no excuse to intervene. It was not exploitation, either, although our policies gave Americans virtual control of the economy of Cuba until Fidel Castro came along in 1959.

The Platt Amendment dates from July 2, 1904 to May 31, 1934. Article III was the decisive one:

> The Government of Cuba consents that the United States may exercise the right to intervene for the preservation of Cuban independence, the maintenance of a government adequate for the protection of life, property and individual liberty, and for discharging the obligations with respect to Cuba imposed by the Treaty of Paris on the United States, now to be assumed and undertaken by the Government of Cuba.

The best expression of American policy—and it was a genuine one—came in a letter from Secretary of State Elihu Root to "Marse" Henry Watterson on March 5, 1908, quoted by Philip Jessup in his biography of the Secretary.

"We don't want Cuba to ourselves," Mr. Root declared; "we cannot permit any other power to get possession of her and, to prevent the necessity of one and the possibility of the other of these results, we want her to govern herself decently and in order."

These hopes were not to be fulfilled, but Cubans would do well to consider who is really to blame—they or we.

This is getting ahead of the story. The Mexicans were the ones who had the best causes for complaint, and they long antedate our turn-of-the-century burst of imperialism.

From the point of view of relations, our early Mexican policy was not conducive to friendliness. "Manifest Destiny," even before it was called that, made it evident enough that the United States was going to covet Texas and all the territory up to the West Coast. That history needs no recounting, nor the dramatic episode of the Emperor Maximilian and the machinations of France, Spain and Britain while we were fighting a civil war.

We had French troops just below our border from 1861 to 1867, and a threat that went deeply into South America. It was the most open and perilous challenge to the principles of the Monroe Doctrine and to republicanism in the New World since the beginning of the century. One might say that the Monroe Doctrine came of age at that time. It was recognized in the United States as a major national policy; it was enforced; it won respect in Latin America and acknowledgment in Europe.

Even Mexico and all of South America appreciated that the United States and Latin America would have to stand together if European intervention was to be blocked. European statesmen could go on scoffing at the Monroe Doctrine, but they knew they could not challenge it with impunity.

Then—in 1910—came the revolution, which Mexicans proudly point out preceded the Russian Revolution by seven years. There also came the violence and anarchy that a profound social upheaval brings, unless or until a strong leader takes over to keep order. The United States being a neighbor, with investments and land holdings worth a billion dollars and more than 40,000 nationals in Mexico, and the American President from 1913 on being an idealist determined to bring the gospel of democracy and morality to all concerned, whether they wanted it or not, it was inevitable that there should be trouble.

The activities of President Wilson from 1913 to 1917 were the most blatant, inexcusable and futile examples of interventionism in the history of our relations with Latin America. He encouraged and armed Carranza and Villa against Huerta in 1913 and occupied the port of Vera Cruz. The mediation of the ABC powers (Argentina, Brazil and Chile) at the time was intended to end with the elimination of Huerta, as it did.

Instead of internal peace and constitutional government, there was anarchy. Pancho Villa deliberately provoked armed intervention by a series of murderous outrages in Mexico and even across the border. General Pershing's forays were as futile as Wilson's policies. Meanwhile, war with Germany was imminent.

To be fair to ourselves, Mexico was, indeed, a difficult neighbor in the post-revolutionary period, and as great power politics go, the United States was patient and forbearing. The turbulent period eased up in 1920 with the election of General Álvaro Obregón, but it was another fourteen years before internal peace was really established under Lázaro Cárdenas, and he provoked the United States, not to say Great Britain, by nationalizing the oil industry in 1938.

Despite all earlier provocations and pressures, the United States Senate unanimously passed a resolution on January 25, 1927, calling for the arbitration of all outstanding issues and thus rejecting intervention.

That was when President Calvin Coolidge had the wisdom to send Dwight D. Morrow, the Morgan firm partner, to Mexico as Ambassador. His diplomacy has ever since been a model of understanding, fairness and practical accomplishment. For most historians, the Good Neighbor policy really began with him.

IMPERIALISM FADES AWAY

With victory in the First World War leaving us so strong and Europe so weak, security was achieved—at least we thought it was. Instead of imperialism there was isolation, disarmament, the liquidation of commitments, The stage was set for the Good Neighbor policy. The Kellogg-Briand Pact of Paris in 1928, which outlawed war as an instrument of national policy, was based on the assurance that no European nation was again going to intervene in a physical, territorial sense in Latin America.

Even in this respect it was unrealistic, but the sense of security was what dictated policy.

From the Latin American viewpoint, the problem was to get the United States to give up its right to intervention. A denial of the right to intervene on behalf of the nationals of a foreign country was brought up at the very first International American Conference in Washington in 1889. The United States did not agree at the time.

The perennial drive for the codification of "American International Law" which is still a goal of the inter-American system, had at its heart the sovereign equality of all states before the law. This principle was unanimously accepted as early as 1916 in a "Declaration of the Rights and Duties of Nations." Article IV states: "Every nation has the right to territory within defined boundaries and to exercise exclusive jurisdiction over its territory, and all persons whether native or foreign found therein."

It was inevitable that the Roosevelt Corollary of "police power" had to be abandoned. "The Monroe Doctrine," as Secretary Kellogg put it, "is simply a doctrine of self-defense."

The pronouncement which is taken as signifying the end of the Roosevelt Corollary never got beyond the stage of a memorandum, but it was published as an official document by the State Department in December 1928. This was the restudy of the Monroe Doctrine by J. Reuben Clark, Jr., then Under Secretary of State to Secretary Kellogg. It restored the Doctrine to its original purpose of defending the hemisphere against European interventions and in the process discarded the Roosevelt Corollary. However, the right of intervention by the United States was not yet abandoned.

During the Hoover Administration the principle of using non-recognition to condemn governments installed by violent revolutions was dropped, at least in theory. Yet a delay by the United States in recognizing the Government of Ramón Grau San Martín in Cuba (Sept. 1933-Jan. 1934) resulted in his collapse by what he aptly called "intervention by inertia." In the same way swift recognition by the United States and the European powers, followed by Latin American recognition, confirmed the Mendieta Government in power in January, 1934. The result was to bolster the real ruler of Cuba, the then Colonel Fulgencio Batista, with the idea that he could and would restore order. This, in effect, installed a dictatorship in Cuba. It was a clear example of intervention by manipulating the diplomatic instrument of recognition.

There is yet to be an accepted policy on the principle of recognition, as Dr. Charles G. Fenwick, Director of the Department of Legal Affairs, Pan-American Union, wrote in a paper for the first American Assembly on Latin America at Arden House.

Dr. Fenwick pointed out that at the Ninth International Conference of America States at Bogotá, Colombia, in 1948, "the United States proposed a general statement that continuity of diplomatic relations was desirable, and that the establishment or maintenance of diplomatic relations with a government did not involve any judgment upon the internal policies of that government. A Mexican amendment clarified the proposal by the provision that the right of maintaining, suspending or renewing diplomatic relations should not be exercised as a means of individually obtaining advantage under international law. Thus amended, the United States proposal was adopted as Resolution XXXV of the Bogotá Conference."

These policies continue to be the accepted principles regulating recognition, although in practice the swiftness or slowness of diplomatic recognition is regarded as approval or doubt or censure.

Long before Bogotá, the Good Neighbor policy received its name. The famous phrase appeared with apparent casualness and without even a particular reference to Latin America in President Franklin D. Roosevelt's first inaugural address on March 4, 1933.

"In the field of policy," he said, "I would dedicate this nation to the policy of the good neighbor—the neighbor who resolutely respects himself and because he does so, respects the rights of others—the neighbor who respects his obligations and respects the sanctity of agreements in and with a world of neighbors."

Professor Bemis, in his "Latin American Policy of the United States," interprets the Good Neighbor policy as being made possible by the disappearance of any danger from Europe after the First World War. This was no doubt a great consideration, but the development of nationalism, the pervading atmosphere of sovereign dignity with its outlet in the League of Nations, the natural reaction to dollar diplomacy and Marine intervention, the growth of industrialism and self-sufficiency, the wave of liberalism—the whole historic conjuncture—would have made something like the Good Neighbor policy obvious and necessary.

If, now, "international communism" were to provide a serious new danger from Europe (or conceivably China) as some Americans rightly feared when Cuba became "Marxist-Leninist," the Good Neighbor policy would be jeopardized only if the United States took unilateral military action. This almost happened in April, 1961, when Cuban exiles, recruited, armed, trained and directed by the United States, invaded Cuba, but President Kennedy wisely refused to commit American armed forces. In 1954, it was indirect intervention by the United States that brought about the overthrow of the pro-Communist Arbenz regime in Guatemala, but there, also, we refrained from direct military intervention with American forces.

In each case, we skated on thin ice under the somewhat dismayed eyes of most Latin Americans, but without falling through. We protected ourselves as much as possible by working with and through the Organization of American States which is, in a sense, the collective expression of good neighborliness. Even though it was felt necessary to take unilateral action when the Russians started to establish nuclear bomb bases in Cuba in October, 1962, the United States sought and received unanimous sanction from the 19 other Latin American states for the naval "quarantine."

THE DOCTRINE OF NONINTERVENTION

In expatiating on the Good Neighbor concept and putting it into practice, President Franklin D. Roosevelt was, with one vital exception, essentially carrying on the policies of Coolidge, Hoover, Hughes, Kellogg and Stimson. President Roosevelt's Assistant Secretary for Inter-American Affairs was Sumner Welles, to whom the United States and Latin America owed so much in the formulation of policy in this happy period.

The feature that President Roosevelt, his Secretary of State Cordell Hull and Mr. Welles added was acceptance at last of the principle of nonintervention. Only then did Pan-Americanism become a complete doctrine. It could not have come sooner because the United States was still in occupation in Haiti and Nicaragua and still utilized the Platt Amendment giving us the right to intervene in Cuba. Moreover, the consistent hostility and rivalry of Argentina, which felt herself to be the legitimate leader of South America, made a true Pan-American policy all but impossible.

By the time of the Seventh Inter-American Conference at Montevideo, in December, 1933, both the United States and Argentina were vying for the laurel of champion of nonintervention. At the meeting, Secretary Hull let the Argentine Foreign Minister Carlos Saavedra Lamas, take the limelight.

Article VIII of the Montevideo agreement declared: "No state has the right to intervene in the internal or external affairs of another."

Secretary Hull still reserved American rights under "the law of nations as generally recognized," but even this last, weak barrier was to be swept away at the Special Inter-American Conference for the Maintenance of Peace at Buenos Aires in December, 1936, at President Roosevelt's orders. This could be done because at this meeting the American governments accepted the principle of consultation and collaboration in disturbances of the peace.

Meanwhile, American intervention or the right to intervene was ended in Cuba, Panama, Haiti and the Dominican Republic. The Platt Amendment not only led us into a number of interventions, but we used the right to control Cuba's fiscal policies. This, at least, had increased American capital investment to a total of about one billion dollars, half or more in the sugar industry, and since sugar was the mainstay of Cuba, control of the industry in effect was control of Cuba's economy, as the regime of Fidel Castro reminded us. The antagonism aroused by the Platt Amendment in

Cuba was in general nationalistic and, in particular cases, the result of the desire of Cuban individuals to manipulate their own financial policies for their private benefit. The antagonism also resulted from the efforts of some politicians trying to get in and divide the spoils of office. It would nevertheless be wrong to underestimate the genuine patriotism and sense of national dignity that impelled most Cubans to demand untrammeled freedom.

In these days it may seem strange for Americans to claim credit for not doing what should not have been done, but it is a fact that the opportunities to annex Cuba were frequent for more than a century, the pressure to do so was rarely absent, and as the world went in those days, it would have been a not unnatural thing to do. United States citizens are therefore entitled to feel some pain when caustic historians, like the Cuban, Herminio Portell Vilá, or young leaders like Fidel Castro who have read only the Cuban historians, talk of the Platt Amendment as if it were an instrument of Yankee imperialism at its worst.

After a last intervention in Cuba (in 1933 to get Machado out, and in January 1934 to install a government run by Batista), the United States Senate (May 31, 1934) abrogated the Perpetual Treaty of Relations of 1903, including the hated Platt Amendment. We retained the lease on the naval base at Guantánamo Bay.

This was an impressive demonstration of the acceptance by the United States of the principle of nonintervention. Cuba was strategically of enormous importance, and it was the Latin American country where our investments were then the heaviest.

The mistake made by the Cubans after Machado (and the United States has its share of the blame) was not to have a genuine social revolution. The price paid for this weakness and folly was a quarter of a century of corruption and misgovernment, ending in a period of terrible brutality, civil war and an uncontrolled revolution that has gone communistic.

In 1933, the United States sought to avoid a drastic solution of Cuba's ills. In a sense it was as if a doctor forbade an operation and allowed his patient's illness to get desperate. President Roosevelt sent Sumner Welles to Havana as Ambassador with express instructions to get the murderous and predatory dictator, President Gerardo Machado out, but to ease him out by suggesting he take a leave of absence of the Presidency. Mr. Welles succeeded in August 1933—and the drastic operation on the body politic which was so necessary was postponed until 1959.

A year later—in 1934—the United States abandoned its last treaty rights to intervene in Central America, and the last Marines were withdrawn from Haiti. The treaty giving us rights to intervene in Haiti was allowed to expire in May, 1936. Then, in July, 1939, the United States Senate ratified the treaty with Panama that abolished our protectorate.

Finally, our treaty rights in the Dominican Republic were ended in March, 1941.

The way was prepared to liquidate these last interventions at the Buenos Aires Conference in December, 1936. There were a "Convention for the Maintenance, Preservation and Re-establishment of Peace" providing for consultation, and a "Special Protocol Relative to Non-intervention." The latter—a key document in the relations of the United States with Latin America read:

Article I. The High Contracting Parties declare inadmissible the intervention of any one of them, directly or indirectly, and for whatever reason, in the internal or external affairs of any other of the Parties.

The violation of the provisions of this Article shall give rise to mutual consultation, with the object of exchanging views and seeking methods of peaceful adjustment.

Article II. It is agreed that every question concerning the interpretation of the present additional Protocol, which it has not been possible to settle through diplomatic channels, shall be submitted to the procedure of conciliation provided for in the agreements in force, or to arbitration, or to judicial settlement.

From then on the problem was to be: What is intervention within the terms as understood by us and the Latin American countries? The military power and economic supremacy of the United States were such that whatever we did or did not do influenced the internal affairs of every one of the twenty nations below the Rio Grande. This meant that in a practical sense we were always going to "intervene."

The questions, in these practical, although not necessarily legal terms, therefore became: "What was deliberate and what unavoidable intervention?" "What was acceptable and what unacceptable?" "When were trade and fiscal policies a means of intervention?" "When did the sale of arms keep a government in power against the will of the people?" "Was recognition—or non-recognition—of new governments being used as an instrument of policy?" And so forth.

This is not to argue that the principle of nonintervention was not of supreme importance. It did put an end to direct, open intervention by American Marines, by management of customs, by fiscal controls of national indebtedness, by unilateral action. It put legitimate "intervention" legally and theoretically in the hands of the organized community.

However, it should be noted that when President Eisenhower thought Vice President Richard M. Nixon's life was endangered in Caracas, Venezuela, in May, 1958, he ordered Marines to two Caribbean posts to be in readiness to invade Venezuela. Had they been used, the whole carefully built structure of nonintervention might have come crashing down.

United States action in master-minding the Cuban invasion of 1961 and the open use, by the United States, of economic sanctions against the Castro regime despite treaty commitments that would have seemed to bar such actions have also weakened the concept of non-intervention. In the missile base crisis of 1962 we had the legitimate excuse of self-defense for our intervention.

The non-intervention doctrine still stands, however, and even in the case of Cuba the United States has continually worked—with partial success—to get collective action through the Organization of American States.

Psychologically, and despite real or apparent infractions, formal acceptance of the doctrine of theoretically complete and absolute nonintervention was enormously beneficial. It was the major accomplishment of the Roosevelt Good Neighbor policy.

Pan-Americanism and the United States

By a happy coincidence, the full flowering of the Good Neighbor policy occurred simultaneously with the spectacular rise of German Nazism. It was to prove a valuable countermovement. A dissatisfied and critical Latin America, such as we have had in recent years, could have proved a much more fertile ground for fascism than it was in the Second World War.

As it happened, by the time German Nazism and Italian Fascism had become a serious threat, the Good Neighbor policy, so aptly conceived and so brilliantly carried out, had transformed United States relations with Latin America in a favorable way.

The change, it can be said, was one of spirit. It cost nothing in dollars or material aid. Its essence was to give up rights of intervention, tutelage, and—up to a point—even leadership. The beauty of it, from Washington's point of view, lay in its negative quality. To desist from doing things that we had been doing was relatively easy. There was an element of risk, and specific American interests sometimes suffered, but on balance the policy paid off handsomely.

It was not until this postwar period, when good neighborliness required positive measures of economic and financial aid and a spirit of understanding and sympathy with social and industrial revolutions and with the democratic aspirations that gathered force against the military dictators, that the Good Neighbor policy, as distinct from the policy of continental security, became difficult.

The threat to the Western hemisphere in the 1930's came, of course, from the fascism of Germany, Italy and Japan, and above all, from the imperialism of Nazi Germany. We think so much in terms of international communism now that we are inclined to forget even such recent history as the appeasement period, isolation, and the enemy we fought in World

War II. Had Britain succumbed and the Axis won the war quickly, the threat to the United States and to democracy in the Western hemisphere would have been very great.

Many of us believe that our enemy is totalitarianism, whether of the Right or the Left, especially as the two are so closely akin to each other. The policy followed by the United States until the Kennedy Administration—that we would fight communism at all costs in every country but would not lift a finger to prevent or even oppose right-wing dictatorships —was shortsighted. These dictatorships, strictly speaking, are not fascist, but they are fascistoid, and they do create a climate which opens a way to an upsurge of communism when the dictator is ousted. Cuba has given us a clear demonstration of this rule. The only effective defense against communism is democracy, not dictatorship.

At any rate, getting back to the Second World War, the Good Neighbor policy paid dividends. The United States could act with the knowledge that nearly all the Latin American states would work together, first for a neutrality that gave Britain and France a fair break, and after Pearl Harbor, either for benevolent neutrality in our behalf or, in most cases, for active support. Argentina was an ugly exception under her military officers, among whom Colonel Juan Perón was becoming important. Chile was tardy but came along with us in due course.

The "no-transfer" principle that came into being in 1811, when we feared that Florida might go to Britain or France, reasserted itself in declarations against the transfer of the British, French or Dutch colonies to "another non-American State," as the 1940 Act of Havana put it.

American policy went through a confusing and contradictory period after the break between Sumner Welles and Secretary Hull in 1943. Mr. Welles deserved great credit for the success of the Good Neighbor policy. Few American statesmen had his understanding of Latin American problems. Nelson Rockefeller, Assistant Secretary for American Republics Affairs, after Hull retired in late 1944, was also an excellent and wise influence, but he did not stay long enough to make any permanent mark.

The history of our relations with Argentina then, and until the fall of Perón in 1955, could be used as a classic example of how not to conduct Latin American diplomacy. Although the ruling group was pro-Axis in the war, Sumner Welles rightly argued that intervention would only unite Argentines against the United States and behind the military. Secretary Hull nevertheless got tough, with results that Welles had foreseen.

After a brief period of calm while Nelson Rockefeller was in charge of Latin American policy, there was another setback when Spruille Braden went to Buenos Aires in mid-1945 as President Truman's Ambassador and reopened hostilities. His activities in the presidential election of February, 1946, gave Perón a most effective slogan: "O Perón o Braden" (i.e., "Your choice is either Perón or Braden").

To make matters worse, Washington published a "Blue Book" on pro-

Nazi activities in Argentina which was accurate but which should have been published after, not just before, the elections.

The results of our policies were so obviously bad that a change was necessary. However, we went to the other extreme and appointed one friendly Ambassador after another with the single exception of Ellsworth Bunker who, before Vice President Nixon invented the phrase, gave a mere handshake to the dictator. We ended up with a notably friendly Ambassador, the late Albert F. Nufer, whom General Perón had asked be kept at his post and not transferred.

Argentina ought to have taught the United States that Latin American dictators should neither be attacked nor embraced. Unfortunately, although we stopped attacking dictators at the time we did not stop embracing them.

The other Latin American states would not accept the blackballing of Argentina, as they showed when the Foreign Ministers met without Argentine representation in Mexico City in February-March 1945, on the eve of the United Nations Conference in San Francisco. Argentina had to be invited to the UN meeting.

The Mexican Conference passed what is known as the "Act of Chapultepec." The heart of it was to declare that aggression within the American system, as well as from without, called for collective action by the American republics. A hemispheric defense treaty was suggested. It took form in the Treaty of Reciprocal Assistance signed at a meeting in Rio de Janeiro in the summer of 1947.

Known as the "Rio Pact," its basic provisions for collective security were given permanent form at Bogotá in 1948. The Rio Treaty was the model for the even more famous North Atlantic Treaty Organization. The key agreement is Article 3:

> The High Contracting Parties agree that an armed attack by any State against an American State shall be considered as an attack against all American States, and, consequently, each one of the said Contracting Parties undertakes to assist in meeting the attack in the exercise of the inherent right of individual or collective self-defense recognized by Article 51 of the Charter of the United Nations.

The determination that there has been an "armed attack," meaning an act of aggression, and what to do about it, require a two-thirds vote which thereupon binds all the American republics, except that no member is asked to furnish armed forces without its consent. Thus the single-nation veto power that has so hamstrung the United Nations Security Council is avoided. At the same time, when a meeting was held in Punta del Este, Uruguay, in January, 1962, under United States leadership to condemn the introduction of communism into the Western hemisphere by Cuba, the bare two-thirds vote of fourteen states was not enough to achieve a decisive result. The fact that the four largest and most important nations of Latin America—Mexico, Argentina, Brazil and Chile—did not vote with the majority virtually nullified the effectiveness of the vote, even though a two-thirds majority had been obtained. In the Cuban crisis of October, 1962, they were able, effectively, to invoke the Rio Pact.

The concept of an attack on one being an attack on all was not new in United States thought nor was it reluctantly accepted. The idea was already in the air when President Wilson told a group of Mexican editors in June, 1918: "Let us agree that if any one of us, the United States included, violates the political independence or the territorial integrity of any of the others, all the others will jump on her."

The high point of Pan-Americanism to date came at the Ninth International Conference of American States at Bogotá, Colombia, March 30 to May 2, 1948. It was there that a true constitution of the inter-American system—the Charter of Bogotá—was drawn up and signed. It was to be "the very heart of our hemispheric organization," as Secretary of State George C. Marshall, who headed the United States delegation, put it.

A major reorganization of the procedures, agencies and institutions of the inter-American System was effected, and from that time on the administrative set-up of the hemispheric system has been known as the Organization of American States (OAS).

The conference drew up the American Treaty of Pacific Settlement (the "Pact of Bogotá") which is now one of the two pillars of peace and security in the hemisphere. It provides bilateral procedures to prevent armed conflicts. If they fail, the "Rio Pact" is ready to operate, first with consultation and then, if necessary, with joint action. The bases of the Rio Treaty are incorporated inferentially in the Bogotá Charter.

The Pact of Bogotá provides for procedures of compulsory or arbitral settlement, through a conciliation commission or by reference to the International Court of Justice, or by arbitration if the case is considered as "non-justiciable." *Ipso facto,* the new procedures removed the United States from a role of judge, arbiter or policeman.

Another document of the Bogotá Conference was the "Declaration of the Rights and Duties of Man." It was the first in the hemisphere to embody such social "rights" as education, health, social security, as well as the traditional political rights. There is also a section on the "duties" which correspond to the rights—such as duty to work, to serve the community and nation, to support social welfare.

An "Inter-American Charter of Social Guarantees" was also signed—really a labor code. As such, the United States could not vote for it since it is a field reserved for state not federal power in our country.

The extent to which the Latin American nations have taken part in international organizations since the First World War is a negative but important feature of their relations with the United States. The early inclination was to balance the League of Nations against the power in the hemisphere of the "Colossus of the North," and in time all the Latin American countries belonged.

However, as the League weakened and then failed, and negotiations to prepare for the period after World War II began, the emphasis turned toward an internationalism that included the United States. Thus, Latin Americans took part in the wartime conferences which set up the United Nations Relief and Rehabilitation Administration (1943), the Food and Agriculture Organization (1943), the International Monetary Fund (1944), the International Bank for Reconstruction and Development (1944), the International Civil Aviation Organization (1944), and the International Labor Organization (1944).

It was the United States which barred the Latin Americans from the Dumbarton Oaks discussion preliminary to the United Nations meeting, and they resented that deeply. As a result of their protests, the Chapultepec Conference was held in Mexico City.

The Latin Americans did not succeed in getting what they desired at San Francisco where the "Big Five" (Nationalist China being a hopeful fifth) established their dominance in the Security Council. As a result, they turned more eagerly toward the Inter-American regional system which three years later was to become the Organization of American States. Their chief victory was to get Article 51 into the UN Charter which says that: "Nothing in the present Charter shall impair the inherent right of individual or collective self-defense if an armed attack occurs against a member of the United Nations, until the Security Council has taken the measures necessary to maintain international peace and security."

The Latin American group of twenty was for years the largest single bloc of votes in the General Assembly. The growth of the Afro-Arab-Asian bloc, which now (1962) totals fifty-five seats, and the increase in world members from fifty-one to one hundred ten has reduced the power of the Latin American bloc but has made its votes, by the same token, just that much more valuable to the United States in its conflict with the Soviet bloc. On so-called "colonial" issues the Latin Americans usually line up against the United States when we support our major European allies.

We continually try to make Latin America a part of our global cold war. However, Latin America, from its point of view, is not vitally involved, or at least it did not become directly involved until the Castro regime brought communism into the Western hemisphere. This difference in attitude made for a lot of misunderstanding and irritation on both sides, and leads us into the critical fields of communism and democracy and their role in United States-Latin American relations.

THE COLD WAR IN THE HEMISPHERE

No aspect of United States relations with Latin America has been handled less effectively than the struggle against communism. The peril was—and is—real, but the almost hysterical anti-communism of American policy, especially during the McCarthy era, was neither helpful to us nor harmful to the Reds.

We argued that Latin America was involved with us in the cold war, but we did not and could not make the area a direct combatant, and the Latin Americans on their part did not consider themselves to be such. The Cuban situation has changed the Latin American governmental attitude, although not as much as North Americans would like to believe. As a general rule, we seemed to accept the phony protestations of dictators who won favor in the United States by proclaiming their anti-communism, although they tolerated the Reds at home and fought against the liberals and democrats who were their real enemies. We never appeared to accept the demonstrable fact that dictators prepared the way for a Communist upsurge after their inevitable removal from power.

Our obsession with the cold war led us into an overemphasis on "international communism," so that we have been striking ineffectively at the roots in Moscow instead of the branches in the individual countries. We cannot in our time stop Moscow or Communist China from giving unified directives and common policies to Reds in Latin America as elsewhere, but we can work to weaken, or even break, the links between communism and nationalism in each Latin American nation. We can make communism ineffective by strengthening the democratic forces in Latin America, by encouraging social justice, by doing more to raise standards of living. This is, in fact, what we are trying to do through the Alliance for Progress.

The outstanding example of the United States' anti-Communist policy at work, before the Cuban revolution, was the case of Guatemala, and because it succeeded in its immediate objective it encouraged the Central Intelligence Agency to try to repeat the manoeuvre in the disastrous Cuban invasion of 1961.

A typically oppressive, one-man military dictatorship by General Jorge Ubico y Castañeda, which began in 1930, was overthrown in 1944. The president who emerged in 1945, Juan José Arévalo, was liberal, radical and tolerant of the then unimportant Communists.

The United States could have been patient, understanding, and helpful, and encouraged a regime of the "democratic left" that would have deprived the Reds of any special appeal. This would have required expert diplomacy by one of our good career men in the Latin American field, or the type of inspired "amateur" diplomacy that Dwight Morrow showed in Mexico in the late 1920's and Josephus Daniels in 1938 when President Lázaro Cárdenas expropriated the oil industry.

Unfortunately, the ambassadorship from October, 1948, to March, 1951, was in the well-meaning but completely inexpert and inexperienced hands of a political appointee—Richard C. Patterson, Jr. He knew nothing of Latin America, nor did he grasp the complex social and political forces at work in Guatemala. All he could see was that Communists were gaining ground in the labor unions, in education and among the peasants. His remedy was to wield the "Big Stick," and in the nationalistic, anti-Yankee, radical atmosphere of the times that was exactly what the Communists needed to strengthen their grip and make further progress.

Mr. Patterson became *persona non grata* and left in the same month that Lieutenant Colonel Jacobo Arbenz became President of Guatemala. Under Arbenz the Communists built up their strength to the point of controlling or influencing the social, economic and political development of the country. From the angle of United States policy one must ask why this happened and whether it was inevitable.

One reason for the Communist successes was that they were allowed to monopolize the social and economic reforms which the people were demanding. As a result, to oppose communism was labelled as opposition to much needed reforms. The United States, having failed to encourage the development of democratic social reforms, having labelled such reforms as communistic, and having an open and heavy-handed anti-Communist policy, was tarred with that brush.

Another reason was that American policy left President Arbenz with no supporters but the Communists. He may or may not have wanted it that way—probably not—but if he wanted to stay in power and have a reform program, he had no choice but to turn to the Reds.

The United States policy was aimed at his overthrow. Let us grant that by 1953 or 1954 this was a valid policy. The Communists had become very strong, and Arbenz had proved himself to be dangerously weak, inept, corrupt and inefficient. The problem was then: what was the best way to get rid of Arbenz?

Many close observers of the Guatemala scene were pointing out that the Army had not come under Communist influence and no high army officer was a Communist. In Guatemala, as in most Latin American countries, the military held decisive power. Moreover, the Reds did not have popular support. In other words, no one was going to fight for them.

All this was amply proved by the fact that when Lieutenant Colonel Carlos Castillo Armas, with 500 men, stepped across the Honduran border into Guatemala, the Arbenz regime and the Communists collapsed. The army would not defend either of them, and the people did not rise.

This is not wisdom after the event, because the weakness of the Reds was clear to those who wanted to see. However, in the panicky atmosphere of McCarthyism and the anti-Red hysteria, it was felt necessary to crush the Guatemala Reds by mustering the whole mechanism of the inter-American system; helping the rebels with arms; and building up a tremendous propaganda campaign.

No one can prove now that with patience, expert diplomacy and quiet support for the democratic forces, especially in the Army, the Arbenz regime would have been overthrown by the Guatemalan people. The chances are excellent that it would have been. The policy we pursued left a bad heritage in Latin America; and communism, if anything, gained strength.

Another feature that Latin Americans are not likely to forget was the handling of the issue in the Security Council of the United Nations. By coincidence, Ambassador Henry Cabot Lodge was president at the climactic moment. As such he should have been impartial. In reality, he was the United States delegate defending United States policy.

"It is certainly true that the United States has no connection whatever with what is taking place," Ambassador Lodge blandly said in the debate. He called the struggle "a civil—not an international war"—despite all that Secretary Dulles had said about "international communism" and all the evidence of Honduran-Nicaraguan intervention. In April, 1961, Ambassador Adlai Stevenson was to play a similar and much criticized role during the invasion of Cuba.

The most important development in the Guatemalan affair had already occurred in point of time. It was the passage, under American leadership, at the Tenth Inter-American Conference in Caracas, Venezuela, in March, 1954, of a resolution condemning "international communism." There had been such a condemnation at Bogotá in 1948 in Resolution XXXII on "The Preservation and Defense of Democracy in America," but Secretary Dulles wanted to reaffirm it and spell it out more clearly. It was obviously the only thing that really interested Mr. Dulles at Caracas; and as soon as he pushed the resolution through the decisive committee, he returned to Washington, although the conference had two more weeks to run and from the Latin American angle the most important issues (those on economics) were still to come.

Resolution XCIII was entitled: "Declaration of Solidarity for the Preservation of the Political Integrity of the American States against the Intervention of International Communism."

The key passage read:

> That the domination or control of the political institutions of any American state by the international Communist movement, extending to this hemisphere the political system of an extra-continental power, would constitute a threat to the sovereignty and political independence of the American States, endangering the peace of America, and would call for a meeting of consultation to consider the adoption of appropriate action in accordance with existing treaties.

The great satisfaction of Secretary Dulles over the passage of this resolution has not yet been justified. In fact, the United States again felt it necessary, after the Castro regime turned communistic, to call a hemispheric conference and reaffirm the incompatibility of communism with the principles of the inter-American political system. This occurred at the Punta del Este meeting in January, 1962.

Nevertheless, the Castro Government could not be overthrown by resolutions nor by expulsion from the Organization of American States. There was a willingness on the part of the Latin Americans to condemn what the United States called intervention by international communism in the Western Hemisphere, but not to the extent of doing anything about it. The old fear of intervention by the United States was still alive, and Mexico's emphasis on the right of all American states to "self-determination" has proved effective. The unaminous hemispheric support of the United States in the Cuban missile crisis concerned military self-defense; it was not a condemnation of Cuban communism as such.

The failure of the United States to make any distinction between communism and Russian aggression, between national Communist movements and "international communism" was, in the opinion of this writer, one of the major errors of American policy. Such a distinction was made in the missile crisis for the first time. Communism in Latin America will be as dangerous and repugnant as anywhere, but it will have to be a communism adapted to the special features of Latin American traditions, society, economics, and character. There is a tendency in the United States Congress and in public opinion as formed by the popular press to see all Marxists, radicals, and Communists as stereotypes of what is believed to be the Moscow Red. The truths about Communists and communism are different and far more complicated, and as a result, the dangers they really represent are not met on grounds where they can be defeated.

Latin Americans, who do not see their Communists in our image and who are not afraid of Russia and China, cannot be aroused to the degree of fear and disgust toward communism that is felt in the United States. Moreover, as in all underdeveloped countries, totalitarian methods of transforming economies and industrializing are attractive to many reformers and politicians. Thus it is that we and the Latin Americans often talk and think at cross purposes in dealing with communism, and a somewhat similar error is made when we try to apply our concepts of democracy to Latin America.

In the Dulles resolution at Caracas in 1954, "the faith of the peoples of America in the effective exercise of representative democracy as the best means to promote their social and political progress" was proclaimed, among others, by the dictators of Argentina, Peru, Colombia, the Dominican Republic, Cuba, Nicaragua and Venezuela. Their tyrannies were not denounced in the conference.

Both at Bogotá in 1948 and at Caracas in 1954, the United States was mainly interested in condemning communism. It had to be a Latin American democracy, Uruguay, that insisted upon the inclusion of "all totalitarian regimes" in the condemnation. In the debate at Caracas, the support for Secretary Dulles came primarily from the dictatorships, not the democracies.

What has more significance for the future is the connection made by the United States then and in 1961 and 1962 between the danger of communism and the Monroe Doctrine. In a news conference on his return from Caracas, Secretary Dulles made the point that "President Monroe's declaration against extending the European colonial system in this hemisphere has long since been accepted and made an all-American policy by concerted action of the American States" but "the same could not be said of President Monroe's declaration against the extension to this hemisphere of a European despotic system."

The latter argument was presumably a modern variation of the doctrine of the "two spheres" which so exercised our founding fathers—a democratic, progressive America and a monarchical, reactionary Europe. It is hard to see how the Caracas resolution brought acceptance of the thesis when it was signed by so many dictators.

It was inevitable that the Cuban revolution should call the validity of the Monroe Doctrine into question. Premier Khrushchev, at a news conference on July 12, 1960, claimed that the Monroe Doctrine had "outlived its usefulness and died a natural death." The State Department replied two days later.

"The principles of the Monroe Doctrine," it said, "are as valid today as they were in 1823 when the Doctrine was proclaimed. . . . The principles which the United States Government enunciated in the face of the attempts of the old imperialism to intervene in the affairs of this hemisphere are as valid today for the attempts of the new imperialism."

In the first shocked realization of the extent of the Cuban invasion fiasco in April, 1961, President Kennedy struck out vehemently with a warning that could only have been interpreted as a threat to invoke the Monroe Doctrine.

"Should it ever appear," he said in an address to the American Society of Newspaper Editors on April 20, "that the inter-American doctrine of non-interference merely conceals or excuses a policy of non-action; if the nations of this hemisphere should fail to meet their commitments against outside Communist penetration, then I want it clearly understood that this Government will not hesitate in meeting its primary obligations, which are the security of our nation."

At that time Cuban communism did not threaten "the security of our nation" and unilateral United States military action (which would have been an application of the Monroe Doctrine) was neither necessary nor wise. When it became necessary to take action in October, 1962, there was no need to involve the Monroe Doctrine, but it is still a fact that the Doctrine is a historical heritage with a deep emotional content for Americans. It might be ignored, or we might refrain from applying it, as happened often in the nineteenth century, but it remains a feature of our foreign policy, like a weapon put aside that can be picked up again in an emergency.

The extent to which the Monroe Doctrine has "been accepted and made an all-American policy" as Dulles put it, is an interesting field for study. It is true enough that the Doctrine is now a collective policy, but it is also a unilateral policy so far as the United States is concerned. We have never agreed that any other American nation has a contractual right to invoke the Monroe Doctrine.

In a radio and television address on June 30, 1954, Mr. Dulles made what he obviously intended to be a cardinal argument: "If world communism captures any American State, however small, a new and perilous front is established which will increase the danger to the entire free world and require even greater sacrifices from the American people."

The thesis that a Communist foothold in the hemisphere would violate the spirit of the Monroe Doctrine was not a policy inaugurated by Dulles and the Eisenhower Administration. It was also formulated under Acheson and the Truman Administration. In a speech in Boston on April 26, 1950, for instance, Edward G. Miller, Jr., then Assistant Secretary of State for Inter-American Affairs, said:

"The Monroe Doctrine has not lost its meaning with the passage of a century and a quarter, for today we consider any attempt to extend the Communist system to any portion of this Hemisphere as dangerous to our peace and safety. This attitude is still basic to our policy."

The danger in Latin America comes from the appeal of the totalitarian method (which could be Fascist as well as Communist) in the underdeveloped countries of Latin America. Marxism has strong roots among Latin American intellectuals and the Communist ideology attracts many intellectuals. We also have to fear the ability of the Reds to create disorders and confusion, to discredit democracy and to bring back dictatorial regimes, whether of the Left or Right. In fact, they would undoubtedly prefer the military type which would not lead to American intervention.

Anti-communism by itself was never a policy conducive to winning good will in Latin America. Under the Eisenhower Administration, United States policy tended to be exclusively anti-Communist so far as totalitarianism was concerned. Any government, any dictator—Franco, Salazar, Perón, Pérez Jiménez, Trujillo, Somoza, Batista—could win our favors by professing or even being (as in Franco's and Salazar's case) anti-Communist. This negative policy did us great harm in Latin America.

The Kennedy Administration started off disastrously with the abortive Cuban invasion of April, 1961, but the basic feature of its Latin American policy—the Alliance for Progress—is wisely aimed at supporting the social and economic reforms that should provide democratic and evolutionary solutions to the problems of underdevelopment that plague the area.

Our handicap is in the slow, uncertain workings of democracy and free enterprise compared to the relatively swift, drastic method of the Communists. The latter sacrifice a generation or even two, but the masses in a number of Latin American countries are being "sacrificed" anyway. For them the Red method cannot be worse and does hold what they may think is a better promise for the future. Democracy and freedom have little meaning to the masses—especially agrarian—in underdeveloped regions. To tell a Colombian, or Dominican, or Brazilian peasant, living on a subsistence level, illiterate, often diseased, that he is now a free man is a mockery and a deception. If he and his family live in a hovel in half-starved misery and illness, with a low expectation of life and high infant mortality, he is, in effect, enslaved by his life, nor can democracy reach him or mean anything to him. Communism can reach him and will do so if this socio-economic state of affairs continues many years longer.

ECONOMIC POLICIES

Nothing in the field of United States relations with Latin America has greater importance than our economic policies. Nothing has caused greater conflicts between us or aroused more resentment toward us.

One might fairly say that we solved the major political problems of the hemisphere in collective fashion in the two decades from the late 1920's to the late 1940's. The Good Neighbor policy, the Rio Pact of mutual defense, the Bogotá Charter and all the machinery of the Organization of American States contain many of the answers to the political questions of the pre-1959 period. Our friendly attitude toward some of the dictators was a departure from accepted principles.

The Cuban revolution brought in a new set of political problems by introducing the cold war to Latin America and offering a "Marxist-Leninist" alternative to the democratic, capitalistic, free enterprise system that had been the model for Latin America as it was—and is—for us. The severe economic decline, amounting almost to a collapse, in Cuba in the first four years of the revolution was not universally accepted in Latin America as proof that a capitalistic system is better for underdeveloped nations than a socialistic-communistic one. As President Kennedy has said, it is "our unfulfilled task" to prove this.

He used this phrase in the speech to the Latin American diplomatic corps in Washington on March 13, 1961, that introduced the majestic concept of the Alliance for Progress. This address will undoubtedly rank in history with the Roosevelt inaugural in which the Good Neighbor policy was proclaimed. The key sentence read:

> "Therefore I have called on all the people of the hemisphere to join in a new alliance for progress—*alianza para el progreso*—a vast effort, unparalleled in magnitude and nobility of purpose, to satisfy the basic needs of the American people for homes, work and land, health and schools—*techo, trabajo y tierra, salud y escuela*." [The Spanish is in the speech.]

From the beginning, therefore, the emphasis was on social reforms, although not at all to the exclusion of economic development. The idea—a valid one—was that a time had come in Latin American history when the masses of the people had to be given the social justice they were demanding with such insistence. For this reason, the Alliance was to center on the three main components of social justice in Latin American society—housing, agrarian reform and education.

The President, in his conclusion, frankly recognized that the Alliance for Progress (the capital letters evolved almost immediately) would "transform the American continents into a vast crucible of revolutionary ideas and efforts." The premise from which the conclusion of the Alliance started was that there must be social revolution in Latin America, not of the violent, communistic Cuban type but a peaceful, voluntary, democratic, evolutionary process.

It is important to note that the Alliance program literally is an alliance; it is not a United States program. In fact, the concept was originally Latin American and was to be found in the plan known as "Operation Pan America" put forward by President Juscelino Kubitschek of Brazil in the summer of 1960. Moreover, on the United States side, the basic principles of the Alliance were first formulated during the Eisenhower Administration by the then Under Secretary of State Douglas Dillon at a hemispheric economic conference in Bogotá, Colombia, in September, 1960. What has been added since is the idea of requiring national economic plans from the Latin American countries.

The Alliance for Progress, therefore, is even more a Latin American than a United States program. The social and economic reforms that are required must be voluntarily made by each of the Latin American nations. Our role, vital though it is, can only be a supporting one.

It would be naive not to recognize that the problems posed by the Alliance for Progress are "staggering" to use Mr. Kennedy's characterization. The requirement is nothing less than a transformation of Latin American society and economics. History provides few examples of ruling classes voluntarily giving up some of their wealth, power and privileges. At best, the program will take decades to fulfill. This means that on all sides, and especially in the United States, there must be a great deal of patience and tolerance.

Our economic policies toward Latin America in the past were, in some respects, wrong or unreasonable. This does not mean that Latin American policies were right or sensible. There are many unwise, unsound fiscal and monetary policies for which we are asked to pick up the tab, many requests that are impossible to satisfy, many reproaches that are unjust.

Nothing could be more misleading or more harmful than for us to beat our breasts in penance while Latin Americans are patted consolingly on the back and allowed to believe that their economic and fiscal woes are our fault and not theirs. Hemispheric policies are not made solely at the State Department, United States Treasury and the White House. We cannot guarantee economic or political stability in their countries, and still less can we enforce desirable conditions. We cannot enforce or impose the Alliance for Progress; we can only do our share.

If we concede to some errors on our part, we can point to failings on theirs. They have ridiculously low income taxes; their inflationary spirals can be stopped, or at least reduced by their own means; they could make it more attractive for American private investors; they could invest their own savings to better account in their countries and send less abroad. This list could be extended, but two or more wrongs never made a right; and power, wealth, responsibility, maturity in these fields, and self-interest all call for a continuing study and readjustment of United States economic policies toward Latin America. In two respects there is something special about these relations.

The first is that economics and politics are more closely intertwined in the hemisphere than elsewhere. The Marshall Plan no doubt affected internal politics in every European country. It was, for instance, a reinforcement of democratic institutions against communism. But Europe had the social and industrial structure, the managers, the skilled workers and the internal markets to absorb economic aid without any *great* effect on the course of politics.

The underdeveloped Latin American countries with their narrowly based economies, their small ruling classes, their business and land-owning interests who play a preponderant role in the conduct of affairs and hence in politics, and the great proportion of the economy owned or controlled by the state, make certain that there is no way to handle economic questions apart from politics.

The other special feature is that in recent years and for the first time Latin Americans are giving priority to economic objectives. This feature goes from top to bottom, from the big businessmen striving for industrialization of essentially agrarian economies to the workers and peasants who now demand social justice with an insistence that makes this popular urge the leading force in Latin America.

The fact that those striving for industrialization, higher standards of living and social justice are on the whole, less well trained, less mature, fewer in numbers and less able than they ought to be to achieve their goals, is a handicap, but it does not alter the validity of their aims or the intensity of their demands. In the same way, Latin American development programs may give economists gray hairs, but the fact remains that Latin Americans are obsessed with the process of development, as Professor Carlson points out in his paper, and they feel that if they adhere to North American standards, they might never develop.

One of the basic complaints of Latin Americans is that United States economic policies do not take the facts, the possibilities, the political necessities and the psychology of the Latins into account. The tendency has been to treat a loan, let us say, to Chile or Brazil just like a loan to Britain or France. For the International Monetary Fund to draw up a fine, sensible, orthodox stabilization plan for Argentina may be its duty, but for the United States to demand that the shaky government of President Arturo Frondizi accept and put into effect this plan may be politically unwise. The circumstances being what they were in Argentina, the Frondizi government could not carry out the plan and stay in power.

President Kennedy's Secretary of the Treasury, Douglas Dillon, has shown an understanding of the socio-economic problems in Latin America that had been lacking. His tenacious, intelligent championship of the Alliance for Progress has done much for what might be called the economic image of the United States in the hemisphere.

Another aspect to be concerned about is the question of whether our economic aid does not—or did not—often help dictators to remain in power. The late Lawrence Duggan warned the United States in his last book, *The Americas,* "to take care that its economic and military aid to Latin America is not used to bolster semi-feudal oligarchies whose domination means continued backwardness and instability." Nowadays Premier Fidel Castro of Cuba is making the same argument in his propaganda war with the United States.

It is understandably hard for Americans to realize that grants-in-aid, Point Four, P.L. 480 loans and grants of agricultural surpluses, even at times Export-Import Bank loans, arouse a sense of shame, a feeling that a country is a recipient of charity, a fear of "imperialism"—in short, anything but friendship. There is some gratitude, but also some resentment.

The Latin American desire for public rather than private credits and investments is based in part on recollections of American practices now abandoned, and in part on their experience with private enterprise in their own countries. Latin American capitalism usually benefits a few investors at the top; it does not result, as with us, in a high standard of living for all. Latin American businessmen and landowners do not, as in the United States and similar economies, bear a fair and adequate burden of corporate and income taxation. They have not, in general, shown the degree of civic responsibility expected nowadays of business leaders in advanced democracies. As a result, the concept of "free enterprise" does not carry the appeal or the conviction that it does in the United States.

Sometimes American investors, exercising free enterprise, drive the local firms out of business by their superior methods and know-how. This is not a triumph for American technology. The local firms might have done as well if we sent technicians and advanced the capital. Foreign capital that displaces internal capital is not welcome.

In addition, we are still plagued by ghosts of the past and still paying for the sins of our pioneering investors. History (or perhaps one should say Latin American interpretation of history) is usually a handicap to present relations.

We will never be free of the well-worn charge of "economic imperialism," sometimes merely designated as "Yankee imperialism." The accusations are that the United States, or its protected citizens, invested in Latin America in order to exploit natural wealth, employ cheap labor, make high profits and withdraw those profits to the exclusive benefit of American investors. As part of this process some big American operators were charged with making and unmaking governments and bribing officials to get favorable laws, concessions or contracts.

To the latter accusation some American investors of the past would have to plead guilty. They, in turn, could argue that in those days there was no other way of doing business in some Latin American countries and that, on balance, American business activities were salutary to the nations concerned. In any event, these practices are now negligible, if not ended, except in the eternal and ubiquitous field of bribery.

The basic accusation of economic imperialism is serious because it is still a widely used weapon of anti-Yankee propaganda, and it is believed by many Latin Americans who should know better.

The phrase "dollar diplomacy" is surely one of the most unfortunate ever uttered by an American president—in this case Taft. He literally meant it as a diplomacy aimed at achieving and encouraging the progress of American business and investments in Latin America, "an effort frankly directed to the increase of American trade," as he put it.

However, with a few unimportant exceptions, the national power of the United States was never used to further such purposes, let alone impose them on any Latin American nation.

Our government did virtually nothing to help American investors who lost hundreds of millions of dollars in the 1930's through defaulted dollar bonds of Latin American governments. When President Lázaro Cárdenas of Mexico nationalized the oil industry in 1938, expropriating much valuable American property in the process, President Franklin D. Roosevelt was not sympathetic or helpful to the oil companies. The intervention of the United States against the pro-Communist government of President Arbenz in Guatemala was not at all done on behalf of the United Fruit Company, which long had an inordinate control over Guatemalan affairs.

These instances could be multiplied. One could equally draw up a long list of the abuses of Latin American governments against American businesses and investors even before the wholesale expropriations of the Castro regime in Cuba. They often brought protests from Washington but until we cut off the Cuban sugar quota in July, 1960, we did not resort to economic sanctions.

The principle always insisted upon in modern times is that while nations have a right to expropriate foreign property under their own laws, there should be prompt, just and adequate compensation. In effect, Latin American governments have got around this by promising adequate compensation and then stalling, and at best paying a small part of the true value of the property expropriated.

The question of who exploited whom, by and large, is therefore not facetious. There are those who would argue that Latin Americans did more exploitation of the money and property of North Americans than the reverse—at least until recent years. Even today, private investors run the same old risks with the same necessary lack of protection from the United States Government, as the Cuban revolution demonstrates.

One essential role of government is in the fields of trade and investment. In our capitalistic, private enterprise system of economy, and in a democracy, the government can do little to control the activities of private firms abroad. It can encourage and provide incentives for investment; it cannot order a firm to put money in this or that country or project. Moreover, the purse strings of the government are in Congress, not the White House or the State Department.

At the same time it can be argued that many projects would neither be good economic investments for private interests nor for the international banks, but would increase the total economic productivity of Latin America. If we say that a more prosperous Latin America is our goal, then we must sometimes make investments by government action.

At the Bogotá Conference in 1948, Secretary Marshall stated a basic contention of the United States:

> My Government is prepared to increase the scale of assistance it has been giving to the economic development of the American republics. But it is beyond the capacity of the United States Government itself to finance more than a small proportion of the vast development needed. The capital required through the years must come from private sources, both domestic and foreign.

Generally speaking, it has done so, but the complaints of the Latin American countries are based on degree and proportion. They want greater government participation and proportionately fewer private investments and less emphasis on free enterprise. In the matter of how much the United States Government could do, the demand has naturally been for "more." Whether there could or can be "more" will always be debatable.

"I have the feeling that there is a very limited understanding of the tremendous responsibilities and the equally tremendous burdens that the Government of the United States has been compelled to assume," Secretary Marshall said at Bogotá.

The most heated discussion at that meeting was put in the form of an Ecuadorian proposal calling upon the United States to take action to maintain a "parity" relationship between the prices of raw materials and the prices of manufactured goods. This was in the same field as the perennial desire of the Latin American nations for stability in the prices of their raw material exports.

The United States steadfastly refused to be drawn into this tricky ground, but the Nixon experience of 1958, with its shocking evidence of hostility, led to a partial reconsideration of policy in this as in other fields.

An interesting factor to note in considering the economic relations of the United States with Latin America is the consistent unanimity of the latter in seeking to protect itself against price fluctuations, and the equally consistent efforts of the United States in seeking to avoid commitments. The fact that the United States squanders billions of dollars maintaining "parity" for its own agricultural products and continually supports by quotas, tariffs and subsidies the prices of domestically produced materials, like oil, steel, lead, zinc and copper, has not helped our case in Latin America.

When it comes to price stabilization we tell Latin Americans to go to the market place for fair and correct economic prices. They say that in World War II we had no such ideas and then demanded stabilization at the lowest levels. This is in addition to the fact that, as they see it, we do not practice what we preach.

More and more economists are calling attention to the fact that the method of regulating the prices of commodities by the unrestricted competition of the world market operates to the detriment of the underdeveloped producing and exporting nations. These countries get windfalls in times of war, but at other times they face the necessity of selling to buyers whose natural objective is to pay the lowest possible prices.

Fourteen of the twenty Latin American nations produce coffee, and some of these—Brazil, Colombia, El Salvador, Costa Rica, for instance—live primarily on exports of coffee. The United States does not produce coffee, and Latin Americans believe that we would like to see the price hover around 30 to 35 cents a pound—where it has been in recent years. In 1957 it was around 60 cents. The difference cost Latin America as a whole about $1,000,000,000 on the average each year. This was more than all the international agencies could lend Latin America in any given year.

The question of coffee production and prices, the complexities of controlling the world market in the face of African competition, the possibilities of Latin American producer nations diversifying their economies, shifting to other products and industrializing, are all technical problems that cannot be discussed here. For our purposes (the study of United States relations with Latin America) it must suffice to point out that the coffee-producing nations have resented American policies in the past. The partial validity of these resentments was recognized after the Nixon trip when we reversed our policy and agreed to join a group studying the possibility of strengthening coffee prices. An international agreement made in 1962 to hold back surplus stocks from the world markets, and attempts to reduce production have improved the situation, but the problem of over-production is always serious.

Secretary Cordell Hull's reciprocal trade program, while global in scope, nevertheless had an important application toward Latin America. The concept of holding tariffs and import quotas to minimum levels by recip-rocal agreements, of refraining as much as possible from the use of ex-change controls, sanitary regulations, clearing arrangements and such barriers to trade, was bound to benefit Latin America, with its underde-veloped raw material economy. It is when we fail to live up to these ideals by such measures as the import quotas on lead and zinc that Latin Amer-icans complain.

A new source of anxiety for the Latin American countries, as for us, is the fear that the European Common Market will reduce or restrict ex-ports to Western Europe. The United States is using its best offices to minimize this threat.

In general, there has been a greater understanding of Latin America's economic problems in recent years, and especially in the Kennedy Admin-istration.

In August, 1957, Secretary of the Treasury Robert B. Anderson firmly told a Latin American economic conference that there were enough bank-ing and credit institutions in existence and that they were all wasting their time in suggesting a development loan bank. After the Nixon trip, Under-Secretary Douglas Dillon proposed just such a bank, which is now operat-ing successfully. Nothing had changed—except the realization that our policy was resented.

An emphasis on long-range economic policies is something that Latin Americans have always stressed. However, American economic philosophy and practices in government investment have always centered on specific projects and the year-to-year appropriation of money to finance them. To get money from Congress for a five-year, seven-year or ten-year plan is al-most impossible. Witness President Eisenhower's and President Kennedy's struggles to get even two- or three-year commitments for their foreign aid programs. The Alliance for Progress, at least, is a ten-year program.

It is tempting to feel that we are struggling with the problems of satis-fying the insatiable, and so to throw our hands up in despair. Latin Amer-icans want to achieve high standards of living, productivity and industrial-ization quickly. We must not expect great results in telling them to be patient, to follow orthodox economic practices, to be thrifty, to accept austerity, to balance budgets, restrict credits, control wages, live within their means. To demand that these countries put their houses in order before they can get the help they need (and the International Monetary Fund comes close to doing just that) may be economically right, but it may also be politically wrong.

The so-called "paradox of rising expectations," about which so much is being written, operates in Latin America as in other underdeveloped areas, and it works in favor of the Communists. A subsistence living was apathetically accepted for generations, but as the standards of living are raised, demands and expectations increase at a still faster rate. The orderly process of capitalistic growth cannot quickly satisfy these demands any more than the totalitarian method. The myth, the promises, and the real accomplishments of the Russian and Chinese Communists are nevertheless tempting. The newly-educated increase faster than the jobs to satisfy them. These "intellectuals" are impressed by the Communist managerial system under which they think they could become an élite.

The strains, the stresses, the ferment, the explosive pressures, the instability, and many other forces pushing and pulling and tearing away at the social structure of twenty different countries surely proclaim the hopelessness of applying economic orthodoxy to Latin America.

The American private investor has a right to say what he considers fair or unfair, good or bad, and a right to invest or withhold his investment, and can tell the countries under what terms he will do so. This is not intervention, nor is it Yankee imperialism. The expropriations by the Castro regime in Cuba and the threat of other revolutions in Latin America, reduced private investments from the United States and increased the flight of capital from Latin America. The international banking institutions, for their part, are responsible to the multi-national subscribers and must follow fairly rigid lines of financial orthodoxy.

The United States government cannot safely take the same attitudes because of political factors. When the Russians begin to enter the Latin American economic field in a big way, as they are expected to do sooner or later, they will have no hesitation in risking economic losses for political gains.

Statistically, the imposition of import quotas on lead and zinc by the White House in 1958 did not hurt Mexico, Peru and Bolivia very badly; psychologically it was a great loss to the United States in the whole hemisphere. It is in this nebulous field of "political economy" that the United States has been especially weak.

We really want to be helpful, but on terms that the Latin Americans say are beyond their strength or experience to meet. This is an argument we are now hearing in connection with the Alliance for Progress. On our side we cannot raise hopes beyond what we are realistically in a position to meet. The Communists can get away with such tactics, but we could not.

FROM NIXON TO CASTRO

It was first realized that greater efforts must be made to meet Latin American desires and needs when Vice President Nixon made his now

famous trip to South America in April and May, 1958. This was in some
ways a turning point in postwar history so far as relations between the
United States and Latin America were concerned. It forced the United
States to review and alter some policies. It opened our eyes and at least
inaugurated an effort to create an economic Good Neighbor policy.

However, it was the brutal shock of the Cuban revolution and the realization of what it represented in Latin America that has been the defini-
tive impulse behind the new orientation of United States policies toward
the area. The Alliance for Progress is an attempted answer to the challenge of the Cuban revolution, so much so that Latin Americans ironically
dubbed it, "The Castro Plan."

One might argue that the Good Neighbor policy was so successful because it was confined to the political field; it cost nothing. The old idea
died a hard death. When Secretary Dulles took office in 1953, he told an
associate: "I want an imaginative program for Latin America, but one
that does not cost any money."

The Nixon experience was a great surprise to Americans, both in and
out of the Government. It should not have been so, which proves that both
our State Department and our people were ill informed.

The prevailing attitude before the trip was no doubt that expressed on
March 5, 1958, by Assistant Secretary of State for Inter-American Affairs
Roy R. Rubottom at a hearing of the Senate Committee on Foreign Rela-
tions. Senator J. William Fulbright, Democrat of Arkansas, asked:

"Do you believe, Mr. Rubottom, that there is widespread discontent in
Latin America with United States policies?"

"No, sir, I do not," Mr. Rubottom replied.

Two months later the Assistant Secretary was an eyewitness to Mr.
Nixon's unhappy experiences. The answer that was attempted then was
to blame it all on the Communists and to argue that the hostile elements
were small minorities. This was true enough so far as the agitators were
concerned, but it ignored the fact that they could not have aroused so
much furor if the atmosphere had not been ripe for expressions of hostility.

In any event, it is an ill wind that blows no good. The courage of Mr.
and Mrs. Nixon, and above all his intelligence in grasping the true reasons for the treatment he received, won him the admiration of the Latin
Americans and gave the right direction to American policy.

His formula—that for dictators the United States should have only a
handshake and for democratic governments an *abrazo,* a warm embrace
—is now a historic pronouncement. It was picked up by Dr. Milton Eisenhower after his trip to Central America later in 1958, and endorsed by
President Eisenhower. Unfortunately, it proved easier to say than to do.

The dramatic developments in Latin America since the Vice President's
trip proved that he had acted like a magnet to draw out a mass of resentments, desires and unrest that were just below the surface and had there-

fore escaped the superficial viewer. This was why the explosive reaction toward him in Lima, Peru, and Caracas, Venezuela, came as such a surprise to the American people and to some of our diplomats.

So far as the Cuban revolution is concerned, it would be wrong to interpret it simply as an example of communism at work, or in terms of an expression of sudden resentment and defiance of the United States and a fierce desire for independence from American economic domination. In reality, the communism came after the revolution got under way, while extreme nationalism, with its customary corollary of anti-Yankeeism, pre-existed the revolution in Cuba by generations. A lot of chickens came home to roost in 1959.

The Cuban revolution was, and is, the result of a profound and complicated mass of historic, social, economic and political factors. It was the explosion at the end of a long internal process, and it was also the Cuban answer to the inflammatory forces and pressures at work in our turbulent era—above all nationalism and the clamorous demand for social justice that is agitating the whole underdeveloped world.

The Communists do their best to make use of this ferment to their ends, just as we do on behalf of the free world. But communism is not the cause of upheavals like the Cuban revolution. In Cuba, it has been the strategy used by the leaders to carry out their basic goal, which is a social revolution of a type introduced to the modern world by the French Revolution.

The Western hemisphere had known only two social revolutions before Cuba's—Mexico's, which began in 1910 and might be said to have ended in 1940, and Bolivia's, which began in 1952 and is still continuing. The United States did its best to nullify the Mexican Revolution in its early stages and was hostile to its aims until the reconciliation set in with Ambassador Morrow in the late 1920's. On the other hand, we have consistently helped the Bolivian revolution.

There is, therefore, no American policy for or against revolutions of this type in modern times. In the case of Cuba, both the Eisenhower and Kennedy Administrations went on record as approving the aims of the revolution. The White Paper put out by the State Department on April 3, 1961, conceded that "the character of the Batista regime in Cuba made a violent popular reaction almost inevitable. The rapacity of the leadership, the corruption of the government, the brutality of the police, the regime's indifference to the needs of the people for education, medical care, housing, for social justice and economic opportunity—all these, in Cuba, as elsewhere, constituted open invitation to revolution."

It was the White Paper that gave the most effective expression to the thesis that the Castroites "betrayed the revolution." This intense and profound sense of betrayal was behind the remarkable wave of defections that led to a steady stream of Cuban exiles to our shores.

The civic resistance to the Batista dictatorship was largely conducted by middle and upper class elements who accepted certain promises and programs that came from rebel headquarters in the Sierra Maestra. These were that there would be drastic social reforms, but in a democratic framework, restoring the Constitution of 1940, holding elections and respecting all the civic freedoms.

The development of the regime into a dictatorship, the growing influence of the Communists, the radical nature of the economic policies which victimized the middle classes as well as the big business and landowning interests—these and other well known developments resulted in a flood of exiles to the United States that has had no equal in the history of our relations with Latin America.

The quarrel of the United States, as such, with the Castro regime rests mainly on two features: the confiscation of American properties and, above all, the involvement with communism and the Soviet bloc. There were other features—the executions in the early months of the revolution, the growth of a sort of police state, the efforts to subvert other Latin American nations, the abusive language used by Fidel Castro and his associates against us—but these were not decisive.

On their part, the Cuban leaders were shocked and bewildered by the reaction to the executions and the hostility shown by the American press, radio and television from that time onward. They were resentful of charges of communism before they were justified, bitterly critical of the way the United States permitted enemies of the revolution to use Florida as a base for airplane forays against Cuba, and then both frightened and resentful as evidence reached Havana of our preparations to support an invasion of Cuba by the exiles.

These, too, could be considered secondary features of the Cuban attitude toward the United States. The basic features lay in the long pent up resentment against American domination of the Cuban economy; American support or acceptance of the disgraceful corruption and inefficiency of Cuban governments and society; the pro-Batista policies of the Eisenhower Administration, and a conviction from the beginning that the United States would do all it could to frustrate and even destroy the revolution.

The results of these clashing policies and emotions were the implacable hostility that continues between our two countries. The attempted invasion of Cuba in April, 1961, was so inept, so hopeless, so completely mismanaged (as was freely admitted afterwards) that it greatly strengthened the Castro regime and greatly damaged our reputation in Latin America and the rest of the world. On the other hand, the impressive and successful reaction to the missile base threat in October, 1962, restored much of the ground lost and was a great setback for the Castro regime.

However, neither development changed the basic situation. Premier Castro, although disillusioned by the bungling and partisan greediness of the old-line Cuban Communists, against whom he turned in the spring of

1962, remains completely dependent economically on the Soviet bloc and professes to be a confirmed "Marxist-Leninist" who is leading Cuba to the supposed paradise on earth of the Communist ideal.

The United States, for its part, remains determined to bring about the overthrow of the Castro regime. Insofar as the Cuban internal political situation can be separated from the Russian military threat, we have wisely abjured the use of military force and are relying on an economic embargo and what diplomatic isolation we can squeeze out of the Organization of American States.

The American demand, in effect, is for "unconditional surrender." As Secretary Rusk put it, the United States will never negotiate with a Communist regime in the Western hemisphere. We continued to say that we would not "tolerate" a Communist regime in this hemisphere, but the fact remained that we were doing so.

The dissatisfaction over this state of affairs in the United States was general. In 1960, long before the invasion fiasco, Adolf A. Berle, Jr., one of our leading lawyers who has been concerned with Latin American affairs for thirty years, wrote that the Cuban situation "inescapably reflects a failure of American foreign policy." This is beyond dispute, but history will have to decide why. Meanwhile, the lessons that Americans must draw from the Cuban revolution are disturbing and challenging.

Whatever we think about this event and its extraordinary leader, the revolution clearly ranks as one of the most important developments in the history of our hemisphere, and Fidel Castro has become a figure of worldwide fame.

A new era has begun in the Western hemisphere. We will continue to be the "Colossus of the North," exerting enormous influence and pressures by our wealth, strength and security requirements, but we will never again exercise the degree of hegemony we held for almost a century until 1959.

In these times, poor and weak countries can defy the rich and wealthy nations with impunity, at least in the free world. The days are gone when we can use our Marines as instruments of American foreign policy or guardians of American commercial interests.

Another lesson to be drawn from the Cuban revolution is that our ideological monopoly in the Western hemisphere has, at least temporarily, been broken. However much the Latin American nations fell short of their aims in practice, they did model their constitutions on ours and sought economic development by variations of our capitalistic, free enterprise system.

The fact that the Castro regime permitted a virtual collapse of the Cuban economy in applying its version of socialism, which Premier Castro later described as "Marxism-Leninism," has not destroyed the appeal of the totalitarian method for many Latin Americans seeking solutions to the problems of underdevelopment and social injustice. Although it has worked so badly, there is obviously a great attraction in the Castro formula: seizure of all properties, centralization and planning of all activities, political and economic independence of the United States, radical social reforms (especially in housing, education, health and child welfare) and the elimination, so far as possible, of corruption in government and business. As far away as Algeria, "Castroism" became the avowed aim of the Ben Bella faction of the National Liberation Front.

The Cuban revolution offered what amounted to an alternative to the capitalistic, free-enterprise system. Recognition of this fact and of the validity of these revolutionary aims led the United States and the democratic leaders of Latin America to the Alliance for Progress. The hope is to foster economic development and social reforms by methods used in the developed nations of the West. Put in another way, it is an effort to meet the challenge of communism (or it could be a Right-wing, militaristic type of fascism) by satisfying, or offering the hope of satisfying, Latin American demands for social justice, industrialization and higher standards of living.

The ideas involved in the meaning and impact of the Cuban revolution on the hemisphere are necessarily being presented here in simplified form. The realities are enormously complicated; the alternatives are not clear-cut; and the development (whether by evolution or revolution) is a matter of decades or generations. Yet, the problems that Latin America faces, and that the United States faces in its relations with Latin America, can only be understood when reduced to essentials and ultimate objectives, and when the conflicts are carried to their logical conclusions in extreme alternatives. The Cuban revolution did bring about a polarization of ideas in Latin American politics.

It had the paradoxical result, on the one hand, of confusing and blinding many North and Latin Americans by the intensity of the emotions it aroused, while on the other hand it clarified many issues and problems in Latin America and called attention to them with shocking force. Ambassador Stevenson was not alone in the United States in recognizing the effects of the Cuban revolution.

Certainly, that blow to our complacency, pride, indifference and good intentions put an end to a constant complaint against us by Latin Americans: that we neglected them. This charge—that the area was "neglected" by Washington—was heard at times during the Truman Administration—so much so that in his electoral campaign of 1952, General Eisenhower promised that Latin America would not be neglected if he were elected.

In his first foreign policy speech as Secretary of State, on January 27, 1953, Mr. Dulles stated that the Truman Administration "may have somewhat neglected South America and taken it for granted that we could forget about South America for a time and then go back again and find everything the same as it was before." (He, of course, meant "Latin America," not "South America.") In reality, Latin America was probably never so "neglected" in our history as in the five succeeding years until the Nixon experience.

The term is a relative and elusive one. What it boils down to is resentment that not enough high American officials and Congressmen visit Latin America or concern themselves with Latin American affairs. There is also resentment over the fact that the axis of our major interest is east and west and not north and south.

In January, 1928, when sending his instruction to the American delegation to the Sixth Inter-American Conference at Havana, Secretary of State Frank B. Kellogg could write: "It is an established principle of our international policy that among the foreign relations of the United States as they fall into categories, the Pan-American policy takes first place in our diplomacy."

This is no longer true and the fact was driven home at the time of the Marshall Plan, which did not include Latin America. As a matter of fact, the resentment then was misguided, because in 1948 we had to meet specific and immediate dangers in Europe and could do so with a relatively short-term program. Our problems in Latin America are of a permanent and continuing nature.

There has been far less reason for Latin Americans to complain of "neglect" during the Kennedy administration. Here again, our cynical neighbors to the south are inclined to give credit to Fidel Castro. Latin Americans will probably never forego the pleasure of plucking feathers from the American Eagle's tail, as Winston Churchill put it.

It would be naïve to consider the perennial manifestations of anti-Yankeeism in Latin America as entirely logical or reasonable phenomena. There is a great deal of emotionalism involved. The contemporary phenomenon of nationalism is xenophobic. Just as it was anti-British in the Middle East, so it is naturally anti-Yankee in Latin America. The Communists, of course, take advantage of these feelings and encourage all destructive manifestations of nationalism.

A basis for anti-Yankeeism had been laid by history. Economics now play a major role. The enormous disparity in per capita income and national wealth between North Americans and Latin Americans causes a natural envy and resentment. Our power, and its inevitable, inescapable, all-pervading influence in the hemisphere, naturally makes us a target and a scapegoat. Add the universal, human weakness of self-pity and buck-passing, and one gets a formidable array of emotions, all tending to blame the United States for the ills of Latin America.

One must avoid both extremes of denying the validity of Latin American resentment or blaming ourselves for whatever is wrong in the region. In any event, the reality and strength of anti-Yankeeism are what count, not whether it is just or unjust and reasonable or unreasonable. It is in many respects a formidable and destructive manifestation with which the United States must constantly deal.

In his studies on the causes of hostility toward the United States in Latin America, done for the State Department, Professor S. Walter Washington of the University of Virginia, defined the resentment that counted as "only those feelings of hostility toward the United States government or people that result in, or are believed capable of resulting in, support of economic, political or military action against the United States or the interests of the American people as a whole."

It should be noted that there is no consideration here for hostility toward Americans as Americans in Latin America. There is none. North Americans find nothing but courtesy and hospitality in going around the area, and nothing but friendliness if they live there. When a leader like Fidel Castro in Cuba, for instance, attacks the United States, he is not in his own mind being "anti-American"; he is being anti-State Department, anti-U.S. government, anti-United States policies, anti-U.S. business.

The course of recent events has made our record a costly one. Since 1955, Argentina, Peru, Colombia, Venezuela and Cuba got rid of their dictatorships, while General Anastasio Somoza was assassinated in Nicaragua and Generalissimo Trujillo in the Dominican Republic. In each case the people had the knowledge that the United States not only did not act as if it preferred democracy, but showed favor to their dictators.

What was permissible in the years before the World Wars, when dictators were almost taken for granted, became poor practice as well as bad morality. Secretary of State Elihu Root could refer to President Porfirio Díaz, dictator of Mexico in 1907, as "one of the great men to be held up for the hero worship of mankind" and everybody could smile indulgently, but when Secretary of State John Foster Dulles decorated the Venezuelan dictator, President Marcos Pérez Jiménez, with the Legion of Merit on behalf of President Eisenhower in 1954, it sent a profound shock through the whole of Latin America.

Government apologists plead the necessity for "nonintervention" when dealing with dictators, and they also deny that there ever has been any favoritism shown toward these dictators. In his report to President Eisenhower after his trip to Central America in July, 1958, Dr. Milton Eisenhower indignantly labelled these charges as "a gross misconception" and blamed the Communists for their propagation.

Americans must not lay this flattering unction to their souls. The Communists are not the only Latin Americans who make these charges nor are they the inventors of them. They are merely making use of weapons we put in their hands, for there is only too much evidence that there has been favoritism by Washington, and there have been policies of "nonintervention" which, like the notorious "nonintervention" in the Spanish Civil War, greatly helped one side.

Examples of United States officials from President Eisenhower down and of United States military officers showing unnecessary or exaggerated friendliness to Latin American dictators, are numerous. The most famous was the already mentioned award of the Legion of Merit to Pérez Jiménez in 1954. Not long before his fall, the United States Navy named the Venezuelan dictator "Honorary Submariner." The former Ambassador to Caracas, Fletcher Warren, a career officer, wrote to the sadistic Venezuelan police chief, Pedro Estrada, from his post in Ankara, wishing him success against the citizens who were fighting for Venezuelan liberty in January, 1958. Mr. Warren's successor, Ambassador Dempster McIntosh, was openly friendly to this same "Himmler of the Western Hemisphere"—which did not prevent the White House from choosing Mr. McIntosh as Ambassador to Colombia in June, 1959.

In 1953, the Peruvian dictator, General Manuel A. Odría, received the Legion of Merit. Early in 1955, United States Secretary of the Navy Charles S. Thomas, publicly compared General Perón in a ceremony in Buenos Aires to George Washington, and José de San Martín, Argentina's greatest hero. At Perón's request, a friendly ambassador, Albert F. Nufer, was kept in Buenos Aires, although a transfer had been announced. At the request of General Gustavo Rojas Pinilla, dictator of Colombia in 1954, Ambassador Philip W. Bonsal was timidly moved from Bogotá to La Paz, Bolivia, by the State Department. United States ambassadors in recent years were excessively friendly to the former dictators in Nicaragua, the Dominican Republic and Cuba.

With these and other known examples of favoritism to dictators, how can the State Department expect to convince Latin Americans that the United States has not been friendly to dictators? There has, however, been a decided change in attitude under the Kennedy Administration, whose record thus far shows a courageous willingness to act positively on behalf of democracy.

The attitude of ambassadors on the spot is less easy to control. It seems clear that any policy of aloofness can only be what Assistant Secretary of State William B. Macomber, Jr., called "a general guiding principle." This was in an exchange of letters with Representative Charles O. Porter of Oregon in 1959. The State Department, wrote Mr. Macomber, could not give any "specific instruction" on the conduct of ambassadors.

In other words, the problem is one of choosing ambassadors who will refrain from "embracing" dictators, and that seems to be impossible. In general, the State Department would be safer with career officers whose experience would make them realize the effect of their social as well as official activities. However, Fletcher Warren, who was so friendly to Pérez Jiménez in Venezuela, was a career diplomat of long experience, whereas Ellsworth Bunker, who handled Perón so cleverly as President Truman's last Ambassador to Argentina, was a businessman and political appointee.

American statesmen always excused a policy of friendliness toward dictators by invoking the doctrine of nonintervention. In reality, this had nothing to do with Latin American criticisms, which were aimed at an effusive, undue cordiality, at our refusal to restrict our policy toward dictatorships to what was necessary, and our failure to be positively favorable, as a general policy, to the democratic nations and forces in Latin America. This would not be considered as "intervention" in an objectionable sense by the vast majority of Latin Americans.

In November, 1961, we actually sent naval units to make a show of force outside the Dominican capital when a return of the Trujillo family was threatened—and virtually all Latin Americans approved. In July, 1962, came the even more daring and emphatic reaction of the White House to the military seizure of power in Peru. President Kennedy immediately suspended diplomatic relations, cut off Alliance for Progress and military aid, and condemned the coup d'état in very strong terms. Although this policy was not effective, the gesture was significant.

The policy of nonintervention is deceptive if it is taken in its strictly legal sense. In theory, as an ideal and, to a considerable degree in hard practice, it is not only good, it is necessary. The Latin American nations wanted it and are the first to complain when there is deliberate and open violation of the nonintervention policy, even when it is aimed against Communist influence, as in Guatemala in 1954 and in Cuba in April, 1961.

However, there is a zone where the policy of nonintervention, in its practical sense, is bound to be a fiction. In conducting our own policies we are influential, usually very influential. This is true whether our policies are positive or negative, whether we do anything or nothing. "When the United States sneezes, Latin America gets influenza," as a frequently used quip puts it.

When we bolster a shaky regime like Bolivia's, as we have done for the past decade, we are intervening in the internal affairs of that country since, obviously, the revolutionary M.N.R. regime would have collapsed a long time ago without our help. When we are unnecessarily friendly to dictatorial regimes, we are also intervening. When we sold arms to General Batista, we intervened in Cuba, and when we put an embargo on arms sales in March, 1958, we intervened in a different way.

We cannot, in short, shirk our responsibilities merely by pleading "nonintervention." It is a good doctrine, but, in affairs of policy, it is not a dogma; it is not an absolute. It can be applied only up to a degree.

The way we use our power or refrain from using it is what counts. Unadulterated power politics, as employed by the Soviet Union within the Communist bloc, has gone with the wind in this hemisphere. We simply cannot do what we please in Latin America—which is as it should be. But this is far from meaning that we can do nothing.

A major feature of our influence in Latin America, especially in connection with dictatorial regimes, centers around our policy of sending arms to the area and United States officers to train local forces. This often has the effect of positive intervening.

The ability to supply or cut off arms to a Latin American government became one of the major instruments of policy in this century, even though our military people have always refused to recognize this obvious fact, and our State Department has often underestimated its importance.

The first time an embargo was used to further our foreign policy in the hemisphere was in Santo Domingo in 1907 when arms were forbidden to Dominican rebels. In 1912, President Taft received formal authority from Congress to put an embargo on arms to Mexico in order to protect the regime of President Francisco Madero, and later President Wilson lifted the embargo in order to permit the rebellious forces in northern Mexico under Venustiano Carranza and Francisco ("Pancho") Villa to overthrow the unfriendly regime of President Victoriano Huerta.

In contemporary times our arms policy has been operated within the framework of the Mutual Security Act of 1951. Succeeding acts kept to the same objectives. The basic purpose of this law is:

> . . . to maintain the security and promote the foreign policy of the United States by authorizing military, economic and technical assistance to friendly countries, to strengthen the military security and individual and collective defense of the free world, to develop their resources in the interest of their security and the national interests of the United States, and to facilitate the effective participation of those countries in the United Nations system for collective security.

Although the arms and military aid were explicitly granted in Latin America "to promote the defense and maintain the peace of the Western Hemisphere," they were used by dictators to keep themselves in power.

"Each country is being occupied by its own army," as ex-President Eduardo Santos of Colombia once said. Arms have usually meant mischief in Latin America, not defense and not protection of the people. Selling arms to a Latin American general is a little like selling narcotics to a drug addict. "There is no greater unknown quantity in the sale of munitions today," Professor Germán Arciniegas, the Colombian historian and educator wrote, "than machine-guns consigned to what may prove to be the wrong address." The military coup in Peru in July, 1962, was carried out by officers trained in the United States, using machine-guns and tanks we sold them.

The United States is now training anti-guerrilla forces at a base in Fort Bragg, N. C., and in Panama to counteract the epidemic of guerrillas encouraged by the Cuban example and Cuban subversion. Such activity is applied exclusively against Left-wing and pro-Communist guerrillas. In Cuba, we help guerrillas against the Castro regime. The policy is frankly a feature of our anti-communism, much as it is in Vietnam. If Latin Americans had any objection it would, as usual, be the danger of bolstering dictatorial or reactionary regimes against popular revolutionary movements.

The employment of American military missions to train officers in the use of the arms we furnish has also brought a good deal of criticism in Latin America, although with less justice. Since arms are furnished, it is natural to provide for their best use. The fact that German military missions trained the armies of Argentina and Chile up to the Second World War, inclined those governments toward the Nazis. When we sell warships to South American countries which can so ill afford them, as we did in 1958, the Pentagon argues that if we refused to do so, these nations would buy the vessels from Britain or France. That may or may not be so, and it is hard for a nonmilitary mind to see that it makes much difference. The political effects of selling costly warships even at a bargain, are unfortunate for us. At best they are little more than expensive toys to placate naval officers who might otherwise cause internal trouble.

The outstanding example in recent years of the harm we can do with our military missions occurred in Cuba. The Batista dictatorship was exceptionally brutal and corrupt. The popular opposition to it was overwhelming. We did finally put an embargo on arms to the regime in the spring of 1958—but we left the military missions. Our officers in Cuba went on hobnobbing with some of the most hated associates of Batista, and our officers in Washington dined and decorated these men. The bitterness that this caused in Cuba was incalculable. To the Cubans we were teaching Batista's henchmen how to kill other Cubans—and honoring them in the bargain.

The United States Government was in a dilemma. We had the choice of intervening by leaving the missions in Cuba or intervening by taking them away. By withdrawing them we might have hastened Batista's collapse; by leaving them there we favored a cruel and predatory dictator and built up a great deal of extra resentment against the United States.

This was bad diplomacy and the wrong choice for a simple reason. Had the United States Ambassador in Havana and the State Department been as well informed as they should have been, they would have known as early as July, 1958, that as things were going, Fidel Castro was virtually certain to win. This—again—is not wisdom after the event. Whatever Ambassador Earl E. T. Smith may have thought of Fidel Castro (and all Cubans knew he was contemptuous of the rebel leader) it was the poorest sort of diplomacy to end up on the losing side.

So when the revolutionaries of the 26th of July Movement entered Havana, they captured, so to speak, the American military mission; and

Fidel Castro told them that since they had taught the Cuban army so badly, he would have no use for them.

If there were some way of making sure that arms sold to Latin Americans would be used only for purposes of hemispheric defense, as our twelve military pacts in the area specify, there could be no objection to the procedure. The 85th Congress in 1958 added the stipulation to the Mutual Security Act that: "Internal security requirements shall not normally be the basis for military assistance programs to American Republics." In the 1959 Act, in order to make the point quite clear, the word "normally" was expunged.

Whether or not internal security is "the basis" on our side, armies are still the makers and breakers of governments in most Latin American countries, or they are at least in a position at all times to intervene decisively.

PRESENT AND FUTURE

It is too soon to say, but it is conceivable that we are seeing a revolutionary process in Latin America as important as the Era of Emancipation in 1810-1824. The region is responding to the same revolutionary urges to be found in all the underdeveloped areas of the world. Essentially, it is a struggle to achieve social justice and economic development by the quickest possible means.

Until the Cuban revolution came along, the process everywhere seemed to be a drive for some degree of democracy. Dictator after dictator was bowled over, starting with Perón in Argentina in 1955. As we can see now, the trend was only superficially political; the deeper meanings were to be found at the social and economic levels, if all these can be separated. Really profound transformations take place in a nation or region when the social fabric is broken. This is what happened in the French Revolution and that is why France, not the United States, is the historic model for social revolutions ever since. We made our social revolution gradually by an evolutionary process that is still continuing in our efforts to integrate the Negro.

Democracy is more than a political manifestation; it is also social, economic, cultural, racial. It is not enough for a country to throw out a dictator and hold democratic elections. Argentina has been proof of that. In March, 1962, her military forces intervened to impose their will, nullifying a fair election.

In 1820, Secretary of State John Quincy Adams, during his previously noted conversation with Speaker of the House Henry Clay, shrewdly remarked: "So far as they are contending for independence, I wish well to their cause; but I have not yet seen and do not now see any prospect that they will establish free or liberal institutions of government." It is, indeed, a long road.

Throughout the Bogotá Conference in 1948, a special preoccupation for the recognition of democracy was noted, and the general feeling was embodied in a number of the resolutions adopted and in the Charter itself.

"The solidarity of the American States and the high aims which are sought through it," says the Statement of Principles, "require the political organization of those States on the basis of the effective exercise of representative democracy."

Among the final documents was a resolution (Number XXXII) on "The Preservation and Defense of Democracy in America." It promises, among other things, to proscribe "international communism or any other totalitarian doctrine" and to uphold "the dignity of man as an individual."

Protection of human rights was stressed in all the postwar Inter-American Conferences, with special emphasis on "representative democracy." For instance, Resolution XXV at Caracas in 1954, "Declares: That it is the continuing desire of the American States that there may be a full exercise of fundamental human rights and duties, which can only be achieved under a system of representative democracy."

Delegates of the dictators of the Dominican Republic, Cuba, Nicaragua, Venezuela, Colombia, Peru and Argentina, blandly signed all these pious declarations. So did the few remaining dictators in dealing with resolutions drawn up by later conferences of the Organization of American States, such as the Meetings of Consultation in Santiago, Chile, in August, 1959, and Punta del Este, Uruguay, in January, 1962. The more recent meetings were directed toward Cuba and "Communist intervention" in the Western hemisphere.

At best these recurring declarations could be taken as expressions of enduring ideals, but it was always doubtful whether the democratic forces needed such lip service and whether the dictators paid the slightest attention to the documents they permitted their delegates to sign.

The attitude of the United States on the question of democracy, at least ideally, was well expressed by Secretary Acheson in a speech to the Pan-American Society of the United States on September 19, 1949. It has an obvious Jeffersonian flavor:

> What I have said should not be construed as blind adherence to the status quo. We oppose aggression; we do not oppose change. Indeed, we welcome and encourage change where it is in the direction of liberty and democracy. . . . We always deplore the action of any group in substituting its judgment for that of the electorate. We especially deplore the overthrow by force of a freely elected government. In such situations we do not cease to hope that the people will regain the right to choose their leaders.

> We realize, however, that the attainment of the democratic ideal in any country depends fundamentally upon the desires and efforts of the people of that

country. The nature of democracy is such that it can be achieved only from within. Democracy as we endeavor to practice it is a continuing development toward political maturity—not a formula to be imposed upon a nation by a self-appointed ruling class, as is the case with certain other forms of government. [We can add the corollary: or to be imposed upon a nation by the United States.]

At the Caracas conference in 1954 we made the following reservation: "The United States of America, in signing the Final Act reiterates that the most effective way to promote human rights may be by education, example and publicity."

The use of the permissive tense, "may be," is appropriately dubious, and while the suggested process would be exemplary, it would also be long range, at best. Behind it is a fear of the revolutionary process, which is a basic in contemporary American policy. We are still echoing Woodrow Wilson's dictum that democracy "is built up by slow habit."

Our faith in the workings of free elections cannot be based on experiences in Latin America in the first three decades of this century. We did our best at one time or another in all the Caribbean countries and in Mexico to encourage or force "democratic elections," but the results were consistently unsuccessful.

The incumbent could almost always manipulate the election to suit his candidate, or to get himself reelected. Most baffling of all was the fact that for the United States to favor a candidate was often tantamount to the "kiss of death." The classic example in this century of trying to defeat a candidate and thereby helping him to get elected, as previously stated, was the role played by Ambassador Spruille Braden against Juan Perón of Argentina in 1946. It is still more discouraging when nations hold fair and democratic elections (as Argentina did on March 18, 1962, and Peru on June 10, 1962) and they are nullified by the armed forces.

This is not an argument against free, fair and democratic elections. Obviously, this is what we must hope, pray for and applaud on all possible occasions. The mistakes of the past lay in trying to influence elections and even pick candidates, or at least to insist that no anti-American candidate be allowed to run, as we did in a number of Caribbean elections. The policy was a failure then, and it is an impossibility now. We should also avoid a tendency to encourage elections for the sake of elections. Ambassador Smith did so in Cuba in November, 1958, although the election was an obvious farce.

The problem has been how to propagate democratic ideals in Latin America, and how to make them more than pious expressions. In this connection, it is worth digressing slightly to note the role that the United States press can play in influencing policy toward Latin America and in the Latin countries themselves.

The influence of important newspapers on the State Department and on

Congress is obvious. A newspaper like *The New York Times* also has an extraordinary effect within Latin America. Often it is possible for a newspaper to say things editorially that the State Department would like to say but cannot, for diplomatic reasons. Nothing could be further from the truth than to think that our career officers in the State Department prefer dictators, or have any higher opinion personally of a tyrant like the late Generalissimo Trujillo of the Dominican Republic than *The Times* and other newspapers. The difference is that the newspapers can say what they think, and in so doing they generally express the true opinions of the American people.

Our military and our businessmen naturally want stability. It provides the climate in which they can best operate. Insofar as the State Department thinks in terms of Latin American support in the United Nations and of pro-Yankee governments, it, too, wants stability.

But stability that sustains an antiquated social structure or that keeps military dictators or oligarchies in power is a lid clamped down on an explosive brew. During all this postwar period when the cold war was priority Number One to us, Latin Americans were having their dynamic social, economic and political upheavals. These were priority Number One to them. Our emphasis on anti-communism at best got lip service— and the loudest service from the military dictators whose only concern was with their internal enemies. As stated before, it was the liberal, the democrat, the fighter for freedom whom they most feared. Most of the dictators —Perón, Pérez Jiménez, Batista—made their accommodations with the Communists.

Latin Americans were not and are not looking to us to lead a crusade against communism, but to help them meet their real and pressing social, economic and political problems.

It is true that our struggle in the cold war is a defense of freedom, democracy and the rule of law which protects the weak, Latin America included, as well as the strong. However, it has been neither easy nor convenient for Latin American leaders and intellectuals to comprehend and accept this fact. Its effects have been remote from them. They would see the benefits of what we do if they were deprived of our shield, but since the danger seems far away, and since they know we are defending ourselves and our own way of life first and foremost, they are not impressed.

The Cuban revolution has made a considerable dent in Latin American complacency. Cuba has brought the cold war directly into the Western hemisphere; it gave a fillip to the Communist movements in every country; and it provided an example of a variation of communism inside the hemispheric family of nations. None of this, however, has been enough to win unanimous support for United States anti-Communist policies insofar as they are aimed specifically at Cuba. The unanimous backing we received in the Cuban missile crisis in October, 1962, was a measure of self-defense; it was not directed against Cuba's internal politics.

THE UNITED STATES AND LATIN AMERICA

Their own immediate problems are overwhelming. Latin America is in the process of upheaval. It is one of the most dramatic and explosive movements in all history. An industrial revolution, urbanization, the growth of a middle class, a population explosion unequalled anywhere in the world, a political ferment that is introducing all the revolutionary doctrines of modern times, a social revolution in which the masses who accepted ignorance, poverty and disease as the natural course of events are now demanding and beginning to get equality of opportunity, education, health and a higher standard of living—all these and other dynamic forces are creating a situation comparable in its way and in the impact it is going to have on the Western world, to the European Renaissance.

This is the age of "rising expectations." With it comes a grass roots pressure for basic and revolutionary changes in social and economic fields. It is hard to live with such insistent, unruly forces. We see the Latin Americans trying to do more than they have the experience, skills or capital to do. They are in a hurry. They are impatient with themselves and with us. Sometimes they are irritated, aggressive, resentful; and their nationalism with its context of anti-Yankeeism leads them to cry out and at times to hit out against us. Boring from within, egging them on every moment, are the Communists.

The Alliance for Progress is the attempted answer that we and the liberal, democratic elements in Latin America are offering. However, the demands it makes on the ruling classes who must share some of their wealth, privileges and power, are frightening, while for the insistent masses the program seems too slow and uncertain. It is put in terms of a ten-year plan, but at best it will take decades, and perhaps generations. During the process, Latin America will be a turbulent region, in a continual state of ferment. A renaissance is a rebirth, and birth is notoriously painful and messy.

Such is the hemisphere in which our policies must be made. Latin America cannot be conjured away by neglect, abuse, or an underestimation of its importance. It will not operate in a vacuum or even in a form of isolationism. There it is, wonderful and terrible, and such as it is, we must deal with it—and they with us.

We need more understanding and tolerance all through the United States Government and public opinion than we have today. Perhaps Latin Americans should not feel the way they do, but the fact remains that their political, social and economic structures are such that no other attitudes can be expected or are even possible.

It is often said nowadays that North is North and South is South, and in many respects the twain are never going to meet. We cannot expect Latin Americans to be like us. The reverse is also true; but we are the stronger and politically the more mature, and therefore we are the ones who must make the greater adjustments.

Here, on our doorstep, we face one of the greatest problems of the modern world—the disparity of wealth between the have and have-not nations, the developed and the underdeveloped, the rich and the poor. The gap is widening, not narrowing. We get much richer, and they a little less poor.

A wise statesman, the late Liaqat Ali Khan, then Prime Minister of Pakistan, in a speech at the Massachusetts Institute of Technology on May 26, 1950, put the problem graphically:

> I suddenly see the United States of America as an island—a fabulously prosperous island, where God has showered his plenty—but, nevertheless, an island. And round this island I see the unhealthy sea of misery, poverty and squalor in which millions of human beings are trying to keep their heads above water. At such moments, I fear for this great nation as one fears for a dear friend.

The cry of the poor and oppressed against those who live in "the houses of ivory" has been heard in the West at least since the days of the Prophet Amos, and now we hear it resound from the Rio Grande to Tierra del Fuego.

The problem of how to face and deal with these pervading demands for social justice in all its forms is a first priority for Latin America today. The manifestations are complicated, but the bases are simply demands on the part of the underprivileged masses of the area for a better life.

The maldistribution of wealth is spectacular almost everywhere—the few rich, living often in a luxury that United States millionaires could not afford, and the great mass of poor living at a subsistence level. The modern world does not regard such conditions as natural or inevitable or as the will of God, Allah or Providence.

The millions who accepted poverty and misery as unavoidable no longer do so. They also know that the capitalistic, free enterprise system of economy is not the only one. They hear that Cuba is now making a "socialistic" revolution. They learn that the Russian masses and the Chinese masses did not have the blessings of foreign capital investments, but that their governments for the first time in history did something for the material well-being of the peasants. That two generations of Russians and the present generation of Chinese have been sacrificed in the process does not impress a Colombian or Brazilian or Guatemalan peasant who asks how he and his family could be any worse off than they are today.

Industrialization and agrarian reforms, jobs and land to till, schools and hospitals, decent homes to live in, decent clothes to wear, relief in old age or illness—this is what the Latin American demands today with an insistence new in his history. Fortunately for all of us, he is now seeking it, except in Cuba, through relatively democratic institutions, but if democracy does not give it to him, he will either fall a prey to the demagogy of right-wing military dictators or he will turn to communism. The revolution he demands, as President Kennedy has said, must be granted voluntarily or it will be sought violently.

The United States failed to ride the tidal wave of democratic idealism that swept over Latin America in the 1950's. In fact, we often seemed to oppose it by favoritism to dictators. The price being paid for this miscalculation is fortunately not too high. This history cannot be rewritten and the scars will remain, but the damage is reparable.

If, however, we buck that other tidal wave that is labelled "social justice," we will pay a very heavy price indeed. The accommodation will not be easy. Social revolutions like the Cuban one hurt powerful American interests which, in turn, bring pressure on Congress and restrict the State Department. Economic orthodoxy might, temporarily, have to be put aside. Men—probably a younger generation of men—imbued with passionate ideals of social justice, with extreme nationalism, inexperienced and blundering, impatient and sensitive, are the leaders with whom Washington will have to treat.

The difficulties of dealing with Latin America in the postwar years were underestimated, but we are entering a period in which the problems will be far more difficult, delicate and critical.

A new era is also beginning for American business in the Latin American world. The nationalism that continues to be so strong is forcing more and more North Americans out of their work and jobs and life in the Latin countries. The Cuban revolution called attention to the threat of other similar revolutions in Latin America and private investors have become understandably frightened. The future of foreign-owned public utilities has become especially dubious in Latin America.

Walking along the razor's edge between intervention and nonintervention, leadership and partnership, is always going to be supremely difficult. The influence of the United States, because of our wealth, power and Latin America's need of aid, must in any circumstances constitute a form of "intervention." The problem is to make it an influence that Latin Americans desire. Leadership is necessary since we have the money, the goods, the know-how, the nuclear weapons, the world power, the prestige, the democratic traditions and practices that Latin American countries either lack or do not possess as a whole or in large measure. The goal of this leadership is to win trust, loyalty and support, and to set an example that will make all men of good will and democratic ideals in Latin America want freely to follow us.

In many respects we have been going counter to the stream of Latin

American history. We have gone astray since the great days of the "Good Neighbor" policy when we and they were surging forward together. The Alliance for Progress, in its aims, is a brave and noble effort to find a common ground on which North Americans and Latin Americans can again move ahead. It is having a difficult and somewhat discouraging start, but it is a plan of vast scope and long range. To expect it to work quickly and easily would be foolish. We are prepared to give much for it, but we should never overlook the fact that we are asking far more of Latin America.

American policy makers will forget to their peril that Latin America is demographically a young region. The population explosion means that where the average United States citizen is 29.5 years old, the average Latin American is 21.5. The boys and girls who fought and survived in Argentina, Colombia, Venezuela, Cuba, the Dominican Republic, are the ones who will direct the futures of their countries. Even where older and more experienced democratic leaders are showing the way, they must satisfy the aspirations of the younger generations. They must beware that their moderate, progressive, pro-Yankee, "democratic Left" policies do not take effect too late for the impatient youth and workers and peasants of their countries. It may be later than all of us think.

Youth is constitutionally impatient, over-sure of itself, imbued with high ideals that are not always practical in our imperfect world, courageous to the point of rashness, indifferent to the sufferings and discomforts of maturity and age. In Latin America the young are extremely nationalistic, and that means either outright anti-Yankeeism or a willingness to disregard the consequences of plucking feathers from the American Eagle's tail.

A wise policy will recognize what Arturo Morales-Carrión, the Puerto Rican official who became U.S. Assistant Secretary of State, described as

> . . . the strength and intensity of their purpose, and their high and passionate devotion to a new way of democratic life, to good and honest government and to an emerging sense of unity with other liberal groups across national boundaries. . . . The United States should begin to attune its ears to the democratic clamor in Latin America. It should not expect the upcoming generations to behave like British parliamentarians. It is a tough generation. They will not be easy to deal with. No profit-making philosophy will persuade them. No rosy propaganda will win them over. Only the conviction that freedom is something to be shared by all, that democracy is not a word but an active, living faith, that one must always look beyond a government to the people, will provide a true basis for heart to heart understanding.

For many Latin Americans this problem of understanding on the part of North Americans deserves first priority. They see the need for a new spirit that will revolutionize our mutual relations as the Good Neighbor policy did in the 1930's. The Alliance for Progress has not yet done this.

Understanding can only come with knowledge, and it would bring sympathy and patience. There has been a gap between us which does not exist with Europe. These are, in truth, our neighbors and yet they are more remote from our feelings and thoughts than the nations separated by the Atlantic Ocean.

Our press and news magazines give much less space to Latin American than to European news. As a result when a big story breaks like the Cuban Revolution, there is such widespread ignorance and misunderstanding that the whole picture is distorted almost beyond recognition. This could not happen if a revolution occurred in Europe.

Where is the new spirit to be found? In sharing and helping the democratic resurgence; in accepting and even encouraging the social revolution, which is a wave now engulfing the area; in "Good Partnership" as President Eisenhower put it; in an "Alliance for Progress," in Mr. Kennedy's phrase.

There are no panaceas, no easy solutions, no dogmas, no formulas, no all-wise, omniscient conferences to settle the problems of our relations with Latin America. It is a field that embraces twenty-one countries at different stages of progress and maturity, different in size, population, wealth, race, history, traditions.

Humility might almost be a first requisite for the student, the diplomat, the Congressman, or the man-in-the-street. There are no "experts" on Latin America; there are only degrees of ignorance. Yet those who work with open and friendly minds in this vast field will not, in Bolívar's sad phrase, be "ploughing the water." The reward for the North American and for the United States Government could be a rich one.

Perhaps the wisest progression would be thus: sympathy, knowledge, understanding, helpfulness, patience, patience, patience. . . .

The American Assembly

*Since its establishment by Dwight D. Eisenhower at Columbia University in
1950, The American Assembly has held Assemblies of National leaders and has
published books to illuminate issues of United States policy.*

*The Assembly is a national, nonpartisan educational institution, incorporated
under the State of New York. It was the official administrator of the President's*

Commission on National Goals, which reported to President Eisenhower late in 1960.

The Trustees of the Assembly approve a topic for presentation in a background book, authoritatively designed and written to aid deliberations at national Assembly sessions at Arden House, the Harriman Campus of Columbia University. These books are also used to support discussion at regional Assembly sessions and to evoke consideration by the general public.

All sessions of the Assembly, whether international, national or local, issue and publicize independent reports of conclusions and recommendations on the topic at hand. Participants in these sessions constitute a wide range of experience and competence. The following institutions have cooperated or are scheduled to cooperate with the Assembly in sponsoring sessions across the country and abroad.

University of Arizona
University of Arkansas
The Associated Colleges of the
  Midwest
Aspen Institute
Battelle Memorial Institute
Brigham Young University
Brown University
University of California (Berkeley)
University of California (Los Angeles)
Cleveland Council on World Affairs
University of Colorado
Creighton University
Dallas Council on World Affairs
University of Denver
Drake University
Duke University
Emory University
University of Florida
Foreign Policy Assoc. of Pittsburgh
University of Illinois
Indiana University
State University of Iowa
The Institute for Strategic Studies
  (London)
The Johnson Foundation
Kansas City International Relations
  Council
Lawrence College
Michigan State University
University of Minnesota

Minnesota World Affairs Center
University of Missouri
University of Nebraska
University of New Mexico
North Central Association of Colleges
  and Secondary Schools
Occidental College
University of Oklahoma
University of Oregon
The Principia College
University of Puerto Rico
William Marsh Rice University
Ripon College
Southern Methodist University
Southwestern at Memphis
Stanford University
St. Louis University
Town Hall of Los Angeles
University of Texas
Tufts University
Tulane University
United States Air Force Academy
Vanderbilt University
University of Vermont
University of Washington
Washington University
Western Reserve University
University of Wisconsin
World Affairs Council of Northern
  California
University of Wyoming

American Assembly books are purchased and put to use by thousands of individuals, libraries, businesses, public agencies, non-governmental organizations, educational institutions, discussion meetings and service groups. The following are completed, continuing or future subjects of study by the American Assembly.

1963—THE UNITED STATES AND LATIN AMERICA (SECOND EDITION)
 —THE POPULATION DILEMMA (JULY)
1962—AUTOMATION AND TECHNOLOGICAL CHANGE
 —CULTURAL AFFAIRS AND FOREIGN RELATIONS
 —THE UNITED STATES AND THE FAR EAST (SECOND EDITION)

1961—ARMS CONTROL
 —OUTER SPACE

1960—THE SECRETARY OF STATE
 —THE FEDERAL GOVERNMENT AND HIGHER EDUCATION
 —GOALS FOR AMERICANS

> *Library, clothbound edition, $3.95*
> *Spectrum, paper bound edition, $1.95*
> *Available from better booksellers and Prentice-Hall, Inc.*

The following titles were published by The American Assembly. Prices indicate books which can be obtained by writing to The American Assembly.

1959—THE UNITED STATES AND LATIN AMERICA (FIRST EDITION)
 —WAGES, PRICES, PROFITS AND PRODUCTIVITY ($2.00)

1958—THE UNITED STATES AND AFRICA (FIRST EDITION)
 —UNITED STATES MONETARY POLICY ($2.00)

1957—ATOMS FOR POWER ($1.00)
 —INTERNATIONAL STABILITY AND PROGRESS

1956—THE UNITED STATES AND THE FAR EAST (FIRST EDITION)
 —THE REPRESENTATION OF THE UNITED STATES ABROAD

1955—THE FORTY-EIGHT STATES
 —UNITED STATES AGRICULTURE

1954—THE FEDERAL GOVERNMENT SERVICE
 —THE UNITED STATES STAKE IN THE UNITED NATIONS

1953—ECONOMIC SECURITY FOR AMERICANS

1952—INFLATION

1951—UNITED STATES-WESTERN EUROPE RELATIONSHIPS

Regular readers of The American Assembly receive early copies of each new Assembly study and are billed subsequently. To enroll as a regular reader please write:

Prentice-Hall, Inc., Englewood Cliffs, N.J.

A SPECTRUM BOOK

Some Other SPECTRUM BOOKS

S-32 COMMUNIST CHINA'S STRATEGY IN THE NUCLEAR ERA,* Alice Langley Hsieh
S-41 GOVERNMENT AND POLITICS OF THE MIDDLE EAST,* Maurice Harari
S-44 THE AMERICAN LABOR MOVEMENT, edited by Leon Litwack
S-54 CONTINUING CRISIS IN AMERICAN POLITICS,* edited by Marian D. Irish

Classics in History Series

S-CH-1 FRONTIER AND SECTION: SELECTED ESSAYS OF FREDERICK JACKSON TURNER,* Introduction and Notes by Ray Allen Billington

S-CH-2 DRIFT AND MASTERY: AN ATTEMPT TO DIAGNOSE THE CURRENT UNREST, Walter Lippman, Introduction and Notes by William E. Leuchtenburg

S-CH-3 THE NEW NATIONALISM, Theodore Roosevelt, Introduction and Notes by William E. Leuchtenburg

S-CH-4 THE NEW FREEDOM: A CALL FOR THE EMANCIPATION OF THE GENEROUS ENERGIES OF A PEOPLE, Woodrow Wilson, Introduction and Notes by William E. Leuchtenburg

S-CH-5 EMPIRE AND NATION: JOHN DICKINSON'S "LETTERS FROM A FARMER IN PENNSYLVANIA" AND RICHARD HENRY LEE'S "LETTERS FROM THE FEDERAL FARMER," * Introduction by Forrest McDonald

S-CH-6 THE SUPREME COURT AND THE CONSTITUTION,* Charles A. Beard, Introduction by Alan F. Westin

S-CH-7 SOCIAL DARWINISM: SELECTED ESSAYS OF WILLIAM GRAHAM SUMNER, Introduction by Stow Persons

S-CH-8 WEALTH AGAINST COMMONWEALTH, by Henry Demarest Lloyd, edited and with an Introduction by Thomas C. Cochran

* Also available in limited clothbound edition